Deeper LEARNING

Deeper LEARNING

7 Powerful Strategies for In-Depth and Longer-Lasting Learning

Eric Jensen • LeAnn Nickelsen

CORWIN PRESS
A SAGE Company
Thousand Oaks, CA 91320

For information:

Corwin Press
A SAGE Company
2455 Teller Road
Thousand Oaks, California 91320
www.corwinpress.com

SAGE Ltd.
1 Oliver's Yard
55 City Road
London EC1Y 1SP
United Kingdom

SAGE India Pvt. Ltd.
B 1/I 1 Mohan Cooperative
 Industrial Area
Mathura Road, New Delhi 110 044
India

SAGE Asia-Pacific Pte. Ltd.
33 Pekin Street #02-01
Far East Square
Singapore 048763

Printed in the United States of America.

Library of Congress Cataloging-in-Publication Data

Jensen, Eric, 1950-
Deeper learning: 7 powerful strategies for in-depth and longer-lasting learning/by Eric Jensen and LeAnn Nickelsen.
    p. cm.
Includes bibliographical references and index.
ISBN 978-1-4129-5203-3 (cloth)
ISBN 978-1-4129-5204-0 (pbk.)
    1. Learning. 2. Learning strategies. 3. Learning, Psychology of. 4. Teaching.
I. Nickelsen, LeAnn. II. Title.

LB1060.J452 2008
370.15'23--dc22   2007042020

This book is printed on acid-free paper.

          11   12   10   9   8   7   6   5   4   3   2

Acquisitions Editor:	Allyson P. Sharp
Editorial Assistant:	David Andrew Gray
Production Editor:	Cassandra Margaret Seibel
Copy Editor:	Barbara Coster
Typesetter:	C&M Digitals (P) Ltd.
Proofreader:	Scott Oney
Indexer:	Jean Casalegno
Cover Designer:	Lisa Miller

Contents

Preface

The field of education is like the swinging of a pendulum: first it goes in one direction and then it goes in the opposite direction. Right now the pendulum has swung way out toward a focus on reading and math and getting the highest test scores. Educators have complained that today's curriculum is a "mile wide and an inch deep." We happen to agree with that analysis. But without the tools to do something about this broad and general curriculum, frustration can occur. Both of us value learning. We want to develop learners who know how to learn, love to learn, and are very good at it. The by-products of loving learning and diving into content at deeper levels are long-term memory of concepts, passion for learning, and good test scores. That's what makes this book different from many others.

This book is not focused on being trendy. It's about teaching in ways that develop deeper learning rather than superficial learning. Just as important, it's about learning that sticks. You're introduced to a simple instructional model, the Deeper Learning Cycle (DELC). It guides you through a sequence of learning that enables all your students to be successful in the classroom. Since students come to the learning situation with different concepts and skills, you can't teach them all the same way. The DELC points out the way for individual students at different points in the learning cycle. Just as important, you can also see in this book the application of the leading edge of brain research.

Acknowledgments

No one has worked harder and more thoughtfully on this material than my writing partner, LeAnn. I appreciate her caring and commitment to helping educators, and she just keeps getting better every year. Countless teachers have benefited from her expertise, and it truly comes through in this project. Thanks, LeAnn!

Eric Jensen

I would like to thank my coauthor, Eric Jensen, for this wonderful opportunity to share my ideas and learn from the expert! What a fabulous experience it has been!

I would like to dedicate this book to my wonderful family: my husband of 15 years, Joel, who is simply the best coach, friend, husband, and father, and who challenges me to think at deeper levels. To my school-age twins, Keaton and Aubrey, may you have a passion for learning and sharing it with others.

I would like to thank my parents, Jim and Dolores Heim, who encouraged me to be a teacher. I have wanted to teach since I was in the sixth grade. My mom was an incredible teacher!

I would like to thank my lifelong colleague and friend, Linda G. Allen, who is a wonderful processing partner and gave me so much feedback on my teaching ideas and presentations. Thanks for your feedback and input on Four-Choice Processing, the Deeper Learning Cycle Lesson Plan Template, and so many other ideas.

I would like to give special thanks to my cooperating teachers and long-time friends I met when I student taught years ago: Laura Smith and Sharon McClelland. You were the best to learn from!

I would like to thank the following school districts for being so awesome to work with on a regular basis and for their feedback on some of the ideas in this book: Waynesville Elementary School in Ohio (Jean Hartman—what a principal you are!), Centerville School District in Ohio, Olathe School District in Kansas, Ridgebury Elementary in Connecticut, Grapevine-Colleyville School District in Texas, Gardner-Edgerton School District in Kansas, Mason School District in Ohio, and Woodland Elementary School in Ohio. Thank you to Staff Development for Educators for the wonderful support and opportunities you have given to me to share this information with teachers nationwide.

Last, but most important, I want to thank God for His strength to complete this book and continue on with my other responsibilities. I could not have done this without Your help!

LeAnn Nickelsen

We appreciate all the hard work and expertise of our amazing and talented editors Allyson Sharp, Barbara Coster, David Gray, and Cassandra Seibel. You were able to manage and organize a lot of different files. Your suggestions, questions, word choice, and eye for detail were invaluable! Thank you so much!

Eric Jensen and LeAnn Nickelsen

About the Authors

 **Eric Jensen** is a staff developer with a real love of learning. As a former teacher, he has taught at all levels, from elementary through university level, and is currently completing his PhD in psychology. He cofounded SuperCamp/Quantum Learning, the nation's first and largest brain-compatible learning program, now with over 50,000 graduates. He authored *Teaching With the Brain in Mind, Enriching the Brain, Brain-Based Learning,* and 22 other books on learning and the brain. He's currently a member of the Society for Neuroscience and the New York Academy of Sciences. He was the founder of the Learning Brain Expo and has trained educators and trainers for 25 years worldwide in this field.

Currently, he does conference speaking, staff development, and in-depth trainings. To purchase any of his 24 books or attend trainings, go to www.jensenlearning.com or e-mail diane@jlcbrain.com. Twice a year, he offers the Learning Brain Expo with leading-edge presenters in learning and achievement. For more information, go to www.brainexpo.com.

 **LeAnn Nickelsen**, MEd, is a former teacher and currently provides staff development nationally on topics that include brain research, reading and vocabulary strategies, how food affects learning, and differentiated instruction. She was a classroom teacher in three states and won a Teacher of the Year award in Texas. She is known as a teacher's teacher because of her practical, research-based examples that teachers can easily implement in their classrooms. She has a passion for both instilling the love for learning and helping teachers succeed. She currently resides in Ridgefield, Connecticut, and parents her school-age twins.

She is the author of several books, including *Memorizing Strategies and Other Brain-Based Activities* and a four-series literacy set titled *Comprehension Mini-Lessons.* She has written articles for parenting magazines and *The Praeger Handbook of Learning and the Brain.* Currently, she does staff development and may be reached at lnickelsen@comcast.net or her Web site, www.maximizelearninginc.com.

Introduction

How to Use This Book

We hope you enjoy the journey in learning how to help all students experience deeper learning. We also want you, as an educator, to experience deeper learning while you read this book. One way deeper learning comes about is by taking the time to process what is being read. There are several ways to do this, and we won't preach to you about which one is the best or the right way. We do want you to keep in mind this fact: we all need to process things our own way, often several times over, before deep understanding occurs. In the educational context, processing learning can be referred to as "the consolidation, transformation and internalization of information by the learner" (Caine, Caine, & Crowell, 1994). It can be the path to understanding, insights, depth, utility, and, as a by-product, memory.

We provide you with several opportunities to process the reading of this book while you're reading it so you can deepen your understanding of the big concepts in this book. We give you ways to process learning before reading, during reading, and after reading each chapter. With each chapter, we invite you to process the content at each of those points with small groups of teachers. Remember, the learning of information does not come from reading the content but from processing, thinking about, or reflecting on the content. Every strategy we use to help you dive deeper into the content of this book is a strategy that helps your students dive deeper too.

The following table shows you the many ways you can process learning. These activities are meant to deepen your understanding of the content of the book and to provide you with even more processing activities that you can use with your students. This book models what it preaches. Notice there is not a column in the table called After Reading. That's because there's a list of questions to reflect on in each chapter. We have placed these questions at the beginning of each chapter so you know the purpose of that chapter.

Opportunities to Process Learning While Reading This Book

Chapter	Before Reading	During Reading
1	Activating Prior Knowledge Web	Text-Posting Symbols
2	Purpose Questions	Stop-N-Think
3	Four-Choice Processing	Mind Mapping
4	Inscribe and Illustrate	Text-Posting Symbols
5	Evaluating Self With Questions	Favorites
6	T-Chart Question and Answer	T-Chart Question and Answer
7	SQ4R	SQ4R

This book models how to get your students and yourself to deeper levels of learning. We know that you'll have a deeper understanding of the concepts in this book if you experience them and if we model them. Much of learning is about understanding. The big picture of this book is the Deeper Learning Cycle (DELC), illustrated below, with its seven steps that take students to deeper, more meaningful learning. The DELC demonstrates how to implement the steps in a school year, unit, and daily lesson plan. Embedded in the daily lesson plan are the strategies you use to reach your daily objective—the deeper processing activities.

■ THE BIG PICTURE

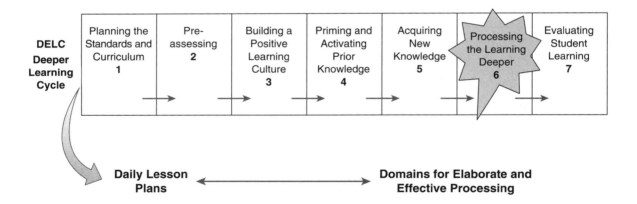

This book begins with an explanation of the DELC. You'll find it easy to understand because your own life experiences confirm it. It walks you through the primary sequential steps of learning. On the more microstrategic level, the Domains for Elaborate and Effective Processing (DEEP) (Step 6) guide each student into the appropriate deeper learning that matches the student's needs with the curriculum and standards. Within those individual domains, there are more specific strategies you can use.

Together, for the first time, you have a clear model for teaching that embraces brain research, the standards, and individual learning differences.

Because we want to model what we preach, we include the big standard of this book (if we may call it that), big questions to support this standard, and individual objectives to achieve this standard. The questions for each chapter help you learn this book content more deeply.

STANDARD: Teachers will dive deeply into the content of this book and process the content in a way that will enable meaningful, applicable content mastery.

When you've finished reading this book, you'll be able to answer the following big questions:

1. How do you facilitate the progress of students toward in-depth learning?

2. How do you organize your time for deeper learning?

3. How do you differentiate these powerful deeper learning strategies to meet all of the students' needs in a daily lesson plan?

This book has the following objectives that should answer the big questions of the book (note that they correspond to the above questions):

1. Explain how the DELC and its powerful strategies bring about student and teaching success. The DELC steps are as follows:
   - Planning the Standards and Curriculum
   - Preassessing
   - Building a Positive Learning Culture
   - Priming and Activating Prior Knowledge
   - Acquiring New Knowledge
   - Processing the Learning Deeper
   - Evaluating Student Learning

2. Incorporate the 10-80-10 rule of thumb so that the components of the Deeper Learning Lesson Plan Template (in Chapter 6) are used to bring all the pieces together and daily implementation can occur.

3. Visualize and incorporate into your daily lesson plans over 45 differentiated, deeper learning strategies that allow students to meaningfully process your content.

This is a journey that makes learning deeper, stronger, more relevant, and often profound. We hope you use the strategies in this book to take students on a journey that many may never get to take. Once you've whetted their appetites for deeper learning, they'll crave it on their own. That's when you know you've succeeded. Enjoy the journey and good luck!

1

Beneath the Surface

Exploring the Deeper Learning Cycle (DELC)

Before-Reading Processing

1. Look at the After-Reading questions and know that these questions set the purpose for this chapter. Put them on the forefront of your working memory while you read so that you know these are the most important ideas in this chapter. If students don't know the purpose of the reading, they'll have difficulty finding the important information in the text.

2. Activating Prior Knowledge Web (Figure 1.1): Answer these four questions based on your background knowledge. Discuss with other teachers in your learning communities if possible.

   • See Figure 1.2 for a web that your students can use with your content to activate their prior knowledge.

Figure 1.1   Activating Prior Knowledge Web

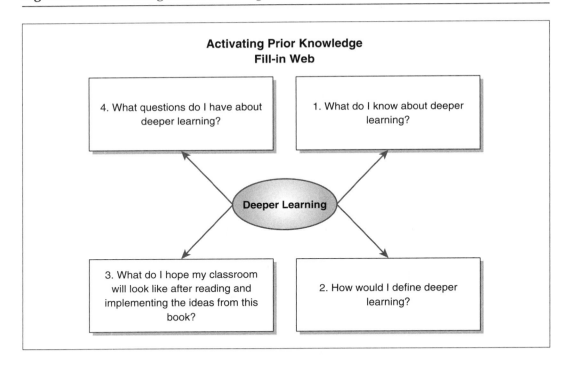

Figure 1.2   Activating Prior Knowledge Web for students

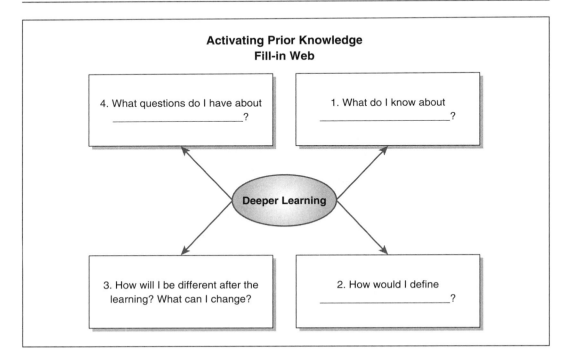

During-Reading Processing

Use the Text-Posting Symbols (Figure 1.3) to metacognitively mark this chapter while you read. This strategy is beneficial for the following reasons:

- It encourages readers to answer questions that arise while reading. Answering questions is what propels readers forward and is what learning is all about.
- It allows readers to efficiently use what is in the book.
- It aids in the metacognition of the reading of the text.
- It allows for deeper processing, so more complex learning occurs.
- It allows for deeper connections to occur: text to self; text to other content; text to historical events; and text to current issues in the world.
- The more you mark, the more you'll learn. The text-posting symbols allow you to process or think deeply about what you're learning while you're reading.

Directions: While reading, use any of the text symbols to mark statements according to your thought processes. For example, if you agree with a statement in this book, draw a smiley face next to the statement. Use as many of these text marks as you want. You can write these symbols in this book or you can write the symbols on Post-it notes. Feel free to create your own set of text-posting symbols to mark your metacognition while reading. See Chapter 4 to see Text in the Spotlight, another form of text posting.

Figure 1.3   Text-Posting Symbols

Directions to teachers: Use these symbols by drawing or writing them in the margin on each page to explain your thinking about what you read. We encourage you to customize your own symbols because you will feel more comfortable using what you have created, but if you like our symbols, please use them! Also, this strategy is not just for your benefit. Please use this with your students while they are reading in order for more complex metacognition (thinking about your thinking) to occur.

? Question that I have

C Confused about text

O Neat word, I want to use this someday (circle the word)

* Very meaningful research to me

☺ I agree!

☹ I disagree

Y I've experienced this before

Post-it notes: Place these along the edge of the page that you plan to use in your classroom. You can refer to that page quickly and easily.

Highlighter marker: Highlight the most important information

After-Reading Processing

The Ultimate Learning Goal:

1. What is your ultimate learning goal for your students?

2. Think of a student who has several of the love-of-learning characteristics described in this chapter. *Activity idea:* List those characteristics of that student.

Varieties of Learning:

3. What is your working definition of learning?

4. How are deeper (or complex) and simple learning similar to and different from one another? Activity idea: Create a T-chart showing their differences.

The Deeper Learning Cycle (DELC):

5. Which step of the DELC are you most excited to learn more about?

6. Which step of the DELC do you know the most about?

7. How does each step of the DELC allow for the success of the next step?

8. How would you rearrange the DELC?

■ THE ULTIMATE LEARNING GOAL

We often get asked the question, "What is your goal for your students?" Without any hesitation, we both say, "I want all my students to love learning so they'll become lifelong learners and apply what they have learned with enthusiasm." A key to a successful society is the fact that citizens build their knowledge of their area of specialty and use that information to improve our society, through better technology, better dams being built, stronger security systems in our airports, quicker and smaller computers, and so on. Therefore, to love learning and to have the motivation to learn deeply is a key to improving our nation and cultivating our personal growth. How is this love for learning fostered in the classroom?

Each chapter in this book contains strategies that feed this powerful love for learning, which is the enabler for deeper learning. They go hand in hand. You can't have deeper learning without a love for learning, and vice versa, you can't have a love for learning without diving into it deeply.

Loving Learning = Positive Affect

The strategy is actually very simple, but not easy. Create a constant stream of positive associations while learning, and avoid any traumatic

Loving Learning = Positive Affect

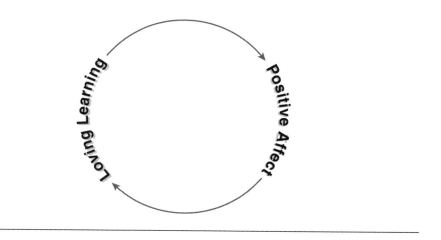

negative ones. Critical feedback is not a problem (for example, "You missed five on this quiz. Notice how all the questions dealt with analogies. Let's walk through that in class tomorrow"). In fact, research supports critical feedback (Stipek & Seal, 2001). In a study of 20 fifth- through ninth-grade classrooms, researchers found that students whose teachers constructively critiqued the quality of their work felt more competent and confident in math than students in classrooms where critiquing was rare. What stunts a passion for learning is when students link up embarrassment, pain, failure, or humiliation with the learning process. Disappointment is okay; it's the trauma that hurts. Stay positive with learners: Do *not* try to toughen them up with harsh criticism or by criticizing them in front of their peers when they're unprepared. Teachers, parents, and peers all play a role in helping students feel confident about their capabilities, responsible for their learning, and supported and respected.

Bottom line, educators have *a lot* to do with children's love for learning, and the more they help them feel competent, the more they'll be self-motivated, which is a precursor to loving learning. First you must be able to recognize which students are experiencing this love of learning and which students you need to focus more on.

Recognizing a Love for Learning

What does a love for learning look like, sound like, and feel like? If teachers want their students to have a love for learning, then they must know the characteristics of this love. Keep in mind that a love for learning rarely exists as a pure state by itself—other factors appear right alongside this self-motivation, such as grades, pleasing others, parents' praise, teacher feedback, opportunities and celebrations for success, positive reinforcement, interest in the topic, opportunities to be engaged, and so on. The following summary shows what a child who loves learning might look like, sound like, and feel like while learning. Obviously, you won't see all these characteristics at once. You might see a few characteristics one day and different ones the next.

Looks like:

- Radiates joy, smiles
- Challenges own thinking—deep analyzing look
- Is actively involved
- Is curious
- Cares about understanding
- Helps other students
- Participates
- Completes assignments
- Doesn't complain
- Pays attention
- Is persistent

Sounds like:

- Asks questions
- Asks, "What if . . ."
- Shares point of view often
- Challenges own and others' thinking and ideas—respectfully
- Asks, "Can we do extra credit on this topic?"
- Says, "I don't get it, but I want to get it"
- Asks for more, more, more
- Asks, "I own a _____. Can I bring it in to show?"
- Asks, "May I tell you what I know about this concept?"
- Is thankful for the learning opportunities

Feels like:

- Their challenge is the right amount
- Success is around the corner
- Says, "I can do this!"
- Accomplishes achievement
- Says, "I'm impressed!"
- Has peace of mind—not stressed
- Has satisfaction from the process
- Is positive about learning opportunities

University of California, Berkeley, psychologist Marty Covington, who studied the academic motivation of 2,500 Introduction to Psychology students, described his self-motivated students this way: "They feel poised and ready to learn, and they seek knowledge above and beyond what's required. . . . They discover knowledge actively rather than acquiring it passively. They wonder more than they worry, and they even say that learning gives them intense and uplifting feelings" (Stipek, interview, June 29, 1999). Deeper learning is all about helping students achieve this love for learning by going deeper rather than just skimming the surface.

VARIETIES OF LEARNING ■

There are some important distinctions at this point. Although an educator's goal is deeper, more complex learning, make no mistake: a substantial amount of learning in school is simple learning. It's the aggregate effects of learning and behavior that count. As you apply the principles in this book, you will see how to help your students learn at deeper levels. Deeper learning may start with simple learning, although it doesn't have to do so. However, in order for most students to dive deeper into concepts, they should be able to grapple with the basics first. The more facts that are known, the more connections can be made.

There are many different types of learning. In your own life, simple learning means you know your own phone number, your home address, and your e-mail address. It means you learn to use bleach only on the whites, not the colored stack of laundry. It means you've learned to arrive at the bank during the times it's open. All of those are learning, and they're simple. Complex learning is the type you engage in when you negotiate a deal, plan your vegetable garden, improvise on a dinner recipe, or troubleshoot your computer. It's the type of learning you engage in to figure out the odds to make a decision on a game show, book a cruise, shop for clothes, or read a book. The world is full of examples of both kinds of learning, and both have an important place in the world.

Some learning at school needs to be simple. Students need to memorize some basics such as the essential facts in a unit, famous historical dates, and a locker number. This simple learning creates the scaffolding for complex learning. Students need a certain amount of background knowledge to think at more complex levels. For example, if teachers want students to evaluate whether or not stem cell research is ethical, they'd better make sure those students know a lot about stem cell research, neurogenesis, animal and human cells, and basic biology. In order for complex learning to occur, simple learning, or building a repertoire of background knowledge, must occur.

What Is Learning?

Learning is the process of acquiring knowledge, skills, attitudes, mental constructs, or values through study, experience, or teaching that causes a measurable change in the brain known as a memory. There are countless ways to describe the specifics of learning (Aguado, 2002). For example, learning could be grouped into that which is taught directly (explicit) and that which is acquired (implicit) by life experience. Most of our learning is acquired (Gazzaniga, 2001). In fact, experienced teachers tell you that most of what students learn was never in the lesson plan.

For example, people "pick up" what to wear based on their observations of others or what's in the media. They pick up how to behave from others around them. Humans "learn" how fast to drive based on the prevailing traffic patterns. This also applies to kids at school. They pick up what behaviors the teacher likes, and they pick up values and skills through experience or observation. With all the possible ways to describe learning, we focus on two that are especially relevant to this book: simple learning and deeper learning of explicit information.

We use a graphic web to explicitly define simple and deeper learning. Both are needed for higher-level processing, but it's important to know the difference so a greater amount of deeper learning occurs. In a classroom, your students should know the difference too. For example, a word and its definition is simple learning. Complex learning might be learning the economic, social, political, and geographic history of a word origin that tracks influences over centuries. Complex learning might include the word's literary proponents, visual aids, and contributions to the language. These factors far exceed the simple word-definition relationship typical of simple learning. All learning should feel good, but complex learning helps students strengthen their self-concept and pride.

Simple Learning

Simple learning doesn't take much effort except for rote memorization. It's definitely needed in the classroom on a daily basis. Some varieties of simple learning are burning your hand on a hot stove; recalling where something happened; knowing the time, people, date, or circumstances of an event; temporal learning; spatial learning; classical conditioning; and rituals and daily routines.

The following web defines simple learning, gives examples of it, gives synonyms for it, compares the pros and cons, and states the requirements for it. There is one caution to remember: too much simple learning could cause boredom.

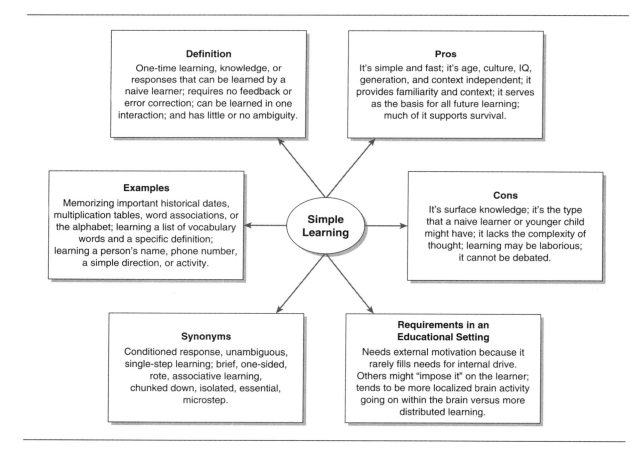

Definition
One-time learning, knowledge, or responses that can be learned by a naive learner; requires no feedback or error correction; can be learned in one interaction; and has little or no ambiguity.

Pros
It's simple and fast; it's age, culture, IQ, generation, and context independent; it provides familiarity and context; it serves as the basis for all future learning; much of it supports survival.

Examples
Memorizing important historical dates, multiplication tables, word associations, or the alphabet; learning a list of vocabulary words and a specific definition; learning a person's name, phone number, a simple direction, or activity.

Simple Learning

Cons
It's surface knowledge; it's the type that a naive learner or younger child might have; it lacks the complexity of thought; learning may be laborious; it cannot be debated.

Synonyms
Conditioned response, unambiguous, single-step learning; brief, one-sided, rote, associative learning, chunked down, isolated, essential, microstep.

Requirements in an Educational Setting
Needs external motivation because it rarely fills needs for internal drive. Others might "impose it" on the learner; tends to be more localized brain activity going on within the brain versus more distributed learning.

Deeper Learning

Now that you have the background knowledge on simple learning, it's time to compare it to deeper learning. Deeper learning requires us to follow multiple rules of operation to complete the task (Feldman, 2000). One must know one microlearning and then add it to other microlearnings to make a complete, complex package. In other words, there are multiple thinking steps to achieving deeper learning with content.

Most complex thinking is not hardwired; it must be taught. Many students lack the exposure, training, and guided experience to think at complex levels. In many cases, teachers assume that students know how to go from Point A to Point B, but in reality many students struggle with steps to deeper thinking. For example, when teachers ask students to summarize what they heard or read, they might give some facts from the reading that really aren't part of the big picture of the information and aren't in any kind of sequential, logical order. To summarize information, students need to practice and understand each of the following microsteps involved in the macrostep of summarization:

- Delete the irrelevant pieces of information.
- Delete duplication of ideas—combine ideas with same subject; be concise.
- Restate information using their own words.
- Use summarization words ("almost all," "in conclusion," "in brief," "the main point," "on the whole," "ultimately," "to sum up," etc.).
- Include only the most important details to support the main idea of the summary.

Summarizing is an example of a skill that requires deeper thinking and lots of modeling of each of the steps involved. The web on page 10 defines deeper learning, gives examples of it, gives synonyms for it, compares the pros and cons, and states the requirements for it. There is one caution to remember: the brain may be fatigued or exhilarated after participating in deeper thinking.

Both simple and deeper learning require diverse, quality skill sets. Initially, your brain may be more activated when deeper thinking occurs the first time. After expert levels begin, it takes less brain activity; typically, greater understanding, greater retention, and more application of concepts and skills are possible. The most characteristic factor of expertise is the connectivity necessary for deeper learning (Abe et al., 2007).

Now that you see the commonalities and differences between simple learning and deeper learning, you should have a clearer picture of what this book focuses on: how to help all students get from simple learning to deeper learning so all students are challenged and successful. The following diagram leads us to the process that enables us to understand and answer this question.

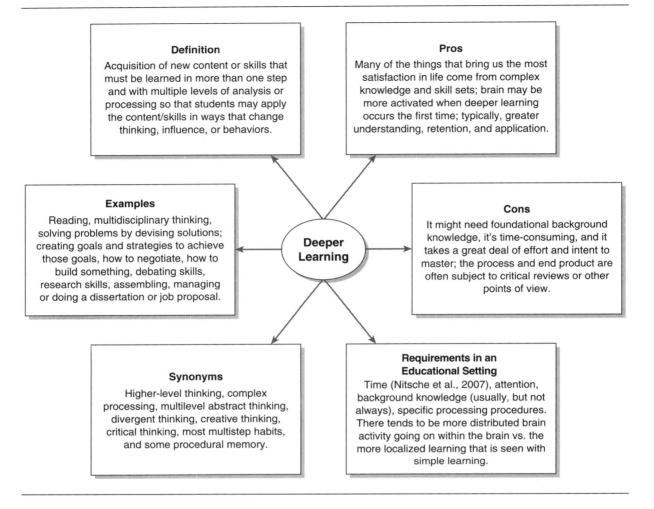

Definition
Acquisition of new content or skills that must be learned in more than one step and with multiple levels of analysis or processing so that students may apply the content/skills in ways that change thinking, influence, or behaviors.

Pros
Many of the things that bring us the most satisfaction in life come from complex knowledge and skill sets; brain may be more activated when deeper learning occurs the first time; typically, greater understanding, retention, and application.

Examples
Reading, multidisciplinary thinking, solving problems by devising solutions; creating goals and strategies to achieve those goals, how to negotiate, how to build something, debating skills, research skills, assembling, managing or doing a dissertation or job proposal.

Deeper Learning

Cons
It might need foundational background knowledge, it's time-consuming, and it takes a great deal of effort and intent to master; the process and end product are often subject to critical reviews or other points of view.

Synonyms
Higher-level thinking, complex processing, multilevel abstract thinking, divergent thinking, creative thinking, critical thinking, most multistep habits, and some procedural memory.

Requirements in an Educational Setting
Time (Nitsche et al., 2007), attention, background knowledge (usually, but not always), specific processing procedures. There tends to be more distributed brain activity going on within the brain vs. the more localized learning that is seen with simple learning.

 THE DEEPER LEARNING CYCLE (DELC)

The DELC (see Figure 1.4) represents how each student can be challenged to arrive at the deeper level of learning. It was created for the following reasons:

- To make teachers and students successful learners at deeper levels
- To give teachers an easy learning tool that describes the steps of deeper learning
- To challenge all students slightly above their ability levels so success can be experienced
- To show processing steps for preparing the learning, during the learning, and after the learning
- To use each step appropriately to achieve deeper learning with all students at their current levels
- To organize learning steps and explicitly define each step for easy application in every lesson plan

The DELC allows teachers to be aware of the research on the importance of each step in the DELC and how that research affects an upper elementary through high school classroom. Each step is introduced below,

Figure 1.4 The Deeper Learning Cycle (DELC)

Planning the Standards and Curriculum 1	Pre-assessing 2	Building a Positive Learning Culture 3	Priming and Activating Prior Knowledge 4	Acquiring New Knowledge 5	Processing the Learning Deeper 6	Evaluating Student Learning 7
*Developmentally Appropriate	*Know Your Students Personally	*Safe, Inspiring Surroundings	*Priming and Preexposure	*Getting the Pieces and Big Picture	The Domains for Elaborate and Effective Processing	*Feedback
*Meaningful Curriculum	*Unit Preassessments	*Positive Relationships Among Students	*Questioning, Discovery, and Discussions	*Getting the Condensed Content	1. Awareness	*Rubrics
*Chunks of Information	*Individual Objective Preassessments	*Positive Relationships Between Student and Teacher	*Making Connections	*Teacher Preparation	2. Analysis to Synthesis	*Mastery
*Units		*Students Vested		*Student Research and Student Sharing	3. Application	*Student Reflection
*Essential Questions				*Books, Text, Journals, or Magazines	4. Assimilation	*Peer Feedback
				*Internet Research		*Self-Reflection
				*DVD or Video, Television		
				*Guest Speakers		

and subsequent chapters give full descriptions of each step. Educators all wish learning could be reduced to a simple, follow-the-numbers formula for learners. Realistically, education is a long way from having anything even remotely close to a formula for all learners that works all the time. What educators do have is a pretty good idea of what's needed at the more basic levels of the learning ladder.

Most teachers, by necessity, are practical. Strategies usually have a greater appeal than theories, generalized understandings, or ideas. But there is a downside. All strategies have an unlimited number of nuances that can make them either succeed or fail. When teachers learn a new strategy, it's assumed that it'll be carried out in a certain, prescribed way. But it doesn't always turn out that way. A really good teacher can make a marginal strategy work, and a marginal teacher can ruin a really good strategy. That's why in this book we strive to balance the principles with the underlying strategies.

If you make a change in a strategy on your own, that's fine, as long as you understand and stick to the overriding principles, the necessary principles. Remember, no one strategy works every time with all groups. And never stick with a strategy simply because someone tells you it works more often than any other strategy. Learn to rotate your strategies in order to find what works best for your particular classroom and students for each school year. There are strategies mentioned in each of the DELC's steps.

The DELC Steps

1. Planning the Standards and Curriculum

2. Preassessing

3. Building a Positive Learning Culture

4. Priming and Activating Prior Knowledge

5. Acquiring New Knowledge

6. Processing the Learning Deeper

7. Evaluating Student Learning

Step 1—Planning the Standards and Curriculum

Teachers always begin with the standards and curriculum. They can create meaningful units of study by placing similar or related objects together for cohesive learning sequences and ease of memory of the information. Wiggins and McTighe's (2005) book *Understanding by Design* explains how to take the lessons and units and create questions that explain the big picture of these objectives. By creating questions for the objectives and units, the brain is able to focus on the more important points. In the classroom, teachers must always have a guide for what they want students to accomplish; this guide is the grade level and subject standards and curriculum. When teachers align the district curriculum with the state standards, the results are typically higher achievement scores (McGehee & Griffith, 2001).

Notice that we modeled this strategy in the Introduction. We gave you the big savvy standard of the whole book, the big three questions you'll be able to answer after reading this book, and the individual objectives for the book that allow you to reach the standard. Teaching toward a bigger picture is definitely deeper thinking, since there are many microsteps that help students achieve the macrostep, the standard. Many times, educators forget or don't take time to relate the daily lesson plan to the big picture, the standard.

Step 2—Preassessing

To help students achieve a deeper level of learning, preassess the students to see what they know about the standards and objectives. How can teachers know where to start teaching students if they don't know what they already understand? There are several types of preassessments that enable teachers to know students' background knowledge better. Teachers explore unit preassessments, individual objective preassessments, and knowing the student as a learner preassessments (likes, dislikes, interests in and out of school, strengths, and growth opportunities). This important information is collected in a variety of ways and is used to determine where teachers should start for activating prior knowledge and processing strategies. Evidence suggests that students with different prior knowledge use dramatically different processing strategies and that a preassessment can help direct students into better learning outcomes (Kieser, Herbison, Waddell, Kardos, & Innes, 2006). In many cases, students with low levels of background knowledge have scattered and unorganized "knowledge trees" in the mind, which means they'll often be poor at causality. They might know the what but not the why or the how.

This second step of the DELC coincides and coexists with Step 3, Building a Positive Learning Culture. When you preassess your students, you're showing them that you care about them and you're letting them know you want to get to know them better so you can serve their learning needs better. Getting to know your students better builds a positive learning culture.

Step 3—Building a Positive Learning Culture (Safe, Supported, and Vested)

Students need a delicate balance of emotions to learn successfully. The ideal emotion is not a flat affect (boredom, apathy, or detachment). The ideal learning state is a fresh, relaxed, yet alert curiosity. While other emotional states can work, there is a very narrow range of states that work for classroom instruction. Students need to be unthreatened and unstressed yet positive and willing to learn (Bishop, Duncan,

Brett, & Lawrence, 2004). Safety, which means limited distractions, is tantamount to learner participation (Dolcos & McCarthy, 2006). Teachers create safety through activities that help gain predictability, freedom from embarrassment or put-downs, and positive social structures. Safety allows the brain to focus on the promotion of learning new information for the future and not organizing resources for ensuring short-term survival. In this book, we focus on

1. Characteristics of a safe, vested, engaged environment

2. Positive relationships—student to student

3. Positive relationships—student to teacher

Motivating students to be in a positive, motivated state of mind so they care about learning helps them dive deeper into their learning. The trusting relationships they have with you and between one another also bring about vested student learning.

 ## Step 4—Priming and Activating Prior Knowledge

Priming and Preexposure; Questioning, Discovery, and Discussions; and Making Connections

You learned how to crawl before you learned how to walk. Before you go after deeper learning, assess well and then help students gather the needed supporting content. To optimize learning, you'll want to teach the skills of processing. Learning is all about connecting the new information learned to an existing neural network in that student. Every student comes to the learning journey with a different schema or background knowledge. The brain is far more effective when people can use the already-created "superhighways" (Altmann, 2002). Unfortunately, many textbooks fail to utilize solid pedagogy to tap into prior knowledge, and a wide range of student responses are based simply on the type of textbook used (Boscolo & Mason, 2000). Because of the background knowledge differences among students, teachers need to use a variety of ways to prime and activate prior knowledge so that the new learning can become connected to each student's existing background knowledge.

The greater the prior knowledge, the easier and faster the learning if the new learning is compatible with the old (Hayes, Foster, & Gadd, 2003). But if the new learning is contrary to the prior knowledge, the existing neural networks become a significant obstacle that should not be underestimated. For example, if a person has a strong prior knowledge about how temperatures affect weather conditions, then the topic of how tornadoes form might be understood more quickly. On the contrary, if a student thinks that the sun is closer to the Earth in the summertime and that's what causes the warm temperatures during that season, that student might struggle with the real cause of the seasons: the Earth's tilt. New approaches and constant revision of learning are necessary. In short, prior knowledge is far more significant as an influence (good or bad) and predictor than most educators give it credit for (Smees, Sammons, Thomas, & Mortimore, 2002).

In DELC Step 4 in Chapter 3 you see that by taking the time to prime your students' brains, you're actually creating snippets of prior knowledge so that the new learning can be more connected to the next step, Acquiring New Knowledge.

Step 5—Acquiring New Knowledge

After students have their networks of neurons activated on a particular topic/subject, it's time to help them acquire the new, related information. This next step is the acquisition of a rough draft, or what researchers refer to as "gist learning" (Wolfe, 2006). This can be done through teachers giving information, students researching information, students sharing what they know, experience, books, the Internet, journals, magazines, interviews, or DVDs and videos. Each brain creates unique neural networks that need creation and activation by coherent, complex learning (Hammer, 2002). Students can acquire information in several ways, but giving choices on how to do that is more motivating. Every brain receives information differently, so at this step, teachers must respect the variety of ways that the brain can acquire information.

While facilitating the acquiring of information, teachers use a variety of strategies. Instructional variety is a key ingredient to successful deeper learning unless every student in your class is exactly the same, with identical genes and life experience. Well, that's not going to happen. In fact, even if it did happen, students would quickly get bored, even if your strategies were perfect. Having a variety of strategies from which to choose is analogous to having a complete set of tools in your toolbox. If you have a variety of tools, you can solve a wide range of household problems. If all you have is a screwdriver, you're pretty limited. In this book, you receive a variety of low-prep, high-impact, ready-to-use strategies to meet the different needs of your students.

Here coherence is the key. It's easy to give or acquire information; the challenge is to make it so coherent that people can understand it. When good teachers make it coherent, learning goes up (Chesebro, 2003). School at times can swamp teachers with a constant sensory buffet, and unless they make some sense of it, they're overwhelmed, baffled, and often frustrated. Part of good teaching is the capacity to explain the concept to someone without background information. If you can't, find another way to explain it. Einstein was famous for explaining relativity: "If you put your hand on a hot stove, two seconds seems like an hour. But if you're with your sweetheart, an hour feels like two seconds." It could be said that people have subject matter coherence when they have the capacity to translate the content into a metaphor, story, diagram, or analogy.

The next step of the DELC, Processing the Learning Deeper, goes hand in hand with acquiring background knowledge. After a small chunk of information is acquired, processing must take place. Once this chunk is understood and mastered, the learner is ready for the next chunk of related information. Then processing time is given for this chunk. This continues until the grand finale processing activity is used to pull all the learning chunks together.

Spencer Bergstrand

Step 6—Processing the Learning Deeper

We could make many assumptions about why many teachers go over the learning quickly and then move on. It might be a lack of time, testing pressure, or other issues. But the bottom line is that students will never get to the mastery level unless they elaborate, process, and explore their material over time. Sometimes people just don't get it the first time because the task overloads their processing systems (Saud de Nunez, Rodriguez Rojas, & Niaz, 1993). The process of elaboration means that students are processing in a variety of ways, depending on what needs to be learned. This is differentiation at its best; processing varies depending on the purpose for that learning. You don't have to give up one of them for another; sometimes several are appropriate.

Getting to the mastery level of all standards is going to take far more time than people have in school. Dr. K. Anders Ericsson, in the Department of Psychology at Florida State University, has studied expert knowledge for decades. He's discovered it takes an extraordinary amount of effortful, motivated practice to get there. That is not typical for a traditional classroom (Williams & Ericsson, 2005).

Deeper learning consists of four domains where students can process content, and typically you engage two or three in a single lesson. They are not leveled, but rather there are simple and complex ways to process within each domain. The domains are

1. *Processing for Awareness*: the consciousness of what's going on; to be cognizant and aware

2. *Processing for Analysis and Synthesis*: the wholes to parts and reverse; separating or combining knowledge and ideas in order to see the parts from the whole and then to put the parts together to form a new whole

3. *Processing for Application*: practicing, doing, or using what was learned in a way to improve self, community, nation, or world

4. *Processing for Assimilation*: the heart of content; personally internalizing the information

We've included 15 to 20 specific processing strategies for each of the domains that work with any content that is taught. You are given descriptions, variations of thinking verbs, end product examples, and then very specific examples of these processing domains in Chapters 4 and 5. Step 6 of the DELC brings Steps 1 through 5 to the total culmination of learning. This step is the key to opening the doors to the mind for deeper learning.

Step 7—Evaluating Student Learning

Most learners do not get complex learning the first time. In fact, there are only two things they *do* get the first time: (1) simple learning (word and definition, 4 × 4 = 16, who was the first president, etc.) and (2) traumatic learning (we learn, but unfortunately we get emotionally damaged). With simple learning, very little feedback is needed ("Is that accurate or not?"). Consider the role of feedback in most complex learning.

Virtually no abstract complex cognitive skills can be learned without feedback. Only through the elaboration process can one ever get some level of mastery. In a way, elaboration is essential for mastery, and the feedback corrects the elaboration (Ilies & Judge, 2005). The brain is not designed to get things right the first time except for exposure to either very simple learning or trauma. Instead, it makes what are called rough drafts, the gist learning mentioned earlier. These are sketchy, highly inaccurate representations of the material that are held either in the working memory or in the hippocampus (temporary holding area) until people have a reason to either forget the learning or elaborate on it (Wolfe, 2006).

Almost universally, data suggest that feedback greatly facilitates improved posttest performance and increased near-transfer performance as well (McCarthy, 1995). Quality classroom activities have feedback built into them. This means students are able to see, hear, and experience the result of what they're doing while they're doing it. It allows them to take in the impartial feedback and adjust. The adjustment to and inclusion of feedback, not the raw memorization of facts, helps make them smarter. This is a reminder that teachers should be careful about the type of activity and the type of feedback students get. We offer many kinds of feedback for your students in Chapter 6.

So how do you evaluate whether or not students have mastered your objectives? Mastery has several components to it. Students should be able to explain and elaborate in their own words what was learned or how to do a skill. They should have a thorough, deep understanding of the content or skill so that it can be used in several different ways rather than in only one way in one subject in one learning situation. You need to create your own definition of mastery after reading this book. We believe mastery occurs after deeply processing the content.

This book dives deeply into each of the DELC steps. If you're still unclear about what deeper learning is, it might help to make an analogy with cooking. Deeper learning is like creating a meal from a new recipe. When you're craving a particular type of food, let's say chicken parmesan, you eagerly search for the perfect recipe. You look at the ingredients and decide if this is the recipe you want to take the time to use. The recipe becomes your standard for the next hour. You study that recipe and prepare for it. You look through your cabinets and refrigerator to see if you have the ingredients and tools to complete this recipe. You also have to read the directions to decide if this recipe is compatible with your cooking ability. This represents Step 2, the preassessment step. While reading the recipe and its step-by-step directions, you activate your prior knowledge by saying to yourself, "I know the perfect parmesan to purchase for this recipe. I also better tenderize the chicken before preparing it. I think I'll use my favorite marinara sauce." This recollection of thoughts of what you have done in the past represents Step 4, activating prior knowledge.

You acquire the information needed for this recipe by reading it thoroughly and even studying the picture. You might even need to ask someone a question about one of the directions. After pulling all the ingredients together and baking it for 30 minutes, you start to savor the scent. You set the table and prepare to indulge in your long-awaited meal. Now it's time to chew the chunks that you placed on your plate so neatly after it was cooked. You decide to take a nibble, but you can't help yourself, and you gobble it up quickly. You digest it and use it for energy to clean up the mess that you just made.

Eventually, with much time, the food can be used to make new cells, muscles, tissues, and so on. You probably didn't think about that last step, but it's very important with deeper learning, and you learn more about it when you get to the domains of learning. Time to evaluate: How was that meal? Will you make that recipe again? Was it perfect? More salt or less salt? More parmesan or less? You can be sure that the next time you revisit that recipe, it'll be better, and eventually the recipe will become a family legend.

Now that you've been introduced to the DELC steps, you dive deeper into these topics so that you have a better understanding of what these seven steps do for your students for deeper learning. Are you ready to experience deeper learning? You received the standards, big questions, and objectives for this book in the Introduction, and now it's time to preassess the audience, which is you, the reader.

A Deeper Learning Preassessment for You

Activity Idea

Directions: On the Preassessment Anticipation Guide (pages 19–20), place a check mark in the Agree or Disagree box, depending on your opinion of the statement that is aligned with the number. Place your check mark in the "Before Learning" section. In the margin of the book on the left-hand side, write why you agree or disagree with the statement. At the end of the book, retake this preassessment to see how your opinions have changed.

Table 1.1   Preassessment Anticipation Guide

Before Learning			After Learning	
Agree	Disagree		Agree	Disagree
		1. Simple learning is a foundational piece for deeper learning. (Ch. 1)		
		2. Preassessment results assist deeper learning. (Ch. 1)		
		3. Deeper learning is the acquisition of new content or skills that must be learned in more than one step and with multiple levels of analysis or processing so that students may apply the information in ways that change thinking, influence affect, or change behaviors. (Ch. 1)		
		4. Taking the time to activate prior knowledge before starting to teach a lesson can facilitate strong connections. (Ch. 1)		
		5. Deeper learning is enhanced when students are highly challenged. (Ch. 2)		
		6. Preassessments are needed in order to create a very meaningful, developmentally appropriate unit that meets the needs of the students. (Ch. 2)		
		7. Research suggests that cooperative learning produces better learning when compared with students competing against each other individually. (Ch. 2)		
		8. Loving learning does not necessarily equal positive affect. (Ch. 2)		
		9. Your overall mood is not as important as other factors when it comes to creating a positive affect. (Ch. 2)		
		10. Priming and activating prior knowledge are the same thing. (Ch. 3)		
		11. The main purpose behind activating prior knowledge is to preexpose the brain to upcoming content. (Ch. 3)		
		12. Processing happens automatically so there is little facilitation that must go on from the teacher. (Ch. 4)		
		13. Rather than think of deeper processing as a taxonomy of thought, teachers should use a variety of processing strategies depending on the purpose for the processing. (Ch. 4)		
		14. Processing all begins in the amygdala, the emotional center of the brain. (Ch. 4)		

(Continued)

Table 1.1 (Continued)

| Before Learning | | | After Learning | |
Agree	Disagree		Agree	Disagree
		15. Too much too fast will last. (Ch. 4)		
		16. Bloom's taxonomy explains how students learn, and teachers should make it a priority to lead students through the taxonomy in its proper order. (Ch. 4)		
		17. We differentiate because everyone comes to the learning situation with different background knowledge, interests, strengths, and growth opportunities. (Ch. 5)		
		18. Students can experience deeper learning even though their background knowledge is not well developed. (Ch. 5)		
		19. There should be about two to four processing opportunities in each daily lesson plan. (Ch. 6)		
		20. Because each teacher has different teaching styles, it is recommended that you start using the processing activities that best fit your teaching style. Then it's very important to branch out and try the others so that you're meeting all of your students' needs. (Ch. 6)		
		21. Thinking through your daily lesson plans enhances deeper learning. (Ch. 6)		
		22. Closures of the lesson are not as important as once thought. (Ch. 6)		
		23. Student vesting is so important that it needs to be at the very beginning of your lesson every time you teach. (Ch. 6)		
		24. One way to manage and implement the processing activities is to create processing baskets for groups of students so they can easily use the supplies needed for the activities. (Ch. 7)		
		25. The Four P's (Purposeful, Pumped, Prepared, and Positive, Emotional Ending) help you create your own processing activities for your students. They are the secret recipe to a good processing activity. (Ch. 7)		

Part I

Preparing for Learning

2

Preparing for Deeper Learning

DELC Steps 1–3

Before-Reading Processing

Look at the After-Reading questions in the third box below and know that these questions establish the purpose of this chapter. Have them in the forefront of your working memory while you read so that you know these are the main ideas in the reading. If students don't know the purpose of the reading, they will have difficulty finding the important information in the text.

During-Reading Processing

Stop-N-Think Boxes (page 61) constitute a graphic organizer that allows you to read chunks of information, process them in a way that is most meaningful to you, and then connect the other chunks in that same reading to one another. Read the whole section under DELC Step 1: Planning the Standards and Curriculum (and all the subheadings in that section), stop, and then choose one way to respond to that chunk of text (see Figure 2.1). Write, web, or draw, depending on your reflection choice, your response in Stop #1 of the Stop-N-Think Boxes. Do the same for Stop #2 after reading DELC Step 2: Preassessing. Continue this with the next section titled DELC Step 3: Building a Positive Learning Culture. In the Stop #3 box, process what you learn from the reading of the section titled How to Structure Cooperative Learning So It's Successful. Then, in the Synthesis of the Stops box, write how all these chunks connect to one another, in other words, a synthesis or summary of this chapter. You're welcome to add more boxes if you need them or subtract boxes that aren't needed.

Figure 2.1   Processing today's lesson: Choice Reflection

Forming the Basics

- Determine the most valuable piece of information you learned.
- Create an outline of what you learned.
- Draw a picture of what you learned.
- Create a web of the details that you learned.
- Predict what information might come next.
- What was the main idea of this information? What details support it?
- List the most important vocabulary words of this concept.
- What are the cause-effect relationships within the lesson?
- List some facts that you learned today.
- Create a who, did what, when, where, why, and how web on the lesson.

Making Connections

- Does this information remind you of anything from your personal life? Objects? Events? Person? Process?
- How does this information connect with other things that you have learned (books, stories, Web sites, current events, famous people, etc.)?
- How would you explain this information to someone 4 years younger or 4 years older?
- How could you implement what you learned in the future (career), in your household, at school, in the community, or in the world?
- How will your life be different now that you know this information?
- Create a simile, metaphor, or analogy of what you learned.

Synthesizing It All

- How would you teach this information?
- What new questions do you have about this information?
- Assess your new understanding of this information. What are your gaps if you feel that you have any?
- Summarize your learning in 10 or fewer words.
- What are you beginning to wonder now that you learned this information?
- What did you rediscover after learning this information?
- If you could change anything about what you learned, how would you change it and why?

After-Reading Processing

DELC Step 1: Planning the Standards and Curriculum

1. How do you and your school ensure that meaningful curriculum and units are taught?

DELC Step 2: Preassessing

2. What type of preassessment would you like to do more of: getting to know your students personally, unit preassessments, or individual objective preassessments?

DELC Step 3: Building a Positive Learning Culture

    3. How is a positive learning culture developed in the classroom?

How to Structure Cooperative Learning So It's Successful

    4. What research supports the effectiveness of cooperative learning in the classroom?

    5. What are five new strategies you can use to enhance the motivational levels of your students?

DELC STEP 1: PLANNING THE STANDARDS AND CURRICULUM ■

We start with the basics. Make sure the curriculum is developmentally appropriate for your students. This step requires knowing your learners well (to be discussed in DELC Step 2). A great resource to use to learn if the content and skills are developmentally appropriate is *Yardsticks: Children in the Classroom Ages 4–14* (Wood, 1997). We also encourage looking through the latest journals about your students' learning development.

To teach for deeper learning, you must know your content and skills that are stated in the standards and curriculum. You also want to know your objectives well and how they relate to one another—this allows you to teach for coherence. Once similar concepts and skills are grouped together according to themes and/or units, the brain is able to see the patterns in the learning versus just teaching scattered, random objectives that don't relate to one another. Many researchers believe that memories hook onto ("attach") related networks of other memories. It makes sense to teach related information for ease of neural network connection. This is called chunking the curriculum, which allows the content to become more meaningful to the learners. By incorporating a list of related objectives into one big unit, learners can see how these microsteps, the daily objectives, create the macrostep, the unit, theme, or big standard.

Planning a Unit of Instruction

Here are some step-by-step sequences for planning a unit of instruction. (These steps are for one particular subject. We want these steps to work in situations in which one teacher teaches, for example, social studies, but a different teacher teaches the math unit. If you teach a self-contained classroom, you'll have more in-depth opportunities to transfer the objectives from one subject to another.)

1. After studying your curriculum, identify concepts, skills, essential questions, and content that correlate with one another or are similar to one another. By doing this, several objectives for the unit are created. Remember, objectives must have the specific content plus a challenging verb of action. There is more information about objective writing in Chapter 6.

Answering the following questions helps you determine what to teach:

What do the students need to know at the end of the unit?

What do the students need to be able to do at the end of the unit?

What terms and concepts do they need to understand at the end of the unit?

What questions (big and small) do they need to be able to answer at the end of the unit?

2.   Using your chosen method of preassessment, gather data to determine the prior knowledge of students for the new content and skills that will be targeted for learning (unit pretest). The pretest should represent the key concepts and skills from each lesson that will be taught in the unit. Write about three to five questions per lesson objective and subdivide them so you know the students' levels of understanding for each lesson objective.

3.   Put all the lesson objectives in sequential order according to students' background knowledge and logical order of the content. You might need to add or subtract some objectives, depending on the pretest results. Ask yourself: What concepts should I teach before I teach the following lesson? By asking this question, you create a brain-friendly sequence of objectives that is in sequential order for better understanding of the big picture of your unit.

4.   Now that the objectives are in sequential order, scrutinize the pretest results to see which objectives need more time and which objectives need less time. Determine which students might need additional differentiated strategies for particular concepts and make note of this important information received from the pretest results.

5.   Create a concept web showing how the terms and big concepts in the unit all relate to one another. See the weather web (Figure 2.2) for an example of how you could chunk the concepts so that the students see the big picture of the unit and also the smaller chunks within the unit.

6.   Create assessments and questions for the objectives. What do you want students to do to show that they understand the questions for objective mastery? What will be ongoing during the unit, and what will be the culminating product? Will the culminating product be differentiated? More about assessment creation is included in Chapter 6.

Let's see how a classroom teacher incorporated these steps in creating a unit on the Civil War.

Example

Fifth Grade: The Civil War Unit

The students will be able to

1.   Sequence the causes of the Civil War by creating a detailed timeline of the events

2.   Sort through the roles that many famous people had during the Civil War by creating a table with the following categories:
   • Famous person
   • North or South side

Figure 2.2 Weather web example

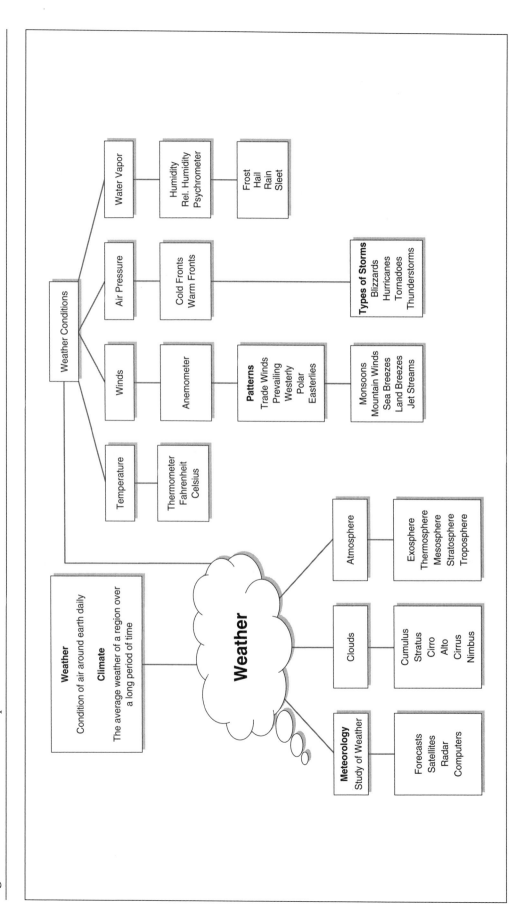

- Something unique about this person
- Major role this person had in the war
- Death information
- Other

3. Create a point-of-view timeline indicating how each side felt during the war in certain battles. Two will be created: North and South Side Perspective (see Figure 2.3 for an example).

4. Compare and contrast through an H diagram a soldier's life in the North and in the South. (Read *Pink and Say* by Patricia Polacco, 1994.) See Figure 2.6 for an H diagram. (Place the differences on the outside columns of the H and the similarities in the connecting box of the H.)

5. Use the WRITE! strategy after reading in their social studies books about slavery. See instructions on WRITE! on page 215 in Chapter 5. Have the students perform a miniplay in their groups too. Then have them write to somebody in the North describing how their life is as a slave in the South.

6. Debate from the points of view of Presidents Lincoln and Davis about the war.

7. Determine the six critical points during this war to research. Six groups should research their topic, create a product, and determine a way to share what was learned with the whole class.

8. Experience the Six Thinking Hats Process: facts, feelings of North and South people, pros of the North, cons of the North, pros of the South, cons of the South, what if questions, and summary of the whole war. See page 197 in Chapter 5 to learn more about the 6 Thinking Hats.

This sequence of events and the example get your unit started. We discuss how to plan each lesson in that unit in Chapter 6. With each lesson, you can change the objectives into questions. For example, if the objective was for students to list in a T-chart the pros and cons of living in the South or the North during the war, the questions you can form from this objective would be: How was living in the South different from living in the North during the Civil War? What land features benefited the Southerners during the war? What land features hindered the Southerners' fighting ability? What land features hindered the Northerners' fighting ability? Answering these questions after the lesson becomes the goal of the lesson. Students are less likely to abandon learning when questions are set on the forefront of their working memories. Make sure the students can see the questions (write them on the dry erase board or chalkboard, or create a PowerPoint), because they'll be asked at the end of the lesson. Tell the students before the lesson, "By the end of this lesson, you'll be able to answer the following questions . . ." This statement relieves stress among students and shows them what your expectations are. These essential questions also set them up for success and help them focus on the most important information during reading, video viewing, note taking, or collaborating.

Figure 2.3   Point-of-view timeline: The Civil War

Perspective: Northerner

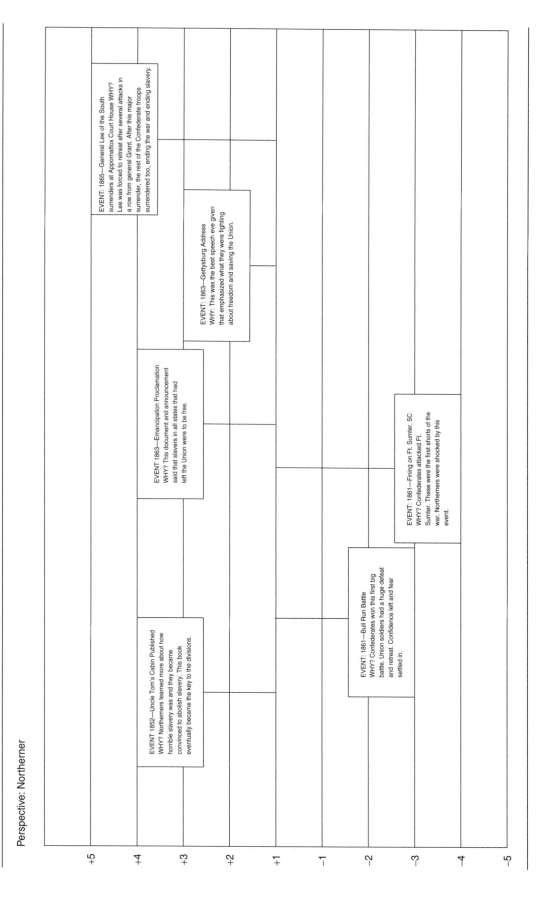

EVENT: 1852—Uncle Tom's Cabin Published
WHY? Northerners learned more about how horrible slavery was and they became convinced to abolish slavery. This book eventually became the key to the divisions.

EVENT 1863—Emancipation Proclamation
WHY? This document and announcement said that slavers in all states that had left the Union were to be free.

EVENT: 1863—Gettysburg Address
WHY: This was the best speech eve given that emphasized what they were fighting about freedom and saving the Union.

EVENT: 1865—General Lee of the South surrenders at Appomattox Court House WHY? Lee was forced to retreat after several attacks in a row from general Grant. After this major surrender, the rest of the Confederate troops surrendered too, ending the war and ending slavery.

EVENT: 1861—Bull Run Battle
WHY? Confederates won this first big battle. Union soldiers had a huge defeat and retreat. Confidence left and fear settled in.

EVENT: 1861—Firing on Ft. Sumter, SC
WHY? Confederates attacked Ft. Sumter. These were the first shorts of the war. Northerners were shocked by this event.

+5
+4
+3
+2
+1
−1
−2
−3
−4
−5

Designing Essential Questions

Every unit needs its own list of essential questions. Your students should be able to answer them before they're comfortable leaving this unit for a new unit. Usually, unit questions are very broad and general. For example, by the end of the unit, students can answer these questions:

1. How did the Civil War change our nation?

2. What are the pros and cons of this war?

3. What are your opinions about this war? If you were Abraham Lincoln, how would you have done things differently?

4. What would our nation be like now if the North had not won this war?

Naturally, the more sophisticated the learners, the more complex your questions can be. The nature of good questions is such that they generate interest, motivation, a stick-to-it mind-set, and higher-level thinking skills. Instead of getting too hung up on trying to figure out the right answers to the questions you want to ask, figure out questions that will be just tough enough to challenge their minds.

Your curriculum can be very meaningful and coherent to your students if you make sure that the unit is created in sequential order and in meaningful chunks that the brain sees as relevant.

■ DELC STEP 2: PREASSESSING

In order to know which objectives to teach in a unit of study, a teacher must know the students' background knowledge on that unit. A preassessment helps the teacher know which concepts or skills need more time, less time, extended learning, or just building the basic background knowledge on. Preassessments decrease the number of surprises for the teacher and the number of students who didn't master the objectives for the lesson. Students often use existing information to connect the new information. This means that to connect learning, teachers must know where the students are in their knowledge and experience of what is about to be taught. Teachers start where students are. Teachers can only do this by giving students preassessments. There are a variety of preassessments you can give to know your students better.

Know Your Students Personally

A Student Synopsis file helps you organize all the valuable information that is needed to guide students to deeper learning. It's as simple as creating a file folder for each student and placing relevant information in it so you can meet that student's needs better when the time arises (see Figure 2.4). Anytime educators need to understand a student better, create choices for projects, reteach a student, find ways to help the student feel like an expert in particular areas, or group students, teachers can look at a summary of how that student learns best. This shouldn't be that much extra work for you, because students in Grades 4 and above could complete these fun inventories on their own and give them to you. Students should know how

they learn best, and these inventories help then
learners better. Some inventories to include
might include information you find at the foll(

- Learning Styles:
  http://www.ldpride.net/learningstyle

Use the characteristics to observe your stuc
Use the strategies to help them one-on-one or

Figure 2.4 Student Synopsis

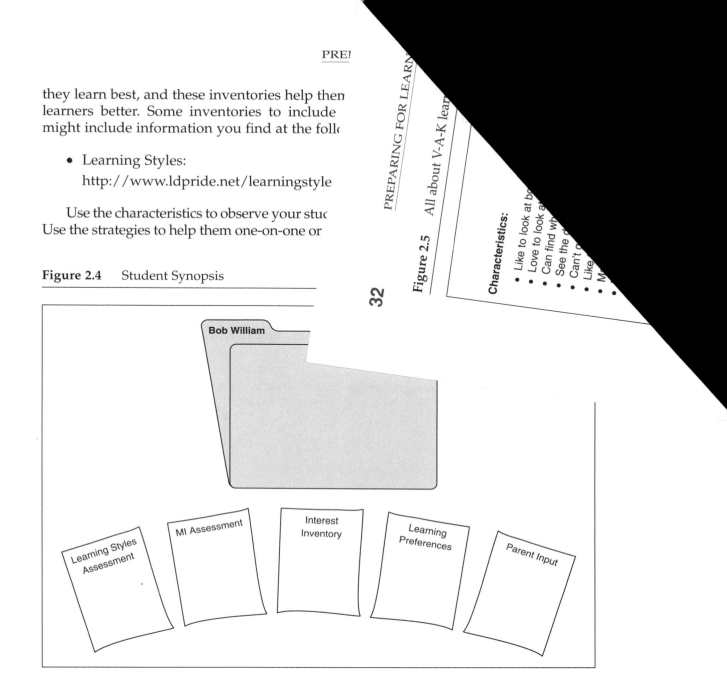

PREPARING FOR LEARN

Figure 2.5 All about V-A-K lear

32

Characteristics:
- Like to look at b
- Love to look a
- Can find wh
- See the c
- Can't
- Like

- Multiple Intelligence Results:
  http://www.mitest.com/omitest.htm (younger elementary)
  http://www.ldrc.ca/projects/miinventory/mitest.html (all ages)

- Emotional Intelligence Results:
  www.queendom.com
  www.authentichappiness.org

- Learning Preferences:
  http://www.learning-styles-online.com/inventory
  See page 62.

- Interest Inventory—Who Are You?
  http://www.outofservice.com/bigfive
  See page 64.

Visual Learners

- ...oks and pictures (would rather read than be read to)
- ...orderly things—demands neat surroundings
- ...at others have lost—remember where things have been seen
- ...etails
- ...et directions orally—need things written down
- ...o work puzzles
- ...y have speech problems
- May watch teacher's face intently
- Need overall view and purpose

Ways to Process Information:

Record, locate, calculate, simplify, imagine, prove, prepare, assess, rewrite, draw a picture of, make a web or mind map, jot down, or draw or use a graphic organizer

Teaching Strategies for Them:

- On worksheets, put a heavy line around items to help pupils to attend to one item at a time or like items
- Allow students to point if necessary; let students touch words while reading
- Have students have a clear tabletop
- Have many routines
- Give one step at a time
- Write down directions on chalkboard
- Use matching games (words and definitions; prefixes and roots, etc.)
- Use charts, graphs, maps—color
- Use highlighters to help keep track of information
- Use mirror to see mouth make sounds of words
- Allow students to work with rulers and number lines
- Use flip charts marked with colors instead of chalkboards; then hang the charts with key information around the room as you present them, and refer back to them
- Mind map information
- Stand still while presenting chunks of information; move around in between chunks
- Distribute copies of key phrases or outlines of the lesson, leaving space for notes
- Use icons to represent key concepts
- Give students overviews of information first before giving the details

Auditory Learners

Characteristics:

- Easily distracted
- Speak in rhythmic patterns
- Learn by listening, move lips/say words while reading
- Dialogue both internally and externally
- Are the chatterboxes
- Tell jokes and try to be funny
- Can win spelling bees if taught Say-Spell-Say method
- Are good storytellers
- Could have poor handwriting or letter reversals
- Know the words to several songs
- Have poor perception of time and space
- Have difficulty listening and taking notes at the same time

Ways to Process Information:

Say it to yourself or out loud, listen to the tape, discuss with a group or partner, tape the response, interview, teach others, explain, debate, create a question, or express yourself

Teaching Strategies for Them:

- Allow tape recordings of books and note taking
- Allow them to repeat out loud what you say (whispering)

- Help them to talk themselves through difficult concepts
- Turn information into a song or rap
- Play music in background during activities (not for all activities, though)
- Use vocal variation (inflection, pace, volume) in your presentation
- Teach the way you test; if you present information in a specific order or format, test the information in the same way
- Use callbacks, having students repeat key concepts and directions back
- Have students, after each chunk of teaching, tell their neighbor one thing they learned
- Develop and encourage students to come up with mnemonic devices to help them remember key concepts
- Use music pieces as cues for routine activities (e.g., circus music for cleanup)
- Decrease any noise distractions
- Use few, precise words while giving directions
- Use the same words if you repeat
- Speak directly to these children
- Have students say punctuation marks as they read to develop awareness of their functions
- Play lots of rhyming and blending games
- Pair student with a visual learner

Kinesthetic/Tactile Learners

Characteristics:

- Are movers—that's how they learn
- Want to touch and feel everything
- Rub hands along wall while in lines
- Put hands on door frames and touch desks while walking
- Often write everything—might doodle often
- Can take gadgets apart and put them back together
- Have many "things" to play with
- Enjoy doing crafts or other things with hands
- Are not clumsy—good at sports
- May be the children making paper airplanes
- Stand close to people
- Point while reading
- Memorize by walking and seeing
- Need concrete objects as learning aids
- Explore new environments intensely

Ways to Process Information:

Label and categorize, show, draw, diagram, simulate or perform a skit, construct, sculpt, create a product, experiment, use manipulatives to explain, point to, or use Post-it notes

Teaching Strategies for Them:

- Use skits, role-playing, plays with content embedded
- Memorize information by linking a movement to it
- Show them *how* to do things
- Allow them to sit on floor and work
- Use props as you teach to spark curiosity and add emphasis to key concepts
- Create simulations of concepts to allow students to experience them
- Give parallel assistance, when working with students individually, by sitting next to them rather than in front of or behind them
- Demonstrate concepts while allowing students to perform step-by-step
- Figure out ways to get them moving—movement should be a part of every lesson
- Provide a timer for when work/study time is over
- Provide a quiet, calm activity after physical activity (e.g., read aloud after PE or recess)
- Teach addition and subtraction on the monkey bars
- Let them clap or tap syllables or numbers
- Create human graphs
- Use manipulatives (tiles, magnetic letters, coins, etc.)
- Use sandpaper letters, felt letters, etc.
- Attach verbal labels on objects in classroom

Unit Preassessments

You can preassess at the beginning of every unit with a unit pretest. This is easy—it's the same as the unit posttest. The purpose of a unit preassessment is to determine what students know, understand, and can do relative to the topic. The unit pretest has two to four questions for each objective covered in that unit. Pretests are taken 3 to 4 weeks before the unit begins so that you can plan your unit better (some objectives need more time spent on them, while other objectives need less time). This allows you to differentiate the lessons in the unit more easily.

Some ideas to shorten the length of grading these unit preassessments follow:

• Have students put the period and number they're assigned to for pretests on their paper rather than their name (for example, 4:14 stands for fourth period, student number 14). This way, you can have students from Period 1 grade the preassessments from Period 4. They learn content while you go over it. This is a great way to prime the brain on what is coming in the unit. Students enjoy grading papers—let them have the opportunity to help you and prime their brains at the same time.

• Do the same as above but allow volunteers to grade them. Again, nobody will know whose paper belongs to whom.

• Make the test Scantron friendly, if you have a Scantron machine, so the machine can grade it.

Quick and Easy Preassessments

If you'd rather not give the students a long unit test, then just give them short, quick preassessments a couple of days before teaching the lesson. This gives you enough time to adjust the lesson accordingly. You might consider the following:

• T or F quiz: Write about six statements about your topic, and students must decide if they're true or false.

• K-W-L: Here is what I *know* about taxes. Here is what I *want* to learn about taxes, and here is what I did *learn* from this unit.

• Venn diagram or H diagram (page 65): Compare and contrast how the Earth orbits the sun and how the moon orbits the Earth. How are these orbits similar and different? (See Figure 2.6 for an example of how to use an H diagram.)

• Historical Event Web (page 66): Have the students place the concept in the middle of a page and brainstorm all they know about this concept in this web by extending the facts and details from the center. Students can brainstorm the who did what, where, when, why, and how of the event to the best of their ability. (See Figure 2.7 for an example of a Historical Event Web.)

• Alphabet Brainstorm (see Figure 2.8): Ask students to brainstorm all the words that go along with your topic. They are to sort these words using the first letter of the word. Example: body unit (A = amygdala, armpits, etc.). Depending on the complexity of vocabulary words they brainstorm, you might change which vocabulary words you expect them to master in this unit.

Figure 2.6 H diagram example

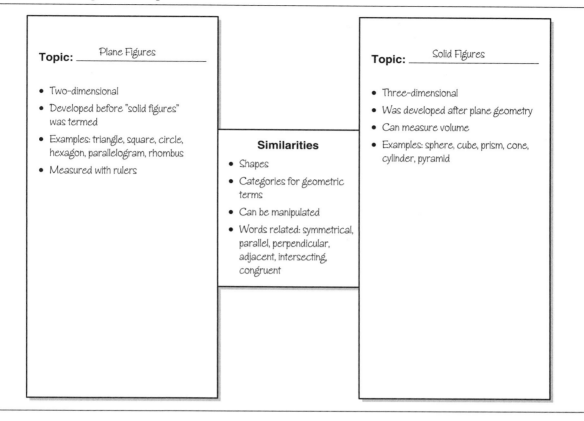

Figure 2.7 Historical Event Web example

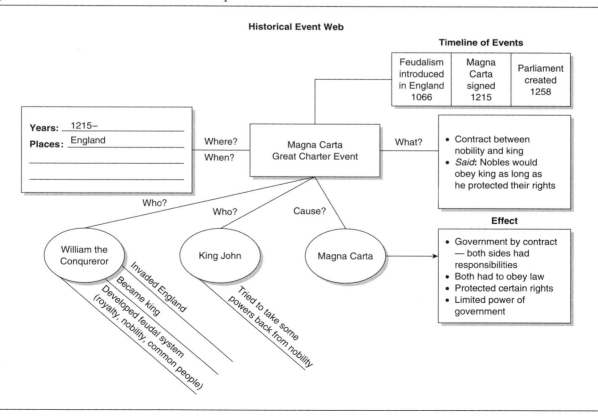

Figure 2.8   Alphabet Brainstorm example

Alphabet Brainstorm

<table>
<tr><td colspan="2">Alphabet Brainstorm
Topic: <u>Human Body Words</u>
*Categorize words that go along with this topic according to their starting letter</td><td colspan="2">Alphabet Brainstorm
Topic: <u>Human Body Words</u>
*Categorize words that go along with this topic according to their starting letter</td></tr>
<tr><td>A = ARMS</td><td>N = NECK, NOSE</td><td>A = ANKLES, AMYGDALA</td><td>N = NEUROTRANSMITTERS, NOSTRILS</td></tr>
<tr><td>B = BELLY BUTTON</td><td>O =</td><td>B = BILE</td><td>O = OCCIPITAL LOBES</td></tr>
<tr><td>C = COLLARBONE</td><td>P = PINKY</td><td>C = CELLS</td><td>P = PITUITARY GLAND</td></tr>
<tr><td>D =</td><td>Q =</td><td>D =</td><td>Q =</td></tr>
<tr><td>E = EYES</td><td>R = RIBS</td><td>E = EUSTACHIAN TUBES</td><td>R = RIBOSOMES</td></tr>
<tr><td>F = FEET</td><td>S = SKIN</td><td>F = FINGERS</td><td>S = SKIN, SMALL INTESTINES</td></tr>
<tr><td>G = GUMS IN MOUTH</td><td>T = TOES, TONGUE</td><td>G = GASTROINTESTINAL, GRAY MATTER</td><td>T = TISSUES</td></tr>
<tr><td>H = HEART</td><td>U = UNDERARMS</td><td>H = HEART</td><td>U = URINE</td></tr>
<tr><td>I = INDEX FINGER</td><td>V =</td><td>I = INTESTINES</td><td>V = VEINS</td></tr>
<tr><td>J =</td><td>W = WAIST</td><td>J = JOINTS</td><td>W = WAIST, WRIST, WHITE MATTER</td></tr>
<tr><td>K = KNEES</td><td>X =</td><td>K = KIDNEY</td><td>X =</td></tr>
<tr><td>L = LIVER</td><td>Y =</td><td>L = LIVER, LARGE INTESTINES</td><td>Y =</td></tr>
<tr><td>M = MOUTH</td><td>Z =</td><td>M = MUSCLES, MITOCHONDRIA</td><td>Z =</td></tr>
</table>

            Jane   **Sally**

- Paragraph writing: Write a paragraph or two about what you know about this concept. Remember to have a topic sentence for each paragraph.

Preassess what the students already know about the concept you're teaching. How do you know where to begin teaching if you don't know what they already know? You must understand where a student is with the existing information for the connections to occur. Preassess to know (a) where to begin your teaching based on your students' background knowledge, (b) how long you might need to spend on a certain concept, (c) how to sequence your objectives for the unit, (d) how to group students, (e) how to decide which students might be able to "clep out of" or be exempted from your unit and work on more challenging projects related to the unit, (f) how to compare knowledge before and after learning, (g) how to find experts, (h) how to see misconceptions before the unit, and (i) how to prime the students' brains for what is coming up in the unit.

DELC STEP 3: BUILDING A POSITIVE LEARNING CULTURE ■

All cells in your body are either in growth modes or protection modes. In growth modes, new dendrites are being produced, new synapses are forming, and new learning occurs. This mode can even happen while you sleep. You want your students' brain cells to be in growth modes in your classrooms. This is done by making sure students are in safe surroundings, in positive relationships with students and teachers, and in positive, motivated states of mind. As teachers, you need to facilitate the building of this positive learning culture.

Culture is the creation, maintenance, or modification of a unique body of ideas, customs, skills, language, and arts of a people or group that are transferred, communicated, or passed along. So how do you help your students be part of this positive learning culture with cells in growth modes versus protection modes? First consider how protection modes are encountered.

In an unsafe, hunker-down, protection mode, our brain is conserving resources, reducing blood flow to nonessential areas, and directing it to large muscle groups. Some teachers call on unprepared learners just to embarrass them or "put them in their place." That's a mistake; when teachers embarrass students, it's likely to cause states of anger or resentment. These strong emotions impair cognitive processing (Simpson, Snyder, Gusnard, & Rachiele, 2001). When a student is anxious or under moderate to strong threat, the capacity to do deeper thinking is highly impaired (Mogg, Bradley, & Hallowell, 1994).

In growth mode, there is the "right" amount of emotion embedded in the learning context. Examples of emotion are curiosity, anticipation, excitement, little confusion, little sadness, and laughter. The student feels safe to take risks, such as answering a challenging question, giving his or her opinion, and volunteering. In short, safety allows the brain to be able to allocate resources for complex understandings. This is critical because our emotions and cognition are interrelated (Gray, Braver, & Raichle, 2002).

To ensure growth mode for your students' brain cells, you must provide them with a safe environment. The following are a few important facets of a safe environment:

- Predictable activities or routines and rituals are in place.
- Rules are in place for location of materials (scissors, etc.).
- There are no put-downs, but instead lots of positive reinforcement.
- Teachers have high expectations for all students.
- Students enjoy the classroom—laugh, smile, are on task, and so on.
- Many opportunities are given for students to share their ideas with other students.
- Appropriate changes are made so that students are successful.
- Students and teachers respect one another's differences and ideas.
- Students seem to have a sense of calm versus being stressed out.
- Students' strengths are honored and valued in the classroom.
- Students have multiple opportunities for choice.
- Celebrations and affirmations occur regularly.

Teacher-Student Relationship

Positive relationships are a must and a "safety issue" for learning to occur. Many students can learn just fine without a close relationship with their teacher. But for others, it's essential. Teachers who understand students' strengths, growth opportunities, background knowledge, interests, and learning preferences can make more relevant connections with their students. If students trust you and know that what you're doing is best for them, they will be motivated in your classroom. This type of motivation is empowering for the student. If you know your students well enough, you will know which strategies are best for them. You will also make sure that each assignment is doable for each student—that means each student will experience success. A positive relationship is also the key to cooperation among your students. Strengthen your connection with your students, and witness the cooperation. When students sense and know that you truly care about them, they are more willing to accept your classroom expectations. Caring is the ability to bring out the best in children by giving positive feedback and encouragement and providing successful learning experiences. Specific attributes that demonstrate caring are listening, being gentle, understanding, having a knowledge of students as individuals, being warm and encouraging, and having an overall love for children.

To care means to know and interact appropriately with your students. Research gathered by James H. Stronge (2002) shows how knowing and interacting with your students affects them:

- Effective teachers said that one key element for their success was consistently emphasizing their care for their students.
- Caring teachers create a warm, supportive classroom culture, which is a key element in caring for students.
- Caring teachers are aware of their students' cultural surroundings at home.
- Caring teachers appropriately respect confidential information.
- Effective teachers work "with" students rather than doing things to and for them.

- Effective teachers give responsibility to their students and treat secondary students like adults when appropriate.
- Effective teachers allow students to own the classroom too—to share in the decision making.
- Effective teachers care about and listen to what their students have to contribute.

Research suggests (Darling-Hammond, 2000) that teacher enthusiasm has a profound influence on student motivation and learning in the following ways:

- There is a direct correlation between a teacher's enthusiasm for the subject matter and student achievement.
- A teacher's enthusiasm for learning his or her current subject matter has been shown to increase student motivation.
- A teacher's participation in graduate studies, which shows a love for learning, may be a source of motivation and may affect student achievement.

Teachers can do several things to foster a positive relationship with their students. Be sure to study the list below and evaluate which areas are your strengths and which areas you'd like to improve.

How to Strengthen Your Relationships With Your Students

1. Listen to your students. Listen to their stories, to their responses in the classroom, to their conversations with other students (as long as they're not private), and to their writing. You learn more about others by just taking the time to listen.

2. Provide students with interest inventories that ask them about their hobbies and how they like to spend their spare time.

3. Greet them at the door and say good-bye to your students as they leave your classroom. Eye contact and smiles are very powerful.

4. Talk with students in the hall while they're switching classes or during lunch while you pop in to get your lunch.

5. Share your life with them. Your writing examples could be about your life. The more real you become to them, the more trust they will have in you.

6. Treat them all with respect. Are there certain students you don't click with? We guarantee it will show—students know. Your biases will come out one way or another. Inequities affect motivation.

Evaluate yourself in the following areas:

Do I have more personal interactions with some students than others?

Is my proximity to my students equal?

Do I smile equally to every student or just my favorites?

Do I give adequate response opportunities to all students?

Do I assume that kids who are different from me are troublemakers?

Teachers could have biases based on gender, readiness levels, race, culture, religion, status, and a host of other areas. A healthy attitude is to assume that all people have biases; some are just more blatant and harmful than others. Give your behaviors a hard look, and you'll see where you can make some adjustments.

These are just a few suggestions for ensuring a positive relationship with your students. Evaluate how caring you are toward all students and which biases you need to work through so that all students feel the positive bond between you and them. Not only the teacher-to-student relationship but also the student-to-student relationship is important for building a positive learning environment.

Student-to-Student Relationships

As students work together in positive ways, they're more likely to take on higher challenges. This can support the process for deeper learning. Relationships are built in the classroom in numerous ways, especially through cooperative learning opportunities. Let's focus on the benefits of cooperative learning according to research and then on how to implement cooperative groups in the classroom.

Why Use Cooperative Learning?

Cooperative learning, as opposed to individualistic learning, has been shown in numerous studies to promote higher achievement across all age levels, across subject areas, and on almost all tasks. If you compare students who are in cooperative groups with those doing the tasks individually and competing individually, the collaborative social strategy produces better learning and works better (Johnson, Johnson, & Taylor, 1993; Walberg, 1999). Early studies suggested that cooperative learning was very effective, and it has been used effectively with all types of students, including at-risk students (Ginsburg-Block & Fantuzzo, 1998) at the elementary level. Other studies corroborate this effect, showing that a quality cooperative learning strategy outperforms random grouping or individual learning (Lipsey & Wilson, 1993).

Teachers may see an increase in students' emotional intelligence skills (Johnson et al., 1993), status, and self-esteem (Petersen, Johnson, & Johnson, 1991). These skills are important because social skills may influence achievement in groups (Chiu & Khoo, 2003). Even when distance learning is used, compared either with individual study or with multimedia approaches, the cooperative learning results are superior (Boling & Robinson, 1999).

Many side benefits of cooperative learning have surfaced in the literature. These include the fact that it may help develop cognitive abilities, improve working memory and everyday decision-making ability, and improve emotional intelligence status and self-esteem. Developing these social skills early in life may also enhance a child's intellectual skills. This is especially important in children who are shy or who are by nature more introverted than their peers. Thus parents and teachers can use the critical balance between mental exercise (i.e., from such intellectual activities as reading, puzzle work, and computer use) and social exercise (i.e., from unstructured play, cooperative or team learning, recess, and informal conversation). Try it out yourself to see the powerful benefits to your students.

Skill Clusterings and Learning

Skill clustering (temporary small groups for a specific purpose) is highly controversial because of the potential implications for academic and life status. One study (Lou et al., 1996) found that students of all skill levels could benefit from skill clustering when contrasted to a heterogeneous grouping (a group of students with varying skill levels). The student groups that benefited the least in a homogeneous ability group are those with low achievement—they do better when placed in multiability groups. In general, there's a serious negative effect when low-achieving students are placed in low-achieving groups for a long period of time (Lou et al., 1996). Understandably, parents want their own children in groups that are either equal to or above the ability level of the other students.

Yet tracking can reduce the peer effect and can be very detrimental to students' self-esteem, according to a RAND Corporation study by Ron Zimmer (2003). After all, students often but not always live up (or down) to the class norms. Temporary low-ability homogeneous groups may be helpful if done well and sparingly for a specific purpose. For example, many students need to be pulled out of regular classes to get small group instruction in comprehension strategies for reading. In a small, lower-skilled cluster, a qualified special education teacher, occupational therapist, or paraprofessional can watch for and listen for responses that a general education teacher may be unaware of or lack the time to observe. This small group professional can also make more specific microsuggestions that will accelerate the learning that can happen in the larger, mixed-skill clustering.

Inclusion classrooms were encouraged by many educators during the last 10 years. Inclusion has its virtues, but we need to remember the power of one-on-one or small group intervention. Often certain students need specific, high-feedback skill building that requires focused attention, motivation, and constant error correction by a content or behavior specialist. The research tells us that without the pullout programs (just the opposite of inclusive classrooms, where students receive much of their support from a teacher other than the regular classroom teacher), many kids struggle for years. Many skilled teachers try to do this with heterogeneous classes while at the same time trying to meet the needs of general education, behaviorally and cognitively challenged, as well as gifted students. It's easy for a school district to tell a teacher to teach in these classrooms, but how many teachers do you know who want to, or can, handle the responsibilities of an inclusion classroom?

The important issue is how grouping is done and the corresponding teacher affect. Some effective teaching strategies may ameliorate the negative social impact tracking may have on self-esteem. In high-quality pullout sessions, children emerge stronger. Any student who is in the lower background knowledge class all day knows it. However, there is no problem when a student is in several groups throughout the week, some lower and some higher. Any temporary negative effects, such as a dip in self-confidence, by being in a lower group are overpowered by the positive feelings of successful new skill building. When low-ability students are placed in a group together for a specific lesson, concept, or skill (temporarily, we repeat, temporarily), sometimes these students are less inhibited from participating, answering a question, or stating their opinions, because they're with other students who have similar background knowledge and won't appear superior. What matters most is how students have grown and how they feel at the end of the day. The take-home message here is that you want the best situation for each student. Some students need intense one-on-one instruction in some subject areas while others need small flexible groups to support their learning.

Heterogeneous Groups

There are many cooperative learning options for teachers to choose from, such as heterogeneous grouping, which is a small group of diverse students. Some of the differences these students might have are readiness, interests, multiple intelligences, and processing style. In fact, most of the grouping in our classrooms was heterogeneous. This type of grouping encourages students to learn from one another's strengths and differences. For example, you could take a student with high background knowledge on the topic of solving division problems, a student with lower background knowledge on the topic of solving division problems, and a student who does well on this concept but still needs assistance and place all of them together in one group to create their own division word problems together. The benefit is that all students can use their strengths to help each other accomplish the goal.

Cooperative learning pioneers David Johnson and Roger Johnson (1999) have a distinct model for cooperative learning. Their model defines one of the key elements of cooperative learning as positive interdependency, because positive time with established peers reduces stress. But a poorly collected, organized, and exercised group of kids could also spiral downhill if social factors like harmony and respect are ignored. Poor social designs increase stress, which produces cortisol. Excess cortisol is stimulated by the perception of negative expectations (Lupien & Lepage, 2001). In a social group, this can lead to impaired cognition, memory, and social judgment.

Putting students together in a relevant social structure is more effective. This means students are likely to engage more in groupings that make sense to them based on content expertise, student roles, or the amount of task relevancy in their personal lives. For example, kids from the same neighborhood may be highly vested in a task on identifying health risks they share in common.

Among those interviewed who are using cooperative social support, the perception is that the academic challenges are more achievable (Ghaith, 2002), and in fact, students do achieve more. Even if the increase in achievement is not always robust, other social values are typically improved (Gillies & Ashman, 1998). The effects of social variables are critical: Are the students isolated or in pairs, teams, clubs, or a whole group? In addition, kids work better with others they feel comfortable with, not a bully or one who they feel is not contributing to the group's chances for success. Any of these factors can influence the student's chances for success, and the potential cannot be either isolated or underestimated. Part of the value of positive social experiences is that they generate peer acceptance and approval. That boost in self-esteem creates hope and optimism, which influence brain chemistry and capability assessments. Use a variety of social structures. Students enjoy having a home "base group" or "family" for the daily or weekly routine and comfort. This can be the group they meet in to start the day at the secondary level and also to end the day at the primary level. This social group doesn't need to satisfy all the students' emotional needs, but it should provide a dependable initial structure for engaging in academics.

In the elementary grades, small classes or cooperative learning groups (usually four students) may be the most appropriate social structure. At the high school level, the use of more varied structures may work better. These include "project teams," or loosely organized pairs or triads for specific short-term goals.

Don't forget the power of heterogeneously grouping students based on their readiness levels. Many times teachers group their students so that a student with a higher level of background knowledge is grouped with a student with a lower level of background knowledge, and by doing so, one could help the other. During this reciprocal teaching experience, there can be a 90% or more retention level 24 hours later. So both students benefit—the one who teaches remembers the information better, while the one who is gathering more information from the other student understands the concept better because it's coming from a peer's mouth.

Now that we've described multiple ways to group students—homogeneously through skill clustering or tiering for particular lessons, or heterogeneously through interest, readiness, or random groups—you're ready to dive into structuring all these groups so they're successful and all students are equally challenged and learning optimally during the group session.

How to Structure Cooperative Learning So It's Successful

Processing *information* can happen independently, with partners, or in small groups. In order for processing *or thinking* to be successful in small groups, you need to structure your cooperative learning with the following three components in mind:

1. Set up a positive learning culture.

2. Hold them accountable.

3. Keep it organized.

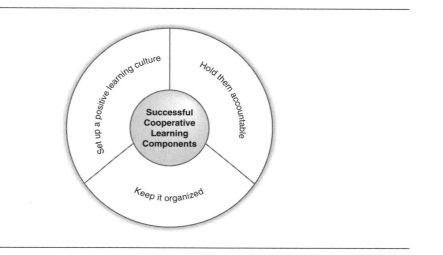

Set Up a Positive Learning Culture

Setting up a positive learning culture in cooperative groups is a must for positive interaction and powerful learning. For students to accomplish a learning goal, cooperation must exist in small groups. The following ideas should assist you in achieving a culture that brings about powerful learning in cooperative groups. A set of group rules or expectations promotes positive interactions between the students, especially if they get to create these rules. A written philosophy about the culture sets the tone for group work, and team-building activities encourage a cohesive, friendly competition.

Empowering students is a great way to promote the intrinsic motivation of all students. We always asked our students to help create the classroom rules. We believe that classroom rules are important, and we also believe there should be another set of rules just for cooperative learning activities so the brain focuses specifically on these rules in groups. Fortunately, the cooperative learning rules always reflect the classroom rules but are more specific for groups. For example, our students brainstormed the way they would want to be treated in cooperative groups. They listed what they would want to hear and see from others in their groups. After much combining, all the rules were grouped into two large categories: respect and responsibility. The specifics were listed under these categories like this:

Respect	*Responsibility*
Help each other (and other groups)	Stay on task—keep group goal in mind
Encourage and compliment each other	Put 100% into your role
Listen to each other actively	Achieve group goal in the time allotted

From these rules, the students created a rubric of expectations that would be used to evaluate how they performed in their small groups. See page 67 for a reproducible called Team Talk that encourages students to evaluate how well their group kept the group rules. Usually the "reporter" of the group writes the responses down for the whole group on the one Team Talk sheet, but all group members contribute their opinions of the ratings.

Written Philosophy

All educators know how important mission statements, or philosophies, are. In fact, some administrators spend so much time creating the mission statement that they forget to create the plan for how to achieve that mission. When a mission statement is in place, the brain knows the bigger picture that all strategies should point to. All cooperative groups, classroom and group rules, behavior, strategies, and values of a classroom can be summed up in the philosophy of the classroom. It's important to ask the students to contribute to this classroom mission statement or philosophy.

Here's an example of a philosophy that was created by a classroom in Alton, Illinois, by Dolores Ann Heim, a retired teacher:

Classroom Team

A classroom is like a baseball team. Some like to catch or pitch to fulfill their dream.

Some hit a home run and some run from base to base. With learning, these differences are things we must face.

We all have different strengths, needs, and learning styles, with lots of different missions and varied learning trials.

We all learn at different rates, such as when we memorize math facts or important dates.

We use these different strengths to help each other out because working together is what it's all about.

Catcher, pitcher, shortstop, they all are important positions, but all think differently and have different missions.

But we're all winners because we give it our all, so let's get ready, get set, and let's PLAY BALL!

"Classroom Team" is used with permission by Mrs. Heim.

This philosophy set the climate for the whole year. All the students signed it, memorized it, and used it throughout each day.

Team-Building Activities

To create a positive thinking culture, each group or team needs to plan routines or rituals for that cohesive bond. Team cheers, team handshakes, or team names are just some of the many ways to keep a team close in order to achieve a goal. Each team should have its own special rituals for when team members are together for their purpose. Since groups change often, the rituals should end when the group has accomplished its goal. These team-building activities energize students to do their best—they feel connected to their group, which can bring about intrinsic motivation among the members.

Group rules or expectations, written philosophies about the expected classroom culture, and team-building activities encourage a positive learning culture in which groups thrive and work powerfully within. Now that they know the expectations, it's time to hold them accountable to utilize this information.

Hold Them Accountable

When you empower students, you see them rise to the occasion. Giving students responsibilities helps them feel empowered. Groups are most successful when students stay on task, and to encourage this, you need to make sure that each student has a specific, different role to play every time the group meets; each group has a specific goal to accomplish; and students know exactly what is expected of them and how they're going to be graded during this group time.

Roles for Students During Group Time

While your students are working in groups, you want to encourage their equal participation. For that to happen, each student needs a responsibility that can be evaluated. Because there are so many responsibilities in groups, students should share the load and have different roles that are needed for a successful cooperative learning opportunity. Some roles might be the following:

- Reader—Reads aloud any passages that need to be read to the whole group.
- Recorder or Scribe—Writes the needed information for the whole group.
- Reporter—Announces to the whole class information that is requested from each group.
- Checker—Checks to make sure that all criteria on the rubric have been met.
- Materials Manager—Ensures that all team members have the supplies they need to do their jobs or roles. Retrieves and returns all supplies.
- Illustrator—Draws or diagrams anything that is needed for the group.
- Scout—Visits other groups to scout out other ideas or answers to questions that the group has.
- Group Leader or Facilitator—Makes sure that everyone understands the directions and their roles.
- Timekeeper—Keeps track of time so the group can accomplish the goal in the time allotted.
- Coach or Validator—Encourages others in their roles so that the group goal can be accomplished—the cheerleader of the group.

This list is just a sampling of some of the roles that your cooperative groups might have. Use the roles that are needed to accomplish the goal smoothly. Remember to encourage students to try out different roles each time their group meets. That way everyone has the opportunity to try out a new responsibility and grow in new ways.

At the beginning of the year, we encouraged our students to brainstorm what each of these roles look like and sound like. After each role was defined this way by the students, we created role cards so that the students could have the cards sitting in front of them to remind them of their duties. Here is an example:

Reporter

Looks Like:

- Encourages the recorder to write certain pieces of information down that can be shared at the end of the group time. Sits next to the recorder to assist.
- Summarizes during the group time when needed.
- If a question is asked by the teacher at a certain point, the reporter is the one to answer once he or she has collaborated with other group members.

Sounds Like:

- Our group enjoyed the following about this group activity:
- Our group didn't understand the following about this group activity:
- Our group learned that . . .
- Our group did a great job at . . .
- Our group could improve on . . . next time.
- Our group's next step will be to . . .
- To summarize our learning:
- Our group was challenged when . . .

Specific Goals to Accomplish

Nothing frustrates members of a meeting more than when there isn't any direction or agenda. In fact, faculty meetings could last forever if an agenda weren't made. There should always be a purpose for group meetings. Students need to know what is expected of them during their team meeting time. In other words, students must know what they should accomplish during the time they have as a group for that particular day. The goal should be posted, and the details of the goal should be listed.

The goal might be that students create a web using the word cards and Post-it notes (for big categories) on the topic of the three branches of government.

The details might be as follows:

Team Name: _____

Roles for this activity: Timekeeper, Materials Manager, Recorder, and Reporter

Graded by: Criteria being met; summary written with support; category correctness

Goal Details:

- ☐ The students will take the word cards, group them according to how similar they are to one another.
- ☐ Then students will label these similar groupings or chunks with Post-it notes, making sure that there are at least two words per category.
- ☐ When all students are content with the web, the reporter will share a summary of the web that the group just created, making sure to justify why words were placed in certain categories.

Keep It Organized

For groups to accomplish their task in the time allotted, the teacher needs to be able to keep all the cooperative learning aspects organized. The following are strategies that many teachers around the United States have used for years to structure their cooperative learning groups.

1. Visualize the whole activity the day before. This allows you to better predict any possible problems that might occur during the activity. Also it ensures that you have all the supplies ready.

2. Have a way to get your students into their groups quickly. Show them a bird's-eye view of where they will be sitting. Just draw with a permanent marker on a transparency a setup of your classroom and write their names with markers on the desks you have drawn that they will sit at, or write their names in the location of the room where you want them to work. Here are some ideas: play a fun song ("Walk Like an Egyptian") for only 15 seconds and tell them to walk like an Egyptian to their location; give them 10 seconds to get to their location by being as quiet as they can—rate them afterward; give them a verb like "saunter" and ask them to saunter to their group location.

3. Have a routine in place for asking questions during group time. For example, you might have the Question Asker as an assigned role in the group. Only this student is allowed to ask the teacher a question after that student has asked at least three other students and checked with another group for the answer.

4. Create a big organizer poster for your cooperative groups. This poster should be laminated and written on only with an erasable marker so it can be used for every cooperative learning activity. This poster should have the group rules that students created, the roles needed for the activity, the goal, time allotted, what to do when group work is complete, where to turn in group work, and a Team Talk evaluation sheet. Team Talk is on page 67 and is helpful for keeping students focused on their roles and responsibilities during the cooperative learning event. See page 68 for the Group Work Expectations poster that will help you organize all of the details of the cooperative learning event.

These three major points—setting up a positive learning culture, holding the students accountable, and keeping it all organized—gives you the confidence that your cooperative learning groups will learn at higher levels during their grouping activities because of the procedures you've put in place.

In many classes, the way cooperative learning is used produces just a fraction of the potential benefits. Used properly, it has far more capacity for change than grouping alone does. The strategy of cooperative learning serves many functions: it is inclusive, social, and active, and it can drive depth of learning while still providing greater feedback. Cooperative learning is one opportunity for students to enjoy the learning process with the content they need to learn and to have an opportunity to foster that love of learning. There are so many benefits to bringing this learning opportunity into your classroom.

Positive, Motivated, Vested State of Mind

Teachers want students to care about their learning. Students get vested when they care about the learning enough to lean forward, listen, take notes, and persist until they succeed. Teachers want students to care about what they're doing in school. It's critical and essential, because when they care enough, *most will overcome nearly any other obstacle* to learning. Without this intrinsic motivation or vesting, you can use advance organizers or monitor instructional time or test until you're blue in the face. But teachers have to face reality: nothing matters *until students care.* This is given such a high status as a make-or-break necessity for complex learning because emotions drive students' attention, their learning, meaning making, and memory, as well as students' decision making, their friendships, work ethic, class effort, participation, and motivation to learn.

Vesting is the emotional drive to learn. Human beings have a brain, which, by design and function, allows emotions to have a significant influence over most of our life (Bechara, Damasio, & Damasio, 2003). Emotions are always found in widely accepted motivational theories. Deci's self-determination theory (SDT) has evolved over the past 30 years and has also been validated by a wide body of research (Ryan & Deci, 2000). Here are the three primary components of Deci's theory.

1. *Emotions:* Positive feelings about *who* (those you work with or you, the teacher) and/or *what* (the relevance factor of the content) *(give people a reason to care).*

   Some examples of this component:

   - Make it personal (something dealing with students' family, friends, neighborhood, or property).
   - Make it urgent (create deadlines).
   - Make it fun (the rewards of either the process or the end point).
   - Put more stakes in the outcome (very strong positive outcome vs. detrimental one).
   - Get the learners to care about you too.

2. *Assets:* Competency, efficacy, beliefs, hope (building student assets is critical to establishing vesting).

   Some examples of this component:

   - Have plenty of affirmations.
   - Track progress to see the capacity to change.
   - Explain how the brain changes to encourage others to try.
   - Tell stories of others who have succeeded.
   - Do skill building in the specific skills needed for the task (writing, reading, planning, problem solving, etc.).

3. *Direction:* Autonomy, freedom, goals, choice (goal-driven learning works for most; our energy needs a direction; for some it's freedom, for others, a clear goal)

   Some examples of this component:

   - Be sure to have students set goals.
   - Allow them to choose from multiple options.
   - Have students also establish a strong understanding of why they want to reach their goals and how their life will benefit from these goals.
   - Track the goals for continuous feedback. Use the reproducible on page 254 to keep track of their goals and the strategies to achieve them.

Because students vary in their "motivational buttons," it's important that you use multiple strategies. The three factors above show up in any motivational study. In fact, the data show that each of these is an independent and significant factor in explaining achievement (Miller, Greene, Montalvo, Ravindran, & Nichols, 1996). Just one of them has a positive influence on reaching goals; achievement is more likely when two or three of the factors are engaged. Any author, researcher, consultant, teacher, or administrator who ignores this fundamental law, this all-essential, affective side, is missing the driving force behind the behaviors of human beings.

For many years Glasser (1986) effectively argued that schools that organize instruction around responsible choice are much better for motivation and learning. The concept of choice sounds exciting to some and frightening to others. If given a choice, will students be motivated to achieve? Some will and some won't. In the Netherlands, a new program allows for significant choice at the high school level. Some students are thriving; others don't even make it to school. It's clear that choice has to be part of a larger academic and social climate that encourages curiosity, striving, and achieving. Another powerful factor for student motivation is hope.

Not long ago, a successful graduate of the Eugene Lang School in the Bronx was making a speech to the sixth graders at a low-income middle school graduation. At the last moment, he tore up his rah-rah speech and made a shocking pledge that he would pay for the college tuition of any of the kids from that class who went on to graduate from high school (6 years away). The parents and the students at this high-poverty school were dumbfounded and ebullient with the explosive meaning of that statement.

During the next 6 years, nothing changed in the curriculum, instruction, or assessment in the schools for those 61 kids. Statistically, 30 of them would graduate from high school, and very few of those would go to college. Yet now these children, who never dreamed of going to college, suddenly had a date with destiny. A few years later, 58 of the 61 kids graduated from high school and went to college. That group of kids gave the school the highest graduation rate it ever had. Hope is a powerful thing for both parents and kids. The benefactor was serious, and years later he made good on his promise. This is a true story, and although a study was never published in a quality peer-reviewed journal, it suggests that hope can make a difference. Some naysayers may be tempted to dismiss the power of hope. Don't make that mistake. Genuine hope, backed by a personal promise of support, is priceless.

We have explored how to create a safe environment, how to enhance the teacher-to-student relationship and the student-to-student relationship, and how to facilitate motivating students to be positive, vested learners in our learning culture. Now here are some specific suggestions.

The Aura of Positive Affect

There are invisible, pleasant components that create the positive affect in a classroom. These components deepen learning and processing, increase motivation in the participants, create positive learning cultures, and overall, just make you want to be there. This is the big picture of education.

Your Presence and Overall Mood

The following quotation by Haim Ginott (1975) explains this most valuable point:

> I've come to the frightening conclusion that I am the decisive element in the classroom. It's my personal approach that creates the climate. It's my daily mood that makes the weather. As a teacher, I have a tremendous power to make a child's life miserable or joyous. I can be a tool of torture or an instrument of inspiration. I can humiliate or humor, hurt or heal. In all situations, it is my response that decides whether a crisis will be escalated or deescalated and a child humanized or dehumanized.

We can't emphasize enough the most important factor in your classroom: *you!* It starts with your presence, your energy, your smile, your encouragement, and your overall mood.

Edgar Allen Poe said, "When I wish to find out how good or how wicked anyone is, or what are his thoughts at the moment, I fashion the expression of my face, as accurately as possible, in accordance with the expression of his, and then wait to see what thoughts or sentiments arise in my own mind or heart, as if to match or correspond with the expression" (Levenson, Ekman, & Friesen, 1990). Swedish researchers found that by observing pictures of a happy face, human beings' facial muscles start to mimic the picture's face, whether it's sad, happy, disgusted, or joyful (Dimberg & Thunberg, 1998). This research suggests that you can catch a feeling from someone else. As teachers, you can change your students' states of mind just by being in a particular mood. Your presence affects your relationship with the students. Three key ingredients for a positive relationship are (1) acceptance—of who and where the child is, (2) connection—you're warmly interested and sensitive or responsive to the child's needs, and (3) supportive—respecting the growing autonomy of the student.

Implications/Examples

- Greet them at the door with a smile and your special way of greeting (high five, side hug, elbow touch, etc.).
- Talk informally throughout the school day about students' interests.
- Have lunch with students every now and then.
- Be aware and comment on the growth of students with positive notes home and phone calls.
- Compliment students on their achievements outside the classroom.
- Try first to understand instead of being understood. Listen to your students wholeheartedly.
- Avoid emotional extremes when dealing with your students.
- Rather than take their bad behavior personally, think what could be going on in their lives to cause such behavior.

Respecting Their Interests

Do you seem to excel in activities and projects when you're more interested in the topic? We think that all would agree that students are more likely to dive into an assignment if they're interested in it. How can teachers stimulate and respect their students' interests in the classroom?

In order to respect students' interests, teachers have to know about them and internalize them. The first step in respecting and therefore encouraging students' interests is to create a Who Are You? Interest Inventory (see page 64) for the students to complete. Ask them questions about what they do in their spare time, what sports they like to play and watch, what books or genre they pick up, and overall, what they really enjoy doing. These questions assist you in understanding your students better and then reaching out to them in a way that encourages a love for learning.

We always encouraged our students to be the ones to choose what they read. Obviously, there is a time and place to choose it for them (classics, novels, historical fiction, etc.). You'll find that students will read more if they're interested in the book. Richard Ryan (Ryan, Connell, & Plant, 1990), a psychologist at the University of Rochester, found that the greater the students' interest and enjoyment in the reading material, the more concepts they recalled from the passage and the better they comprehended the book. A follow-up study also showed that students' interest in material also helped them remember it over the long term.

Giving students choices encourages them to learn more about their interests or to choose strategies they're comfortable with to learn more about a topic. In one research study, students were given the choice between three out of six puzzles to work on. These students persisted longer and expressed more interest in the puzzles than the control group of students who didn't have a choice. Research has validated this concept of autonomy (Deci, Koestner, & Ryan, 1999). While giving choices to students, teachers need to make sure that any and all choices set students up for success, so teachers should take the time to structure the choices for success.

One year, while teaching in Texas, I (LeAnn) had six students who were very interested in horses. I didn't know much about horses, so I decided to take horseback riding lessons with these six students. After several lessons, I understood why they loved it so much. I provided them with horse books to read, newspaper clips about horses, and magazine articles about horses and just talked with them about their continuing horseback riding lessons. I still stay in touch with some of these students. They knew I cared, but most important, I encouraged a love of learning about horses by showing an interest in their favorite pastime.

Eleanor Roosevelt (1983, p. 14) said, "When you are genuinely interested in one thing it will always lead to something else." Keep this in mind while you help students explore their interests and while you respect their interests.

Implications/Examples

- Give your students choices often (homework assignments, which project to do, which questions to answer for research, which book to read, etc.).
- Give students interest inventories so you can match up your lessons with what they're interested in.
- See page 182 for a processing activity called Choosing Your Task: Structured Choices. These choices are for projects that go along with students' understanding of the content at hand.

Enjoyment

Southwest Airlines staff is trained to keep the whole process of flying more fun for the customer. The company's attitude is that when something is fun, you can't stop people from doing it. When you enjoy what you're doing, you don't want to stop. You see students lost in a dream during their learning moments when they're thoroughly enjoying it. They get frustrated when you have to end the activity in order to move on to the next one. There are other benefits from making the learning enjoyable too.

Not only does enjoyable learning elicit intrinsic motivation, but it also can bring about higher standardized test scores and less anxiety. Adele Eskeles Gottfried (1985), a psychologist at California State University, Northridge, found that the more that students enjoyed academics, the higher were their standardized test scores and grades in reading, social studies, and science. She also found that the more kids enjoyed schoolwork, the less anxious they were about it.

It's imperative that teachers make sure that students are enjoying the learning process through fun activities that support the concepts or skills being taught. There are many aspects of enjoyment, but one that definitely belongs in the classroom is laughter.

Humor and Laughter

Humor is creativity plus play. It's finding new, unexpected, creative connections between things. Humor helps students enjoy the classroom and learn more. They also link positive feelings toward learning, which in turn foster a love of learning.

Effective teachers demonstrate a sense of fun and play. They also have a good sense of humor and are willing to share jokes. Learners prefer teachers with a sense of humor—not someone who just tells jokes but someone who has the ability to pleasantly communicate rules and expectations about acceptable behavior from the participants. Instructors are expected to help participants understand when their behavior has reached the extremes of the desirable to undesirable behavior spectrum; of all aspects of teaching and training, audiences most value a presenter's ability to moderate behavior with humor and skill.

Without emotion, learning is very limited. How you bring emotion into your lessons allows the participants to decide if they're interested in the topic, if they want to learn it, if they should believe it, and if they should remember it. These are just a few of the very important decisions that are made based on the emotion of the lesson. A very effective strategy to engage students and to invite them to love learning is to use humor and laughter effectively in the classroom. Some other benefits of using this strategy are a reduction in anxiety, an improvement in student receptiveness to difficult material, an enhancement of creative thinking abilities, an enhancement of recall, an improvement in student-teacher relationship, and healthier teachers. People learn more easily when stress is reduced because they become more emotionally and intellectually open to the learning experience. A well-placed joke or other display of humor not only makes us laugh and feel good but can also, in the right learning situation, promote better attention and recall while creating an atmosphere more conducive to learning.

But studies also indicate that learning saturated with humor and laughter can produce undesired results. Gorham and Christophel (1990) demonstrated that teachers who showed an overdependence on humor were looked upon negatively by students. The key is to have a balanced approach to using humor and laughter in the classroom. Below are a few ideas that should get you started with humor and laughter in your classroom.

Ideas and Strategies to Enhance Humor and
Laughter in Your Classroom

• Open your lesson with a joke or a funny personal story and immediately invite your audience to improve on it or tell a better one. Plan this as your grabber.

• Clip cartoons and jokes and post them around the room or photocopy them on handouts. Be tasteful in your selections—your goal is to amuse, not to hurt feelings or cause anger. Ask students to bring in their favorites as well.

• For special events or to introduce a few minutes of unexpected fun, show clips from movies to enhance the learning. For example, we play a scene from the movie *Father of the Bride* (Shyer, 1991) when we teach about lowest common multiples. When Steve Martin (George Banks in the movie) goes into the grocery store to purchase hot dogs and buns, he gets very frustrated that the bun company puts more buns in their packaging than there are hot dogs in their packaging. He refuses to pay for these superfluous buns and takes them out. Then we ask the students, "How many hot dogs and hot dog buns does he need to purchase so there aren't any leftovers and he doesn't have to open any containers in the store?"

• Surround yourself with funny, playful colleagues. Look for the fun in life and take time to play a little each day.

• Have a set of energizers ready for your students when you see them getting the afternoon blues. Here are some of our favorites:

1. www.ncpe4me.com has great energizers for the elementary and middle school classroom.

2. Have a student lead a group of students into stretches to a funny song.

• Cross-laterals (when one side of the body crosses over to the other side) are good exercises for the brain. For example, put your left elbow on your raised right knee and vice versa; take your right arm and keep it straight while you stretch it over to the left side of your body and vice versa; crisscross them several times; put both of your hands together in front of you with your arms straight; draw a big figure eight while keeping both hands together.

• If you aren't comfortable or especially adept at joke telling or humor, don't try it. Instead, find an appropriate joke and read it to the class or make use of an audio or visual rendering by a professional comedian or cartoonist to make your point. We had Garfield Moments in our classroom where we shared some of our favorite comics by placing them on the overhead projector. Encourage students to bring in their favorite comics.

• Design activities that encourage moments of laughter. Spontaneous humor that arises naturally from the context of the classroom is preferable to canned anecdotes or forced jokes.

• Interject humor into the day by including a humorous twist to the objectives (such as inventing a ridiculous course prerequisite), introducing yourself with a Top 10 list in the style of David Letterman, or inserting funny questions into a test.

• A joke a day keeps the daily doldrums away. Keep a joke book handy and have joke time in the classroom. Allow one student a day to share a favorite, appropriate joke. The student must write it out before sharing with the whole class (just in case it's inappropriate).

• While students are processing with a partner or in a group, have them toss a ball around to show who should be speaking or sharing what they've learned. Whoever has the ball in his or her hand should be the one speaking. Then that person tosses it to somebody else in the group, and it's that person's turn to share what was learned.

• Play music in the classroom that energizes students and makes them smile. Allow students to share what they've learned through a rap or song.

• Take a dance break every now and then: Electric Slide, Cha Cha Slide, Twist and Shout, Boogie Fever, I Like to Move It Move It, and so on.

• After students are in cooperative groups, ask them to do a group ritual such as high-fiveing each other and saying "awesome."

• Have Silly Simile Summary breaks. This is where the students can be as silly as they want and compare what they just learned to anything else (respectfully, of course).

• Teach your students to take a positive statement and make a funny negative statement out of it. For example, "I slept like a baby last night; I woke up every hour and cried." "You look like a million bucks—green and wrinkled."

Challenge and Matched Skill Level

A lesson should be interesting and enjoyable, but it should also have different degrees of challenge for the students. The best learning comes from when teachers match the learning situation with the child's skill level, but slightly above that skill level. This is where the challenge comes in. Research has shown that children are most likely to experience the ultimate state of learning during lessons in which there are clear goals, students receive immediate and specific feedback, and students are working at levels slightly above their ability levels. When given a free choice, kids select this optimum challenge level.

High-achieving students love learning more than other students do, and self-motivated students are more likely to take on academic work that is difficult. They also perform complex tasks such as reasoning, inferring, and understanding more competently than other students. These are just a few reasons why educators must make sure that their lessons are challenging for all students. This is quite a task when classrooms have anywhere from 10 to 40 students with a wide variance of background knowledge. How can teachers make the lessons, concepts, and skills more challenging for all students at all levels? One of the best ways to meet the many different levels in the classroom is through differentiated strategies.

Implications/Examples

- Make assignments more complex if needed.
- Allow students to do projects based on their background knowledge, interest, and growth opportunities.
- The more broad and general you make an assignment for students with greater background knowledge on a topic, the more challenging the assignment could be for them.

Engagement

Many strategies exist to produce an engaged audience. Presentation skills, reading your audience's state of mind and knowing how to change their mind, and kinesthetic activities all keep participants engaged powerfully. Educators need to get them actively engaged in their learning so they become more motivated to learn. One of the best oxymorons out there is passive learning: there is no such thing. You are the deciding factor as to whether or not your students stay engaged.

Powerful Nonverbals

No matter how interesting your topic or lesson might be, to fully engage your audience you must have effective presentation skills. Research on communication indicates that 93% of a message is communicated nonverbally and 7% is communicated verbally (Mehrabian, 1981). What a teacher says may not be as important as how the teacher says it. Educators must understand strategies that help them capitalize on these powerful nonverbals that keep students engaged. These strategies consist of nonverbal communication keys such as facial expressions, gestures, eye contact, voice, and state changes, which all play a key role in helping students be fully engaged during your lessons.

Implications/Examples

- The facial expression that is inviting to students is an open face that displays an excitement and openness to students' comments and questions. Smiles also can help students enjoy the learning more. Deborah Yurgelun-Todd (Yurgelun-Todd, Killgore, & Young, 2002) at Harvard's McLean Hospital has used functional magnetic resonance imaging (fMRI) to compare the adolescent brain's activity with the brain activity of adults. The adults and teens were asked to view a face with fear on it, but 50% of the adolescents confused it with shock or anger, while every adult correctly identified the emotion. The researcher found that when teens processed emotion, they had lower activity in their frontal lobes (prefrontal cortex—the rational center) and more activity in their amygdala (irrational center) than adults. Studies like these suggest that teachers must take the time to teach adolescents to read body language and facial expression, and teachers need to practice using the correct facial expressions and body language to convey a particular message. Theater is a great way to do this. These are learned skills and are very important in conveying correct messages.

- Natural gestures that keep the audience's attention are most effective. Use your hands, arms, and stance to convey important information. For example, when talking about something that happened first, second, and so on, actually stand and use your arms to represent "first," then move your whole body to the left and use a different gesture to emphasize "second," and so on. This shows the separateness of the events and improves the memory of the sequence of events.

- Eye contact invites connections with students, establishes a sense of proximity, can manage discipline problems, and keeps students engaged. When 3 seconds of eye contact are made, students feel like you're really looking at them. The expectation of listening and being engaged is set. Make sure that your eye contact meets all students in the classroom. Teachers tend to have the most eye contact with those sitting in the front, but they must make sure that those sitting around the perimeter of the class are receiving this powerful nonverbal too.

- A monotonous voice is easy to tune out or fall asleep to. Variations of your vocal tone, pitch, and speed help to engage your students. Usually a high pitch shows excitement, while a low pitch indicates seriousness or intensity. The pace should not allow time for students to become disinterested or bored. Students usually are more actively engaged when teachers move fairly quickly through the lesson with opportunities to process the content, ask questions when needed, and be able to practice what was learned. Finally, both lowering and raising your voice can be used to emphasize important information.

State Changes

All these nonverbal communication examples are types of state changes. To keep students attentive, you must be in tune to your students' attention span. When you notice student attention or energy subsiding, change what you're doing. This slight change is called a "state change" and is very simple to implement. Some examples of state changes are the following: change the pitch and tone of your voice, walk to a different location in the classroom, show an object, ask another student to come teach a section of information, put on relevant outfits or accessories, have students stand up or sit down, facilitate a quick energizer, play music, and just do something different and novel.

Kinesthetic Activities

Students are actively engaged when you get them moving or using objects in the lesson. There is a large body of empirical research suggesting the value of play, movement, and recess (Pellegrini & Bohn, 2005; Pellegrini & Smith, 1998) and their positive impact on cognition. Students often get frustrated and antsy sitting too long in their seats. To help them refocus, get them up and moving. A portion of your learners are kinesthetic learners, which means they learn best when the content is embedded into movement or manipulation of objects. Here are some simple examples:

- Ask students to stand up and process versus sit and process.
- Ask students to get the supplies needed for activities versus you handing them out to everyone.
- Create human graphs in the classroom (circle graphs, bar graphs, etc.). Or stand in locations of the room based on opinions; for example, say "Stand in that corner of the room if you think . . ."
- Allow students to sort words from the unit into categories by having them write the words on 3 × 5 cards and creating labels for them. They are creating a web with index cards labeled with important, interrelated vocabulary terms from the unit.
- Use dice, cubes, and spinners as often as possible during lessons. You can easily link content with these objects.

There are many simple ways to keep students engaged in the lesson. State changes and nonverbals such as facial expressions, gestures, eye contact, and voice fluctuation are just a few of the most powerful strategies to keep students fully engaged so that their learning experience can foster a love for learning. Allowing students time to move, get out of their chairs, and be involved kinesthetically with your content are strategies that keep them fully engaged and loving learning.

Examples of How to Build a Positive Learning Culture

- Students need to respect each other's strengths and growth opportunities. Celebrate students' strengths (bulletin board with cards labeled [name of student]'s Expertise). Have them list their strengths on these cards. You can use this information for many other purposes: to help other students with their growth opportunities (students helping and teaching one another), to help students understand their own strengths, to group students accordingly, and to celebrate our differences.

- If there is a bully in your classroom, make sure the school counselor and you have a plan of action to help this student. Learning shuts down when students are fearful. Bullies perceive slights from other people in which no harm is intended. In other words, they misperceive neutral acts from peers as threatening, hostile acts. John Lochman (Lochman, Coie, Underwood, & Terry, 1994), a Duke University psychologist, helped design a bully-proof program in which boy bullies were taught, for 40 minutes, two times a week for 6 to 12 weeks, some social skills. They were taught how some social cues (nonverbals such as facial expressions) they interpreted as hostile were really neutral or friendly. They had direct training in anger control and monitoring their feelings. After the program, Lochman found that the adolescent boys who graduated from the program were less disruptive in class, had more positive feelings about themselves, and were less likely to do drugs or drink alcohol. The longer they had been in the program, the less aggressive they were.

• Have zero tolerance for any and all put-downs. Recognize and praise empathy and kindness. Have your students create a rap or chant about how each student creates the team of players. Use the poem "Classroom Team" on page 45 to build respect for each child's learning differences, strengths, and growth opportunities. Ask students to sign this page as a commitment to respect everyone's differences, strengths, and growth opportunities.

• Make sure students' physical needs are met: thirst, hunger, temperature, proper tools for their special needs (left-handed scissors, pencil grips, etc.).

• All answers and questions are provisional—thinking is always in rough draft form, and you need to accept and respect all questions and answers. Students should feel very safe participating in discussions. Some ways to respond to questions and answers are shown on page 69.

• Be authentic with your students. Let them see your passion for your topic and them. Enthusiasm and a love for learning is bred among the learners who witness these actions.

• Get to know your students just to get to know them. They can tell if you truly care about them. One way students fall through the cracks is when nobody catches them starting to fall. Get to know them so you can catch them before they fall.

• Think about your students first, even before preparing your lesson. Ask yourself the following questions: What interests these students? What causes stress among these students? How can I connect with these students? Are they dealing with a negative emotion right now? If so, how can I divert their attention away from that emotion and onto the learning?

• When you're emotionally vesting your students' lives, they'll buy in to your lessons and your teachings.

• Let the students know that you value their time. At the beginning of a lesson, make sure to answer their number one question: What's in It for Me? (WIIFM?). To answer this question, go through the four questions on page 70 at the beginning of your lessons so that meaning is established. Ask students to contribute to these questions.

• Hold class meetings to discuss classroom behavior (good or negative). Devise plans to continue the good behavior or to stop the bad behavior. Students love having ownership of devising solutions to classroom problems.

• After every cooperative group meets, ask the students to do a quick activity with their teammates. This could be as easy as a high five and saying, "Our team's red hot!" This repetitive motion can, over time, build on team spirit and enthusiasm. Have your students create age-appropriate celebration rituals and choose one to celebrate with after cooperative learning success occurs. They may include affirmations such as "Awesome!" "Way to go!" "What a brain!"

• Give students several Post-it notes and ask them to write three positives and one growth opportunity for each student's project. Place the note near the student's project so he or she can read all the feedback from all of the students.

• Use hope-building activities. Talk to students about the possibilities of their future. Customize what you say for each student, and let them know they can make it in the world. Continually affirm the positives and believe in their capacity.

Positive Learning Culture Questions to Ask Self

• Are the physical, emotional, and social needs of my students thought about and tended to? What do I do to promote safety in all of these aspects?

• Do my students know their strengths?

• Do my students readily ask and answer questions—do they feel safe to do so in my class?

• Do my students like to take risks by sharing new ideas and participating in discussions?

• Do my students feel safe in small groups, or are they intimidated by certain students in the group?

• Are the supplies readily available and displayed safely?

• Is the classroom environment more calm than stressful?

• Do I use a respectful tone of voice with all students?

• Do my students have ample opportunities for choice?

• Do I call the classroom "mine" or "ours"?

• Do I ask for input from the kids on how to plan events or showcase the learning?

• Do I love my job, and does it show?

• Do I catch them being good and positively reinforce the good behavior that I see?

• How well do I know my students and ask questions about their lives?

■ CONCLUSION

We hope you see how important it is to set up a firm foundation for learning. The DELC starts with planning the standards and curriculum (#1), pre-assessing the students who will receive that curriculum (#2), and then building a positive learning culture (#3) so that all students are set up for successful learning. Now that you have processed what you should do to prepare for deeper learning, it's time to dig deeply into the processing of information during the learning. You will explore how to activate and acquire knowledge at deeper levels and then process that information in a variety of processing pathways, depending on what the student is ready for.

STOP-N-THINK

Name: _____ Date: _____

Circle One: Book, Lecture, Video, _____(other)

_____

Stop #1

_____

Stop #2

_____

Stop #3

_____

Stop #4

_____

Synthesis of the Stops:

LEARNING PREFERENCES

Name: _____

Date: _____

Circle one of the following and then explain why you circled it. Would you rather

1. Learn in a small group OR independently?

   Why: _____

2. Listen to music while learning OR have very little noise in the classroom?

   Why: _____

3. Learn new, complex information in the morning OR afternoon?

   Why: _____

4. Draw a concept OR write about it OR web it?

   Why: _____

5. Do math computations (equation solving) OR solve math word problems?

   Why: _____

6. Sit next to a window OR sit up front OR sit in the back OR sit in the middle of the classroom?

   Why: _____

7. Gather information by reading a book OR searching the Internet OR interviewing somebody OR taking notes from the teacher?

   Why: _____

8. Write information OR type information OR speak the information?

   Why: _____

9. Be a leader of a group OR a participant of a group?

   Why: _____

10. Work with a partner OR work with a small group of about three or four?

    Why: _____

Rate the following school subjects with the appropriate number for EACH category:

Interest (I like this topic. I'm curious about this subject. I would like to explore this topic in more depth in my spare time.):

    1 = I just do NOT have much interest in this subject

    2 = I am sometimes interested in this subject

    3 = I am thoroughly interested in this subject

Strengths:

    1 = I am NOT very good at this subject

    2 = I am somewhat good at this subject

    3 = I am very good at this subject

	Interest	*Strength*
Math		
Science		
Social Studies		
Reading		
Writing		
Spelling		
Vocabulary		
Physical Education		
Music		
Art		

WHO ARE YOU?
INTEREST INVENTORY

Name: _____ Date: _____

1. What are your favorite hobbies?	2. What are your favorite books AND types (genre) of books to read?
3. What are your favorite games to play? (board games, card games, etc.)	4. What are your favorite sports that you play? What sports do you like to watch?
5. If you had 2 hours to do whatever you wanted, what would you do?	6. What are your favorite subjects in school, and why?
7. What are your not-so-favorite subjects in school, and why?	8. What career interests you the most?
9. If you went to the library and had to check out nonfiction books, what topics would you choose?	10. What would you like me to know about you? (strengths, growth opportunities, etc.)
11. What clubs or committees are you currently on? Last year? Future ones you plan to be on?	12. Is there something that nobody in this class knows about you? Something unique about yourself? This will be kept secret if you want.

H DIAGRAM

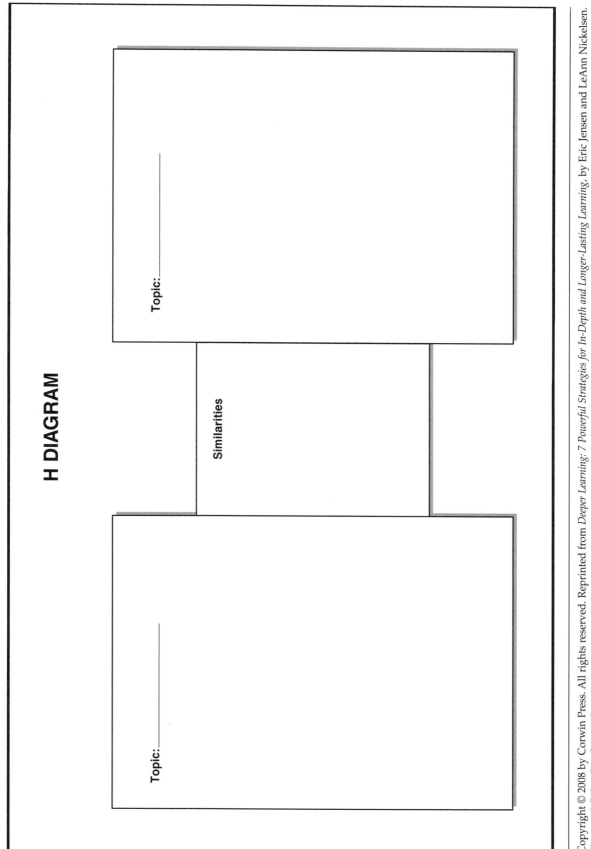

Topic: _____

Similarities

Topic: _____

HISTORICAL EVENT WEB

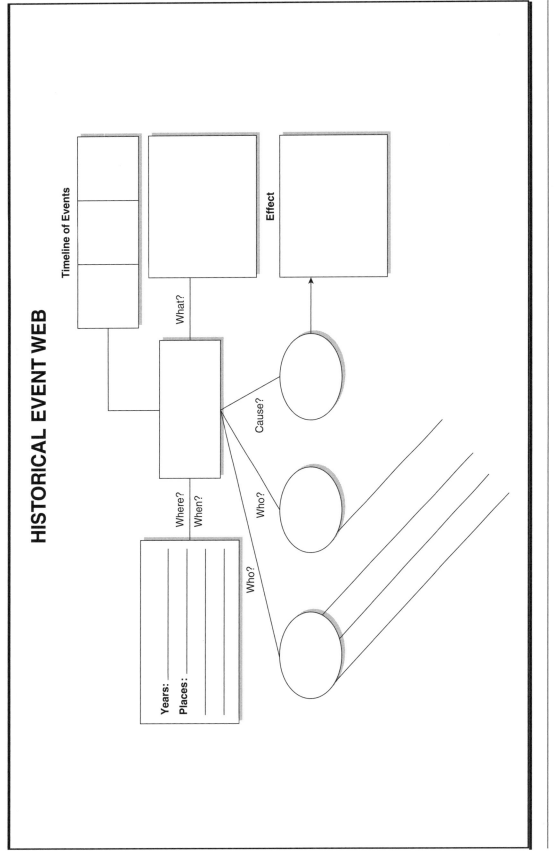

Timeline of Events

Years: _____ _____

Places: _____ _____

Where?

When?

Who?

What?

Who?

Cause?

Effect

TEAM TALK

Names of Students on Team:

_____

_____

Team Name: _____

Criteria	0 = No Way!	1 = OK	2 = Yes!	3 = Awesome!
1. We stayed on task and complimented one another.	0	1	2	3
2. We respected the speaker by not interrupting and by valuing what was shared.	0	1	2	3
3. We helped one another.	0	1	2	3
4. We asked clarifying questions if we didn't understand.	0	1	2	3
5. We actively listened to each other.	0	1	2	3

6. We could do better on the following next time:

_____

_____

7. We really did well on:

_____

_____

8. Specific Comments:

_____

_____

GROUP WORK EXPECTATIONS

1. Respect and Responsibility

   Respect

   - Help each other (and other groups—low voice)
   - Encourage and compliment each other
   - Listen to each other

   Responsibility

   - Stay on task
   - Put 100% into your role
   - Achieve group goal

2. Make sure you understand your role card for this day. Ask any questions you might have.

Roles for Today's Activity: _____

_____

_____

Today's Goal: _____

Time Allotted: _____

When finished:

1. Complete Team Talk Sheet and turn in at the following location: _____

2. Turn in completed group work at the following location: _____

3. Please do the following: _____

Other Instructions: _____

_____

Q-CARD FOR PROMPTING AND REDIRECTING STUDENTS' ANSWERS

CUE: Use symbols, words, or phrases to help students recall the information

CLUE: Use overt reminders such as "starts with," "it sounds like"

PROBE: Look for reasoning behind an incorrect answer or ask for clarity

REPHRASE: Pose the same question in different words

REDIRECT: Pose the same question to a different student if the previous student wants to pass

HOLD ACCOUNTABLE LATER: Later in the lesson, check back with the student who responded incorrectly to make sure he or she has the correct understanding

Q-CARD TO FEEDBACK DURING A DISCUSSION

1. **Make a simple declarative statement.**

   E.g., "Not everything you read is true."

2. **Paraphrase what you heard the student say.**

   E.g., "So you think that . . ."

3. **Describe your state of mind.**

   E.g., "I'm confused about what you're saying."

4. **Invite the student to elaborate.**

   E.g., "Maybe you should give some examples to help us better understand."

5. **Invite the student to ask a question.**

   E.g., "Do you need to ask a question to clarify your thinking?"

6. **Invite the class to ask the student a question.**

   E.g., "Does anyone have a question about Carla's statement?"

7. **Be deliberately silent.**

   E.g., Wait time

SOURCE: Walsh, J. A. and Sattes, B. D. (2005). *Quality Questioning*. Thousand Oaks, CA: Corwin Press.

WIIFM?
WHAT'S IN IT FOR ME?

1. What will I learn by the end of the lesson, or what will I be able to do by the end of the lesson?

2. Why do I need to learn this concept or skill? How will it help me currently and in the future?

3. What do I already know about this concept or skill? How have I experienced it before?

4. How does this concept or skill connect with what we have already learned?

3

Priming and Activating Prior Knowledge and Acquiring New Knowledge

DELC Steps 4 and 5

Before-Reading Processing

Four-Choice Processing (page 93): Complete each square by choosing how to respond in each box about the topic of activating prior knowledge. This activity is meant to activate your prior knowledge on this topic. Through this activity, you have the opportunity to react to the concept of activating prior knowledge in at least four different ways, all of which are your choice. Notice that each box gets more complex as you go along.

Try this activity with your students. Use the Four-Choice Processing reproducible (page 93) to activate their prior knowledge on your curriculum, to process during a lesson about something they just learned, or to use as a review with another student. Four-Choice Processing squares will really get your students thinking at different levels. If a student doesn't have the background knowledge to think at a higher level on the concept at hand, have that student process the concept in Boxes 1 and/or 2.

During-Reading Processing

We invite you to try mind mapping this chapter. We've given you a mind map skeleton of Chapter 3 in Figure 3.1. Photocopy this page so you can try this beneficial strategy. You need Figure 3.1, colored pencils, skinny markers or twist-up crayons, and your imagination.

The beauty about a mind map is that you can design it however you want and in any way that helps you process what you're reading so that you'll remember it better and be able to apply it.

Here are some suggestions to help you create your mind map:

- Write short phrases and major concepts versus sentences.
- Use plenty of color, because it enhances memory.
- Make sure that you draw pictures or symbols to represent what you're learning. A picture paints a thousand words.
- Represent related topics in spokes around the main topic, which is in the center.
- Use arrows or underlining to highlight the important ideas.
- Cluster or group similar facts related to the main topic.

After-Reading Processing

DELC Step 4: Priming and Activating Prior Knowledge

1. What are three purposes for activating prior knowledge?

2. Out of the activating prior knowledge examples, which one will you use soon?

3. What does research say about the benefits of priming the brain for the upcoming learning?

DELC Step 5: Acquiring New Knowledge

4. How can you use the rule of 10–80–10 in your classroom situation?

5. Out of the four ways to prepare for the acquisition of content, which one would you like to focus on?

Figure 3.1 Mind map skeleton of Chapter 3

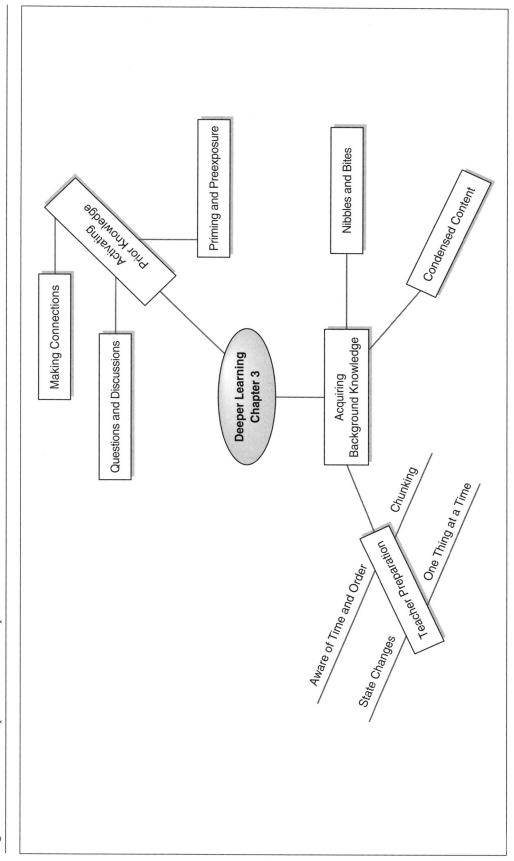

■ DELC STEP 4: PRIMING AND ACTIVATING PRIOR KNOWLEDGE

Background knowledge is what a person already knows. The relationship between students' background knowledge and their achievement is strong; it provides the platform, the schema, and vocabulary needed to succeed (Zull, 2002). If students don't have sufficient prior knowledge to move forward, many of the missing pieces can be integrated into your instruction. There's a good reason to do this: what students already know about the upcoming content is one of the strongest indicators of how well they'll learn the new information relative to this content. This piece of information alone shows the importance of acquiring prior knowledge before being taught. There are several other reasons for activating prior knowledge:

1. To improve opportunities for memory of the concepts and skills taught

2. To make strong connections and to make content more relevant

3. To ensure that students' background knowledge is built by scaffolding

4. To correct students' misconceptions right away or create a plan to do so

5. To foster interest, motivation, and therefore greater opportunities for *success*

Activating prior knowledge is an important step for deeper learning; thus it is Step 4 in the Deeper Learning Cycle (DELC).

Activating Prior Knowledge by Priming and Preexposuring

Airlines often ask families with small children to preboard the plane. Studios and theaters want us to preview a movie. Preexposure is the process of covertly preparing students for future content or skills days, weeks, months, or even years before accountability. If you find yourself frustrated over the lack of content background that students have in the subject matter, you can instead build the pieces of the background while in class through preexposure. This can be a bonanza for teachers, who often get a blank stare from students when they present new information. It could be based on skill acquisition (for example, people prepare themselves to drive a car by driving a tractor, go-cart, or bumper car as a kid). Preexposure could also be based on semantic processes such as objects or verbs (people learn words as kids that they're only allowed to use when they're more "mature"). In a well-planned curriculum, students are getting preexposure all the time. For example, fourth graders can be primed for algebra by working with symbols in basic problem solving. They can be primed for geometry by building models that include exposure to points, lines, planes, angles, solids, and volumes.

When people watch television, producers want to entice viewers to watch the next show. The promotionals for the next show are a form of priming or preexposure. You get the content in the form of highlights and a tease. Priming can happen minutes or even seconds, hours, or days before teaching the unit or lesson. It prepares the learner for the understanding of concepts and gives the brain information to build into a semantic structure later on. It gives improved efficiency in the subject's ability to name a word, an object, and a concept or even perform a skill with some earlier exposure (Martin & van Turenout, 2002). Additional connections may have already been made, so this begins the more complex hierarchy. In fact, semantic priming has been shown to have effects up to a year later (Cave, 1997). Different areas of the brain are involved in different types of priming (Martin, 2001). In either case, the systems and subsystems have turned out to be far more complex than thought earlier. The effects of priming may be stored such that they preserve data as well as or better than if students purposefully learned it.

Priming and Preexposure of Content Examples

Treasure Chest: Find a cardboard treasure chest and fill it with artifacts that go along with your unit. Ask students to add to the components of the treasure chest. For example, on a unit about Native Americans, some students brought in arrowheads they found in their backyards. The teacher placed books, moccasins, leather, and headbands in the treasure chest.

Book Tag: Gather as many picture books as you can about your unit. Allow students to choose a book to peruse. Students look through the book for interesting pictures, captions, and graphs. They should tag a page that has an interesting picture. These tags are used to share with other students.

Peripherals in the Classroom: Create an interactive bulletin board about your unit and post it about 1 week before the unit begins. Students will catch the concept on the run.

Your Ticket In: Give students a rectangular Post-it note before they leave your classroom. Tell them that in order to enter the classroom tomorrow, they must hand you this note filled out with the following (limit the amount of writing to the space on the note):

1. What they know about the topic already

2. An experience they've had with the topic (short story)

3. A neat Web site that has information about this topic and what they learned from that Web site

4. A drawing of what the topic looks like

5. A question they have about the topic

6. Other choices they create

Have students share these the next day, or you do it. The students will see that you value this activity.

Activating Prior Knowledge
With Questions and Discussions

Activating prior knowledge activities are one form of meaning making, but don't forget about the emotional vesting in the form of What's in It for Me?

- Why do I need to learn this?
- How will this concept or skill help me now and in the future?
- How does this relate to what I've already learned?

These questions set the stage for the understanding and meaning making that occur during the lesson. Pose these questions at the beginning and the end of the lessons since the answers are different at both times. Sometimes the students don't know why a concept is important to learn or how they'll use the concept in the future. Just list the reasons for them or allow the lesson to help them discover the purpose of knowing the concept or skill.

Teachers must take the time to activate any relevant piece of their students' background knowledge. Through questioning and discussions, students can activate their background knowledge and learn from others' experiences. Peers have special ways of relating to one another that teachers can't always emulate. Below are some questioning strategies and discussion starters that help students talk about the topic prior to learning.

Questioning and Discussion Examples

Super Sleuth (page 94). This game gives students opportunities to get up, walk to a peer, and ask that student a question on the Super Sleuth board pertaining to the topic at hand. Students place their signatures in the boxes as they're discussed. The questions allow for discussion of what is already known about the topic. The goal is to get nine signatures (there are nine squares with questions in them), one per square, from nine different students. That goal is achieved through discussion about the topic at hand. If you're pressed for time, ask students to just get three in a row, as in tic-tac-toe.

There are different ways to use the Super Sleuth in your classroom:

1. As a review of the concepts that were learned (find someone who can explain the differences between igneous rock, metamorphic rock, and sedimentary rock)

2. As an activating prior knowledge activity (find someone who ate one quarter of a pizza in the last 2 weeks—math; find someone who has been temporarily blinded—1 minute or less—after looking directly at the sun—solar energy unit). See Figure 3.2 for another example of how to use Super Sleuth to prime students' brains with the vocabulary words that you will use in the unit, book, or lesson.

3. As a way to practice concepts (find someone who can calculate 23×46; find someone who can write a complex sentence)

Figure 3.2   Super Sleuth example

Super Sleuth

Find someone who is a **taciturn** person.	Find a good **crony.**	Find someone who is **bundobust.**
Taciturn—disinclined to talk	**Crony**—close long-standing friend, pal	**Bundobust**—well organized
Find someone who considers himself or herself to be a **refractory** person.	Find someone who is **capricious.**	Find someone who is a **philodox.**
Refractory—stubborn	**Capricious**—impulsive, unpredictable	**Philodox**—loves to hear himself or herself talk.
Find an **ardent** teacher.	Find someone who owns a **tulchin**.	Find a **sapient** person.
Ardent—passionate, glowing, hardworking	**Tulchin**—dummy made of calfskin placed beside a cow at milking time to relax cows	**Sapient**—having great widsom and discernment

IIQEE Strategy (page 95). This discussion starter helps students think inwardly first and then ask other students about their experiences with the topic. Each student individually completes the statements that are listed on the IIQEE reproducible: "I think I know the following about the topic," "I am sure that I know the following about the topic," "Questions that I have about this topic," and "Experiences that I have had with this topic." After the first four statements are completed, the students find a student and ask what his or her experiences are with the topic. They swap their experiences *if* they both have one to swap. If a student hasn't had a personal experience with the topic, then the student just writes and learns from the experience of the other student. Having students teach one another is very effective for retention and meaning making. If there's enough time, allow students to find more friends to share their experiences with—it will deepen their background knowledge on the topic. See Figure 3.3 for an example.

Another idea for using IIQEE is to allow this page to become a poster in the classroom without the lines for writing. Give your students each a pad of Post-it notes and ask them to respond to each question on a separate note. Then place all the notes on the poster in the appropriate places. You will share the poster contents afterward and hope to spark new conversations and questions about the topic.

Spin & Activate (page 96). Distribute a 6-spinner (with the numbers 1 to 6 in each pie section of the spinner) to small groups or partnerships. Students take turns answering the questions in the spinner about the topic at hand. The questions work with any content but might need to be altered in minor ways to fit your unique topic. These questions help activate the knowledge or experiences students have had about the topic.

Web-N-Pass (pages 233–236). Create three questions if students are in groups of three for your students to think about that will activate their prior knowledge on the current unit or lesson. For example, if they're learning about the Great Depression, the three open-ended questions might be: Why do you think the Great Depression occurred? What were some of the effects of the Great Depression on the people, government, economics, and environment? What would you have done to solve some of the problems in society during the Great Depression? To see other examples of this activity, please see the Web-N-Pass Application Activity on page 167 in Chapter 5. Ask each student to write a different question on an 8½ × 11-inch piece of paper in the center of the page with a circle around it. After each student has prepared his or her page, let the brainstorming begin. Each student writes an answer to the open-ended question in the center of his or her page. When that answer is written, rotate the pages so that each student answers the question on each of the three pages. They can draw a line from the center of the circle and write their answer on the line. This activity might take about 5 to 7 minutes. The goal is for each student to think about each question and write a response on the page. Then have students read to the whole class each of the answers from their page that they started out with.

Activating Prior Knowledge by Making Connections

Learning is like a ship and anchor. If you don't want the ship to float away, you must anchor it to a strong foundation. If teachers want to make

Figure 3.3   IIQEE Strategy example

> **IIQEE Strategy**
> **"To Activate My Prior Knowledge"**
> **TOPIC:** _____Faults_____
>
>
> I think I know the following about the topic:
>
> • Tectonic plates have something to do with earthquakes.
>
>
> I am sure that I know the following about the topic:
>
> • Inactive faults do not show any movement.
>
> • Faults can be dangerous.
>
> • They change the surface of the earth.
>
>
> Questions that I have about this topic (I want to learn . . .):
>
> Do faults cause earthquakes?
>
>
> Experiences that I have had with this topic:
>
> I have not experienced faults or earthquakes.
>
>
> Experiences that my friend, Billy, _____ has had with the topic:
>
> Billy lived in California and experienced an earthquake.

---

sure that learning sticks, they must make sure it's grounded in a strong foundation of background knowledge of each student. Meaning making becomes more powerful when teachers help students connect what exists within them (prior knowledge or background knowledge) to the new information that's being taught. Below are some specific strategies to help students make more meaningful connections while activating prior knowledge.

MAKE Meaning (page 97). This strategy for quickly activating prior knowledge allows students to make connections in three different ways: What is known about the topic, what has been experienced related to the topic, and how could this topic be applied to the student's life. Each student should complete a MAKE Meaning reproducible. See Figure 3.4 for an example.

Figure 3.4   MAKE Meaning example

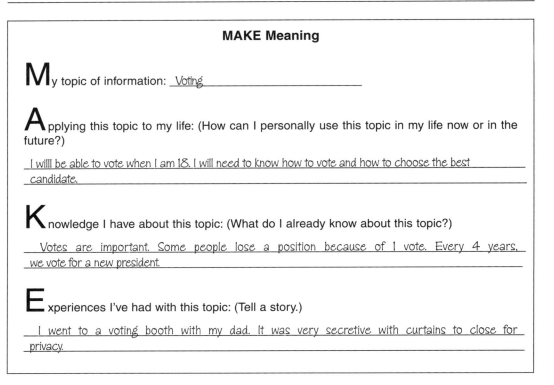

Digging Detectives (page 98). Making connections with content area texts is imperative to the successful comprehension of the book. Digging Detectives allows students to prepare their minds for a topic before reading about it. Students go through a series of questions and book analysis steps before digging deeply into a book. Notice that the questions prime the brain for what the book might be about, but they also help the reader make some connections with content before the reading begins. See Figure 3.5 for an example of Digging Detectives.

Ship & Anchor Connections (page 100). This graphic organizer helps students see how new, more complex words are connected to already known words. It's important to make sure that students see the similarities and differences between these words. The graphic organizer guides your discussion of the similarities and differences between the two words or concepts. It's especially useful while teaching abstract words and connecting them to more concrete words. See Figure 3.6 for an example of Ship & Anchor Connections.

Activating prior knowledge is imperative before teaching begins. There are several engaging ways to activate prior knowledge: by priming and preexposure, by questioning and discussing, and by giving time for students to explore the connections they can make with the content. Now that they have the background knowledge, it's time to learn how to acquire the new knowledge.

Figure 3.5   Digging Detectives example

DIGGING DETECTIVES

Name: _Maria_

Title of Book: _Mexican Immigration_

1. I found the following within my book (check):
- ☑ Table of Contents
- ☑ Index
- ☑ Titles and subtitles
- ☑ Words in boldface type that are defined in the glossary
- ☑ Captions near pictures, diagrams, graphs, charts, etc.
- ☑ Other: _Question Box_

2. What page is your favorite picture on and why is this your favorite? Please describe. PAGE: _13_

    I like seeing people cross the calm water to get to the U.S. – I did not know people want to be in
    America that badly.

3. Write 2 different titles that you see within this book:

    The Challenges of Immigration. Leaving Mexico for Peace and a Better Life.

4. Write 2 different subtitles that you see in this book:

    The Journey From Mexico. Mexicans in the Workforce.

5. Write some questions that you would like answered about this book:

    Did the Mexicans find work right away? Why did they want to leave Mexico?

6. What do you know about this topic?

    We have a lot of good Mexican food in the U.S. because of Mexican immigration.

7. The purpose of reading this book is:

    People choose to immigrate for many different reasons.

8. Let's define and draw pictures of the following words:

Word: Pesticides	Word: fiestas—party; cultural festival.	Word: braceros—Mexican laborer brought to U.S. for short-term work.
Word: immigrate—to come to a new country to live	Word:	Word:

Figure 3.6   Ship & Anchor Connections example

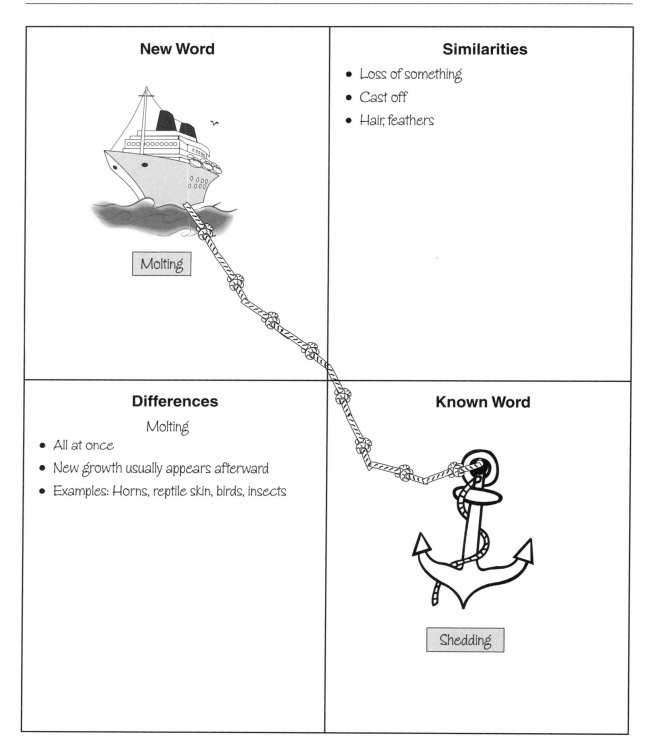

DELC STEP 5: ACQUIRING NEW KNOWLEDGE ■

How do people acquire background knowledge? They typically acquire it by following one of two pathways: (1) through a quick, crash course of quality information or (2) over time, in bits and pieces that amount to quantity. Background knowledge comes into play every day in school. Students are tested on their ability to process and store information and the number, range, scope, and frequency of their academically oriented experiences. The latter play a huge role in our acquisition of information. How can teachers activate prior knowledge if it doesn't already exist in a student? There are two ways: one is by providing plenty of bites of content stretched out over time. The second is to shortcut expert knowledge with condensed models of thinking that could only have been derived from expert knowledge or hundreds of hours of experience. Acquiring background knowledge in a variety of ways is so important in the DELC that it has become the fifth step of the DELC cycle.

The only way this can work in your classroom is to change the model you use for allocating time. If each week you spend 100% of your time on the current unit, you have no time to create background information. Here's the solution: use the 10–80–10 rule. This means that each week you spend 80% of your time on the current unit, 10% of your week preparing students for upcoming units, and 10% revising and bringing back up prior learning. That's much less time for the "in the moment" of the unit learning, but here's why it works out better for you. Students don't get all new learning perfectly the first time. You start building previews and reviews into your schedule and thereby account for the background knowledge time and for the review time. There's less pressure on you or the students to get it right the first time, and with all the pre- and postlearning, students learn it all better with less stress.

Memorable Chart—How to Use Time Each Week

10% of time: prepare for upcoming units; priming and preexposure, preassessments, gathering information

80% of time: teaching current unit

10% of time: elaborate review of past units; connecting new with old (revising)

Getting the Pieces (Nibbles and Bites)

First start with a timeline. If students *need* to know something for a unit in March, do most of your priming in February, though you can start earlier. Remember the 10–80–10 rule.

The 10–80–10 rule of thumb for a daily lesson plan might look like this:

10%—Before the Lesson

• Prepare learners by activating prior knowledge and tying the future information into today's lesson. This might include preassessments for the upcoming unit too. While students are taking preassessments, their brains are being primed for the upcoming unit.

80%—During the Lesson

- Engage learners by grabbing their attention with an amazing story, a unique object, a breathtaking video clip, pictures, quotes, or a minisimulation.

- Frame the learning so that the all-important question of WIIFM? is answered. Framing means to make the content more relevant by explaining why this lesson is important to the learners now and in the future.

- Instruct by modeling, giving examples, reading texts, showing video clips, using the Internet, researching, role-playing, and so on.

- Elaborate on the learning by allowing processing time. The Domains for Elaborate and Effective Processing (DEEP) help students process information at their current levels of understanding. Chapter 4 elaborates on DEEP. During this time, new connections are made, content can become deeper or wider, meaning making and understanding occurs, and trial and error with feedback elicits elaboration of content.

10%—After the Lesson

- Consolidation of information takes place over time. It takes a rehearsal of the information as often as possible to establish strong connections between neurons. Closures are opportunities to connect past information with new information.

To prepare students' brains for new content, the following strategies for building background knowledge should be used as much as possible:

1. Experience as many field trips as possible.
2. Explore virtual museums via the Internet.
3. Provide silent reading time—books galore!
4. Teach vocabulary words—elaborate on them.
5. Activate prior knowledge before lessons and give snippets of information needed before teaching the lesson (see examples at the beginning of this chapter).
6. Provide homework that deals with students' lack of background knowledge on a particular subject.
7. Show pictures related to the topic.
8. Show artifacts connected with the content.

Getting the Condensed Content (Shortcut Expert Knowledge)

Getting the quick capsule version is always a bit challenging, but it can be done. The shortcuts are few and far between, but they're a gold mine for the brain. Anytime you can include one of these, go for it:

1. Provide a working model of the learning (or build one!).
2. Invite expert guest speakers to the classroom.

3. Show video/DVD clips.

4. Scrutinize an overview mind map of the big picture.

5. Support Internet research (see page 151 in Chapter 5 for a WebQuest activity).

6. Use books, journals, and magazines to gather information—research.

Typically, teachers respond with comments such as "I know that's a good idea; I just don't have time." The reality is that you can't afford not to build background knowledge. Without this knowledge in your students' heads, you end up having to constantly fill in the gaps and reteach. Use the 10–80–10 rule.

Teacher Preparation for the Acquisition of Content

When you prepare to teach a lesson, be sure to keep in mind the following strategies: chunk the content, decrease the number of disruptions, be aware of the order of events, be aware of the amount of time you can teach before processing time is needed, and use state changes when needed.

Chunking

Chunking is a process in which the brain perceives several items of information as a single item. Chunking helps the brain see similarities between pieces of information, so that several bits of information can be seen as one. Getting a master's degree or a doctorate can be overwhelming, but when you chunk down the process, you really just need to complete one course. Each course may have 10 classes to attend or two papers to write. Each paper may have two books to read. But starting with one book, you can over time get the degree you want. Chunk each part of the process into smaller and smaller bits until the task seems doable. Then complete another class.

The brain best receives information in little chunks, sections, or groups of similar bits of information. Then the brain needs time to think about, chew on, and digest these chunks of similar information. This "time" is what processing is all about. The brain must have time to process what was just learned. The brain can't process too much information—it needs small, relevant chunks to process. Then additional chunks can be taught or learned and then processed. The brain is constantly making what is being learned meaningful to the learner by relating chunks of information to existing information in that brain. Learning is all about connections.

Break up your content into chunks so that students can digest it better. A chunk is a small group of related pieces of information. For example, if you're teaching a unit about the planets, the geological facts about each individual planet is a minichunk of information. You could break this up into further chunks by creating a chunk for an individual planet's natural resources, formation history, atmosphere, moons, orbit pattern, and size, because these are all related to one another. Chunking aids in making the content small enough to digest properly.

Chunking can be used to make your life easier. For example, a daily to-do list could be broken down into the following tasks:

To Do Today for Family

To Do Today for Work

Phone Calls to Make

E-mails to Write

Errands to Run Today

Schedule of the Day

Your brain puts these similar items together, and life can be more efficient if these items are categorized within larger units of information. For example, having a list of errands on the forefront of your brain while you're in your car saves you time and frustration because all the errands can be completed at one time. When you start to organize your belongings, your brain needs to decide what chunk or category each item belongs in so you know where to place it or store it for easy retrieval and access. People organize based on how similar the items are. For example, they may place all computer items (ink, paper, disks, books, etc.) in one location on a shelf in their study closet or computer desk drawer so they can find them when needed. Chunking is a skill that can save time and allows for more efficiency and for working memory to be freed up for other processing opportunities.

Students juggle a lot of information in the learning process. Depending on the developmental age of students, their experiences, and their ability, students can only handle so many chunks of information in their working memory at one time. Teachers can make each chunk bigger, but they can't increase the number of chunks that can be handled at one time. The capacity of working memory typically develops with practice and age (up until about age 25). Students under age 12 are good with just one item at a time, and those older may be able to hold two to three things at a time. Recent research suggests adults might be able to handle about four items (Cowan, 2001). Most adults experience much more rapid and accurate results when they focus enough to have a strong working memory. It's no different with students: the better the working memory, usually, the better the academic performance; the poorer the working memory, the harder it is to focus on what is most important.

Plan your units and lessons so you're placing similar concepts together. Then give students an opportunity to process each chunk at levels they'll be successful with. Check for mastery after each chunk is learned. Eventually, you'll be able to ask the students to process several of the chunks together so they see how they're relevant to each other. The DELC Lesson Plan Template guides you in your planning of this strategy.

Think of reading as three big chunks of processing opportunities: before reading, during reading, and after reading. For example, below we have included processing ideas that can be used before, during, and after reading. It's important to make sure that students are thinking about their thinking (metacognition) in these three chunks of time. This guide should be with every teacher and student while reading a book.

BEFORE READING

1. Preview the Text

   Do a book walk and find the following:
   Title, main headings, subheadings
   Pictures, graphics, captions, maps, graphs, diagrams
   Boldface type vocabulary (preteach 3–5 words)
   Chapter introduction/Introductory questions
   First and last paragraphs
   Boxed or highlighted information

2. Activate Prior Knowledge

   What do you already know about this subject?
   What experiences have you had in this area?
   Did the book preview remind you of anything?
   Teacher shows an object or picture, shares a personal story, or reads a short story
   that relates to the text in order to help activate prior knowledge anticipatory set).
   Predict what the text might be about.

3. Create a Purpose and a Plan

   What reading strategies do you plan to use while reading this passage?
   What is the purpose for reading this passage?
   What is your monthly personal reading goal?
   Present and generate questions to consider while reading.

DURING READING

Read with the purpose in mind.
Read slowly with Post-it notes handy to mark text (metacognition).
   ✓ I got it! I know and/or understand this.
   ! This is really important or interesting.
   ? I don't understand this, or this does not make sense.
   C This is a connection with my life, other book, and/or world.
Organize text in a meaningful way while reading (graphic organizer).
Use strategies based on reading goal (use think-alouds).
Create questions to answer during the reading.
Clarify vocabulary.
Read with the author's purpose in mind.
Analyze charts and graphs.

AFTER READING

1. Pause and Reflect

   Do I understand what the main topics are?
   Can I explain the key terms in my own words?
   Do the graphics, pictures, and captions make sense?
   How does this text connect with my life, other texts, and world?
   What can I do with this information?
   Check predictions.

2. Reread

   Skimming is a strategy that makes sense when you're looking for specific information.

3. Remembering and Processing the Text (make sure it connects with text read)

   Do something with the text (drawing, mnemonic, jingle, discuss, or any other project
   or product).

4. Discuss future reading goals.

The bottom line is to build background knowledge in small chunks and then show how these small chunks connect with each another to form a bigger picture. Small chunks must exist before you ask your students to process. Units must have related chunks built on top of one another for coherency to occur.

One Thing at a Time

Sit in a chair. Write your name in cursive in the air with your writing finger. After doing that, with your opposite foot create a circle in the air going in a clockwise direction. Now try to do them *both* at the same time. How successful were you? Most likely, your brain was challenged to do both at the same time. It's a bit like driving your car: you're doing many tasks at once. But it wasn't always that way. You can't do two things at once unless one of them has become automatic and you're not thinking about it. This is because it's impossible for the brain to consciously think about two different thoughts at the same time—the brain functions best when it focuses on one conscious thought at a time.

In today's society people challenge the brain to override this rule—they try to force it to think about many thoughts at once—bouncing several unrelated thoughts from one end of the brain to the other. This multitasking can cause stress, exhaustion, and inefficiency.

For example, imagine that you're listening to a conversation with a group of friends, but you overhear your name being mentioned in the group sitting next to you. You look like you're still listening to the original conversation, but you can't help but listen in on the second conversation where your name was mentioned. You have to stop listening to the first conversation in order to hear and comprehend the second conversation. It's impossible to listen to both conversations at the same time—you can go from one to the other, back and forth. This is called splitting your attention.

Selective auditory attention allows you to filter out the other often louder noises or conversation and pay attention to the one that is most relevant at the time. Some students have a difficult time filtering out distracting, irrelevant noises, and therefore they don't comprehend the learning at hand. As much as possible, teachers need to be aware of potential distractions and be ready to cut those distractions out.

Doing two things at the same time is different from consciously processing two inputs at the same time. You can *do* two things at the same time if one of them is stored in the automatic memory. Motor neurons may become so used to being activated in a particular sequence that they fire automatically with little or no conscious processing. For example, most people can ride their bikes while thinking about occurrences. Some people can talk on the phone and clean up their desks too. But to write a thank-you note while talking on the phone would cause some disturbances to the brain, since both tasks need to activate the same part of the brain.

Classroom Implications

Possible Distractions and Solutions

• *Students reading with a partner while others are reading aloud too.* Some students may need to read in a more secluded area so the others won't distract them. Classical music has been known to act like a wall so that the background, disturbing noise isn't focused on so easily.

- *Students studying with the television on.* No matter what any student tells you, no one can watch TV and study at the same time. Students can divert their attention from the TV and switch their attention to studying, but they can't do both simultaneously.

- *Students listening to announcements on the intercom while the teacher continues to talk.* Encourage office staff to have announcements at a certain agreed-upon time and not during lessons.

- *Teachers giving a second set of directions after the students have already started on the cooperative learning group activity.* You might have a chime or a saying such as "New Information Alert!" that gets students' full attention before you start on something new.

- *Students daydreaming while the teacher is talking.* It's normal for the brain to daydream or to tune out the talking person. Just walk near the daydreaming students or do a state change. A state change is doing something different that is novel. The brain pays attention to novelty. For example, stop talking, look up in the air, take a deep breath, and then talk again more slowly or with a different accent. This gets their attention. Silence is an amazing state change too.

- *Students talking to one another while the teacher is talking.* If teachers provide a consistent processing time in their lessons, they'll see less talking in the classroom. Perform an experiment with the students where they have to listen to two different conversations at the same time. They'll probably not be able to recall perfectly all the facts about the two different conversations. Explain to them that when they're talking to others, they can't listen at the same time. Also, the one who is listening to the talking can't listen to two different conversations at the same time either. Simulation, consistent processing opportunities, and high expectations could alleviate the talking.

- *Students writing or copying notes from the chalkboard or overhead projector while the teacher continues to talk or participants seeing a visual while the presenter keeps talking.* The participants miss out on something. When you show a visual of any kind (PowerPoint, transparency, poster, object, book, etc.), always give a couple of seconds for the brain to register what it is before talking or explaining the visual. The brain is always trying to make sense out of what it sees. Once the brain recognizes the visual, it focuses on what is being said versus trying to figure out what the visual is.

- *Students taking notes but not taking the time to think about what's being said.* Remember that learning comes during the processing of the information and not the hearing of the presentation. Have you ever noticed yourself taking lots of notes in your college classroom but afterward not really knowing what you learned? We've been to staff developments where we couldn't tell you what we learned afterward, because processing opportunities didn't exist. This can happen during note taking too.

The following note-taking strategies encourage processing breaks during the note-taking process.

1. Split-Page Note Taking: Create a vertical line from the top of the paper to the bottom so that it divides the paper in half. Students take notes on the right-hand side for about 8 to 10 minutes and then are asked to process that content on the left-hand side of the paper. A few processing ideas are to draw a picture of what was learned, create new sentences using the information, or web the words that were learned.

2. Mind mapping: See the beginning of this chapter for the details of this note-taking and processing activity.

3. Processing Notebook: See Activity for Assimilation in Chapter 5 on page 187.

The bottom line is to set the students up for success by alleviating distractions so they receive one thing at a time. Encourage your students to focus deeply on one concept or task at a time versus juggling too many concepts or tasks that take their toll on the working memory. There's no such thing as multitasking; what it is, is rapid monotasking.

Aware of Time and Order

In a learning episode, if all things are equal, people tend to retain best that which comes first and retain second best that which comes last. People often remember least that which comes in the middle. This is referred to as the beginning, end, middle (BEM) theory.

Many variables, such as novelty, prior knowledge, and emotional information, affect a person's retention of information, but if educators teach in a way that the BEM theory is applied, retention of the content could be enhanced. Making something new, different, or novel enhances memory tremendously.

Students generally remember the first and last learning episodes of a lesson better than the middle, since there is more novelty at these given points of the lesson. The anticipatory set at the beginning of a lesson greatly focuses the brain on the content to come, while the closure of a lesson lets the brain know that something new is about to happen (the lesson will end and something different will occur). The novelty has worn off by the middle of the lesson, therefore creating obstacles for attention. The hippocampus, part of the brain that temporarily stores information, is full by this time as well and needs to process what is in it in order to make room for more information. This suggests that it's smarter to put extra attention on the middle of the lesson, since that part may be less likely to be encoded and retrieved.

Teachers should plan a processing time when they notice inattention in their students, which is usually during the middle of the lesson. For example, students could practice the math skill that was just taught by using their dry erase boards to solve a word problem and show it to you for accuracy, or students might start writing a complete paragraph after learning the parts of a paragraph. You could ask students to turn to a partner and discuss what steps are involved for photosynthesis. When this independent or guided time is complete, the brain is ready for more input. Thus the end of the lesson is a great time to rehearse the learning or objective from that lesson, or the closure. Closures are short processing opportunities for the benefit of consolidating students' memories of the content that was just taught and other already existing information. Closures must be used by every student. Using the BEM theory in the lesson plan enhances the memory of the content for all students.

Classroom Implications

- Teach the most important information first. Avoid using precious beginning time for taking attendance out loud, grading papers, or just small talk.
- Use the middle learning episode for practicing the learning and for meaning-making processing. When you see students starting to lose their attention on the lesson, it might be a good time to have the practice time or processing time.

Make sure each lesson has a closure at the end (another opportunity for meaning making to occur). Closure is when the students summarize what they learned from all the learning chunks from the lesson. The Awareness processing activities at the beginning of Chapter 5 are all types of quick closures that you can use. We like to save the last 5 minutes of class time for closures. In fact, we asked a certain student who is very time savvy to wave her hand in the air when 5 or 10 minutes of class time were remaining. This was a signal to stop teaching and prepare the students for their closure of the lesson. When teaching complex information, teachers should summarize the information first and then ask students to summarize the information.

State Changes

A state consists of three interrelated components: thoughts, feelings, and physiology. It's another word for the mind-body connection—when people think a certain way, the body responds accordingly. When negative, depressing thoughts permeate a mind, usually the body doesn't have enough energy to accomplish much. In fact, depressed people sleep or sit a lot. If children believe that they can't do something, then they won't even try to do it. How people think directly affects what they do or how they respond to things.

Countless stimuli can impact a person's state of mind, such as environment (weather, seasons, no lighting, etc.), school events (nonverbals, bad news, bullies, etc.), and the foods people eat (simple carbohydrates, protein, etc.). In other words, a rainy, dreary day could make people feel a little depressed and not motivated to accomplish much. Seasonal affective disorder (SAD) occurs during the winter with its cold and often cloudy days. Some people respond to winter with depression-like symptoms. A certain negative look from a friend causes some people to feel uncomfortable and worried. Everyday events constantly cause chemical changes in us that make us behave differently. To counteract these feelings, eating more protein may provide the brain with the raw materials to help people feel more energetic and focused.

Try this experiment. Reflect on your day so far by writing down all the little things that happened to you that really grabbed your attention. These things might include the time when the plate fell out of your hands at breakfast or when you didn't see the car coming and almost walked out into the street. How many did you remember? You probably remembered the very emotional, unique, weird things that don't normally happen. These little incidents get our attention, and novelty is one of the best ways to keep the brain focused and attentive. You might be able to call some of the things on your list abrupt, intense state changes. The incidents certainly got your attention and probably changed your state of mind from what it was before the incident occurred.

You might be thinking, "I can't do state changes all day long to keep my students' attention—I'll be worn out." But it can be done with practice, and it's fun to have a class that's giving you back energy. State changes need to be used when you see the students' attention dwindling. Sometimes you do it automatically, such as when you walk near a student who seems to be daydreaming or when you whisper an interesting fact and then repeat it. Some students age 10 and over can process an item in working memory intently for about 10 minutes before inattention sets in. For focus to return, a change must occur in how that student is dealing with the information (state change).

The key to implementing state changes is to be aware of your students' attention spans and signs of inattention as well as to have a number of state changes up your sleeve, ready to use at any moment. One of the most valuable state changes is allowing processing time at the moment when you see many students drifting away. When inattention characterizes the majority of your students, it's probably a good time for a change of state.

Classroom Implications

Teachers can change students' states of mind, which in turn changes their behavior. If your students are slumping in their chairs, ask them to stand up, turn to a partner, and explain the pros and cons of the concept that was just taught. This state change of standing instead of sitting automatically gets the students out of the slumping-chair state of mind. You didn't have to reprimand, force, beg, or get upset. You just had to do something different. A state change is simply doing something different at that time. Some examples are speaking with a lower voice, walking to a different location in the room, putting on an accessory, having another student teach the information, and asking students to stand up and process.

The bottom line is to use a state change for a behavior change or to improve attention.

■ CONCLUSION

DELC Steps 4 and 5 prepare students for the big deeper learning step: processing deeply. Priming and activating prior knowledge sets the stage for acquiring background knowledge. Once information has been acquired, it's time to move into the next DELC step.

FOUR-CHOICE PROCESSING

Topic: _____

1.	2.
3.	4.

CHOICES

Box 1 – Choose One	Box 2 – Choose One
• How would you describe it? • How would you define it? • Which words are related to it? • How could you illustrate it? • How would you summarize it?	• What are some examples of it? • What are the pros and cons of it? • How would you categorize, classify, or group it? • What would you compare it with and why?
Box 3 – Choose One	**Box 4 – Choose One**
• How do you feel about it? • How would you support your feelings? • How does it compare with your life and what you know? • Do you agree or disagree with it and why?	• How would you improve it? • Can you develop a new use for it? • What if it didn't exist—how would life be different? • What solutions can you devise for it?

Super Sleuth

NAME:

> **IIQEE Strategy**
> **"To Activate My Prior Knowledge"**
> TOPIC: _____

I think I know the following about the topic:

_____
_____
_____

I am sure that I know the following about the topic:

_____
_____
_____
_____

Questions that I have about this topic (I want to learn . . .):

_____
_____
_____
_____

Experiences that I have had with this topic:

_____
_____
_____

Experiences that my friend _____ has had with the topic:

_____
_____
_____

Activating Prior Knowledge Spinner

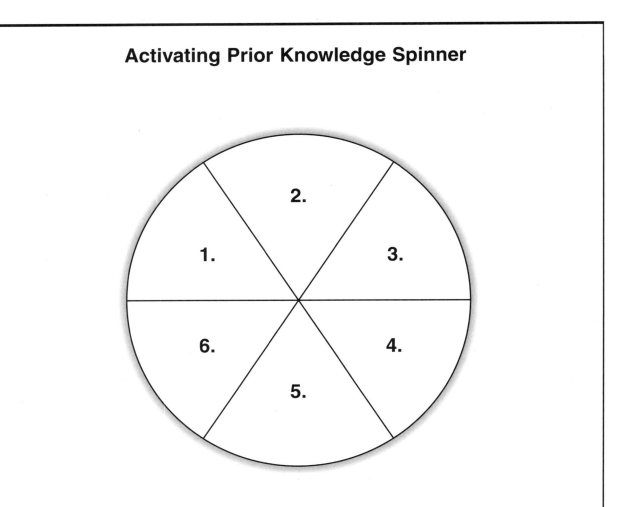

1. What are some facts that you know about this topic?

2. What are some synonyms for this topic? OR Define this topic in your own words.

3. How could you use this topic currently in your life or in the future? OR What questions do you have about this topic?

4. Can you think of a specific example of when you experienced this topic? If so, how did it benefit you?

5. If you were writing about this topic, what information would you include?

6. Why might it be important to learn about this topic?

MAKE MEANING

My topic of information: _____

_____

_____

_____

Applying this topic to my life: (How can I personally use this topic in my life now or in the future?)

_____

_____

_____

Knowledge I have about this topic: (What do I already know about this topic?)

_____

_____

_____

Experiences I've had with this topic: (Tell a story.)

_____

_____

_____

DIGGING DETECTIVES

Name: _____

Title of Book: _____

1. I found the following within my book (check):

   □ Table of Contents
   □ Index
   □ Titles and subtitles
   □ Words in boldface type that are defined in the glossary
   □ Captions near pictures, diagrams, graphs, charts, etc.
   □ Other: _____

2. What page is your favorite picture on and why is this your favorite? Please describe.
   PAGE: _____

   _____

   _____

   _____

3. Write two different titles that you see within this book:

   _____

   _____

   _____

4. Write two different subtitles that you see in this book:

   _____

   _____

   _____

5. Write some questions that you would like answered about this book:

   _____

   _____

   _____

6. What do you know about this topic?

   _____

   _____

   _____

7. The purpose of reading this book is:

   _____

   _____

   _____

8. Let's define and draw pictures of the following words:

Word:	Word:	Word:
Word:	Word:	Word:

After-Reading Response:

_____

_____

_____

_____

_____

_____

_____

_____

_____

_____

_____

_____

_____

_____

_____

_____

_____

_____

_____

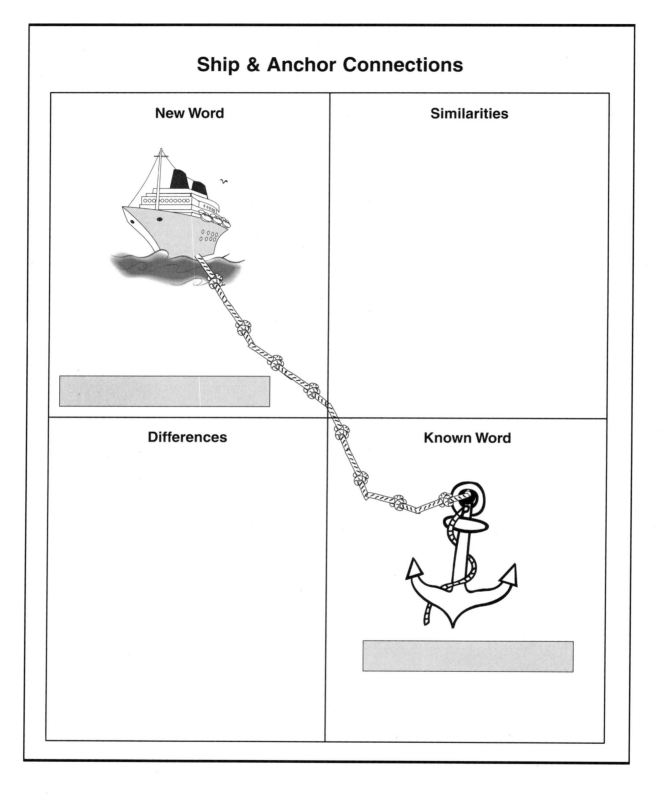

Ship & Anchor Connections

New Word	Similarities

Differences	Known Word

Part II

Processing the Content

4

Processing With a Purpose

DELC Step 6

Before-Reading Processing

Inscribe and Illustrate (page 114 and Figure 4.1): Use the Inscribe and Illustrate graphic organizer to write your own definition of processing and/or draw a picture or symbol of what you think processing is. You can do both or just one—your choice. It's still true that the left hemisphere is more dominant for language and writing and the right is better suited for drawing and illustrating (Magnus & Laeng, 2006).

During-Reading Processing

We introduced text symbols to you in Chapter 1. We're going to show you another way to use these symbols. Use Text in the Spotlight (pages 115) to document your metacognition while reading this chapter. Write the page numbers of questions you have, confusing sections that you encounter, personal connections you made, words that are new to you, and opinions that you have. Also use these for discussions with other teachers. We have included a different Text in the Spotlight for your students' use on page 116.

Figure 4.1 Inscribe and Illustrate example

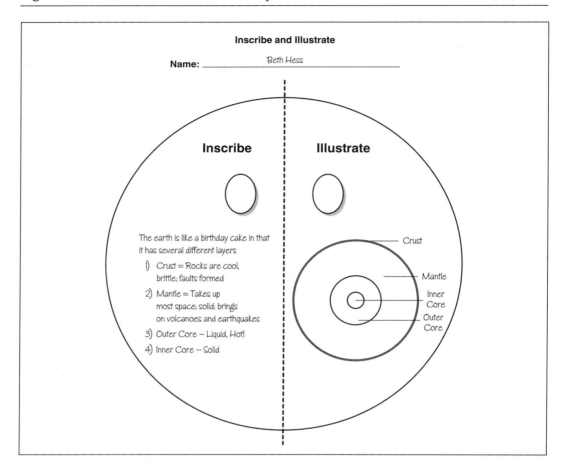

After-Reading Processing

What Is Processing?

1. What is your new definition of processing?

2. If you had to explain to a 10-year-old what processing is and why it's so important for his or her brain, how would you explain it?

3. Complete the following simile: Processing is like _____ because _____.

The Domains for Elaborate and Effective Processing (DEEP)

4. In a nutshell, what are the DEEP?

5. Which domain do you feel your students reach in most of your lessons? Why? What is your strength to which you attribute this?

6. Which domain do you want your students to reach more often? Why? What new strategies might you use in order to help your students reach this domain?

We've elaborated on how the Deeper Learning Cycle (DELC) Step 1 (Planning the Standards and Curriculum), Step 2 (Preassessing), Step 3 (Building a Positive Learning Culture), Step 4 (Priming and Activating Prior Knowledge), and Step 5 (Acquiring New Knowledge) play a part in deeper learning. This chapter describes Step 6, Processing the Learning Deeper, which culminates the deeper learning. In this chapter you learn what processing is, how it works, its location in the brain, the benefits of processing, and the DEEP, which allows students to process at levels at which they're comfortable and successful. After we introduce the DEEP, you are given over 45 deeper processing activities in Chapter 5 that can be used for any content in your classroom.

DELC STEP 6: WHAT IS PROCESSING? ■

Remember the last time you attended a funeral, wedding, concert, picnic, or big sporting event? If you're like most people, you did something after the event. It's likely that you thought about the event or shared your feelings and opinions about it with others. Good or bad, people usually have a few choice comments about life experiences. The bigger the event, the more they recycle the event. In an extreme case, remember how long the events of September 11 stayed in your thoughts, feelings, and conversations? Humans process an event by telling stories about it to others, creating cultural artifacts, or even simply grieving over the loss of loved ones. In that sense, humans all have an innate ability to process life experiences, but at a very simple level. Yet in order for humans to develop their full potential, and certainly to succeed in school, they need the skill set to turn raw information into better quality information. Most students don't have that skill set.

Since "processing" is an unfamiliar word in the field of education, here are some examples. Processing turns oranges into orange juice, trees into lumber, and recycled plastic into new products. Processing turns milk into cottage cheese, metal into a tool, and eggs into an omelet. Clearly, processing has a transformative capacity. As we mentioned earlier, in the educational context, processing may be referred to as "the consolidation, transformation and internalization of information by the learner" (Caine, Caine, & Crowell, 1994). It can be the path to understanding, insights, depth, and utility and, as a by-product, the path to memory.

Where in the Brain?

In our brains, processing turns raw data into stored knowledge, meaning, experiences, or feelings. Processing begins with the thalamus, the input "server" in the brain. All new unprocessed sensory information (except for olfactory data) comes to the thalamus first for initial processing. This same information is also routed simultaneously to the amygdala, so that any perceived uncertainty or threat can get first priority. This routing happens in 100 milliseconds (Davis & Whalen, 2001) and typically helps us to survive any fast and potentially deadly event. The amygdala makes a behavioral response as an immediate next step (before any cognitive or emotional response). If a flying object is moving quickly toward your head, it's a bad time to think about the motives of the rock thrower and a good time to duck fast.

Medial view of the brain

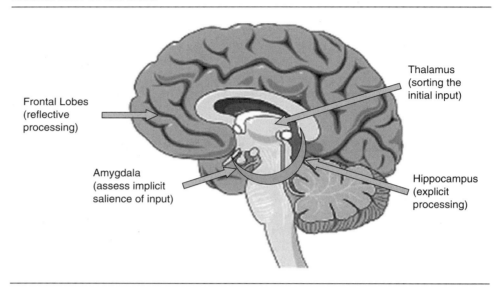

The rest of the data that students are confronted with every day in school needs something a bit more than a visceral response. The brain has routed visual input to the occipital lobe, sounds to the auditory cortex, touch sensations to the sensory cortex, and spatial representations to the parietal lobe. But this early-level processing doesn't give students much cognitively. To get to that, they need purposeful strategies to move forward. The DEEP described in this chapter and Chapter 5 are likely to engage nearly every area of the brain because they engage the emotional, movement, spatial, language, sound, memory, and thinking areas of the brain. This spreads the processing around in ways that include, not exclude, any of the multiple intelligences and learning styles.

How Do Students Process Learning?

It's been said that we're drowning in data and starving for meaning. Educators need to work with students to help them benefit from their experiences and learning. Teachers can support and guide their students' ability to process raw data into coherent, complete, and meaningful learning, as described in this chapter. Here are some examples.

Content can become more concrete by drawing pictures or symbols of the word or by using synonyms. Obviously, the more objects or experiences students are exposed to, the more concrete the concept becomes. Here are a few synonyms for "processing": contemplation, thinking, cognition, reflecting, consolidating, associating, meaning making, connecting, elaborating, rehearsing, reviewing, retrieving, and encoding. The following symbol is helpful in understanding what processing is all about. Every linguistic that is taught should have a nonlinguistic along with it, especially abstract terms like "processing." We hope the following nonlinguistic deepens your understanding of what processing means.

Imagine that the gears above the silhouetted faces represent thoughts inside the brain of each figure. Both figures think about what they learned from a lesson. They do this independently and then share their perspectives. The middle gear represents the new ideas and thoughts that come about from that sharing. The middle gear is very powerful and deep—ideas and thoughts are challenged, new paradigms are created, and neural networks are added to or changed because of this middle gear movement from powerful processing through conversations.

Spencer Bergstrand

After learning content, processing allows a person to reflect, study, evaluate, and create meaning from the content so that many ideas are internalized. Students make the content personally meaningful by making connections with what they already know about the content. One more step then needs to occur in order to maximize the benefits of processing: discussing the learning or content with somebody else. When two people discuss how they make content meaningful, a whole new arena opens up. New perspectives arise, paradigms are changed, opinions are challenged, deeper thinking is required, aha moments are swarming the brain, and the neurons are wiring and firing.

You have been processing while reading this chapter if you are participating in the Before Reading Processing by completing the Text in the Spotlight reproducible on page 115. You also have an opportunity to process after reading this chapter. You learn a lot from all of this independent processing, but we would like to challenge you to have someone else read this chapter and then both of you process together what was learned and how you plan to implement it. We hope you experience the deeper learning from this partner processing opportunity.

Why Students Need More, Not Less, Processing

You can't afford *not* to provide processing time in the classroom. Some signs that not enough processing is taking place are as follows: students and teachers are feeling overwhelmed and stressed; mastery is not shown among a large percentage of students; there is unfocused conversation among the students; there are confused looks, frustration, and giving up among students; and questions are not being asked or addressed. You can teach faster, but students will simply forget faster. A good mantra or rule of thumb is "Too much too fast won't last." The benefits of processing are what true learning is all about. The benefits are as follows:

• Information has a better opportunity for becoming meaningful and therefore more memorable.

• Processing time allows students to think about the learning, pose questions for clarity, and discover those answers to the questions. Questions lead to some of the most powerful learning opportunities. A question not asked or answered is a lost opportunity for lasting learning.

• Processing allows more opportunities for the subject at hand to be elaborated on. Elaboration allows for stronger and fuller connections between the neurons. The chunks of information become more in-depth and therefore allow more opportunities for connections in other subject areas and in application.

- Processing allows for more viewpoints to be considered and learned from. Paradigms change because of processing opportunities, among other factors. Viewpoints are challenged during processing.

- More emotion is attached to the content when processing opportunities are given. Processing gives the students' minds time to connect the content to what they know. Teachers can facilitate ways to bring emotion into the processing of content.

- We are strengthening working memory every time we give processing opportunities.

- While the students are processing, the teacher's mind is given an opportunity to reflect on how the lesson is going. This time can help the teacher make quick changes or rethink how something was taught. It's a time to evaluate how the lesson is going and how to make the necessary changes for success for all students. Not only will the students' brains benefit from processing; the teacher's will also.

Try it in your classroom to see the benefits. Also, try reading this book by processing each section you read. See how much more you learn when you process chunks of reading by participating in the During-Reading activities in this book. The information becomes more meaningful, more deep, and therefore more memorable and applicable.

■ THE DOMAINS FOR ELABORATE AND EFFECTIVE PROCESSING (DEEP)

By now you should be ready to sink your teeth into the real nitty-gritty of how to process. But first we need to make a distinction: not all processing is the same. Asking your students to "just process" the material is too vague and can even be a waste of time. There is no one-size-fits-all, and you should have different processing strategies to fit different students and different situations. The four domains of the DEEP are broad categories for different types of thinking. Ultimately, the strategies in these domains are part of the daily lesson plan.

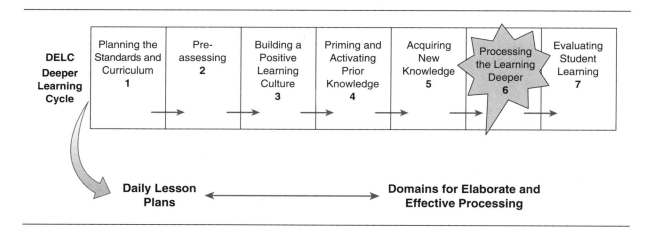

There's an understandable tendency to use the "default" form of processing hierarchy of Bloom's taxonomy. The short version looks like this:

Bloom's Taxonomy

Level	Type of Thinking	Example
HIGH	Evaluation	How do you feel about investing American money in space exploration?
	Synthesis	How would you improve the space station that is currently in outer space?
	Analysis	Which planets are most like the Earth? Which categories would you use to sort the similarities between all nine planets?
	Application	How can the study of planets in our solar system help our world?
	Comprehension	What adjectives might you give to each planet to describe its unique characteristics?
LOW	Knowledge	What are the nine planets in our solar system?

Unfortunately, this presumed hierarchy doesn't mesh with current brain research. We're grateful to many educators and researchers, including Spencer Kagan and Robert Marzano (Bloom et al., 1956; Kagan, 1994; Marzano & Kendall, 2006), who have described the mismatches, and there are many. A common criticism is that it is not a good match to how we actually think. The following are a few examples of the differences between the old and new research:

OLD SCHOOL: Higher-level skills are always based on lower-level skills.
NEW: Many of our higher-level skills operate independently from lower-level skills. In fact, if brain damage impairs lower-level skills, often higher ones are preserved. This doesn't mean that all deeper learning doesn't require simple learning; it does mean that some learning is independent of simple learning (O'Kane, Kensinger, & Corkin, 2004).

OLD SCHOOL: In order to evaluate, one must have higher-level thinking skills.
NEW: Evaluation can occur without higher-level thinking. Many evaluative processes in our brain happen too fast for thinking; we just "know." As an example, our amygdala evaluates incoming stimuli and activates other neural structures involving racial out-groups in less than a second without any formal education (Hart et al., 2000). Hart and colleagues' study showed that unless we have prior experience with an ethnic group, our brain instantly makes an evaluation that the person we're seeing is "of concern" and we should stay alert. Without any data to support this decision, the brain is saying that it's better to be safe than sorry and people should err on the side of caution regarding outsiders.

OLD SCHOOL: Higher-level thinking requires simultaneous lower-level engagement.
NEW: So-called higher-level thinking often occurs without lower-level engagement. Using our deductive reasoning, we primarily engage brain structures in the right hemisphere, but we engage no lower processes.

Higher-level thinking skills are independent of them. A classic example is a high-IQ student who has had damage to certain so-called lower-level thinking parts of the brain (Murai et al., 1998; Treffert & Wallace, 2002) but is nonetheless perfectly able to function at higher-level thinking tasks. The more "basic" or lower structures were dysfunctional, yet the high-IQ subject was able to perform at a high level. This often happens with head injuries.

OLD SCHOOL: Each level is more complex than the level below it. **NEW**: Each of the steps can be simple or complex. A good example is the experience we've all had of meeting "the guy in the diner" (or bar, or pub, etc.). Often this person is quick to evaluate and judge just about every person, every event, and any politician or ballot measure. Supposedly the higher-level thinking such as evaluation requires higher-level thinking, but in reality it can be either simple or complex. This highly opinionated short-order chef, bartender, or waitress has got an opinion (evaluation) on everything. But he or she may have little or no complex reasoning in coming up with the evaluation. In fact, any level of thinking can be simple or complex. A recall question can be complex when it involves space, person, time, day, context, and so on. It can also be placed in a historical, financial, geographic, or political context. In short, a simple question can remain simple or become complex depending on how the listener treats it. The commonly held notion of a vertically stacked taxonomy is not only intuitively incorrect; it doesn't hold up under scientific or evidence-based scrutiny (Marzano & Kendall, 2006).

There are several challenges in the Bloom model. First, as outlined above, it doesn't match up with how our brain actually processes. Second, it's often posted on walls in schools but rarely used. This may be because it can be intimidating and there is a lack of staff development for teachers in how to use it. Finally, the processing has to be simple and integrated into daily instruction for all learners. Kagan (1994) uses the cooperative structures model, and it has many merits. We use the DEEP model processing structures described in Chapter 5. The suggestions made below include multiple approaches. In each type of processing (we call them thinking domains), teachers can make the activity simple, moderate in difficulty, or very challenging. The tiering notes help you do this. Not surprisingly, there are many ways to sort and group the actions of processing. Here are four different yet generic domains for processing. Each of these serves a different purpose, and each supports the others.

After what you've learned in earlier chapters, you'll be able to assess the skills and background knowledge of your students. Then you can decide if your students are meeting the standards and expectations for their grade and class levels. Once you've done both of these, you'll be able to say which of the following processing domains you want to begin with. Typically, you'll use two to three of these processing pathways in one lesson. Just because there's no goal in the NCLB standards for a certain type of processing doesn't mean it's worth ignoring. Give students the tools to succeed in life, regardless of the constraints.

The reproducible on pages 117 through 120 helps you see the details of each of the processing domains, and the table helps you compare and contrast the domains. Notice the symbols that are used to represent the type of processing. The symbol is a nonlinguistic that helps you get a better grasp of the abstract term. Text in the columns (a) describe the domain and give a symbol, (b) give variations of the domain name, (c) describe the end product that you see when students are processing in this domain, (d) list a possible range of questions that can be asked, and (e) give specific processing activity titles (the actual activities are explained in Chapter 5).

Domain 1: Awareness

While you read this, what noises are you aware of? Are you aware of the humming of air conditioners or heaters? Are you aware of a leaky faucet, dripping every now and then? There are certain noises that surround people, but they just aren't aware or cognizant of them. Awareness is the consciousness of what's going on around us. It means to soak up the environment by observing it, feeling it, and listening to it. Once you're aware of something, in most cases you're able to recognize it, recall it, identify it, describe it, and remember it.

The Awareness domain is like an appetizer: it's what a guest digests at the beginning of a meal. The appetizer tells the stomach that it wants more and is ready for more. The Awareness domain prepares the brain to want more depth and width to the topic that was just introduced or brought to awareness.

The end result of being in a state of awareness could be any of the following: interest or knowledge can be heightened; definitions and basic background information can be understood; feelings, sounds, and observations can be explained; and the brain can be better prepared for more elaboration, more detail, or more chunks of information. Deeper learning doesn't necessarily occur in this domain, but this domain enhances the other domains of learning in which deeper learning is experienced.

There are several questions that enhance the awareness of the environment around you. These questions are listed from simple to complex but could easily change, based on the content that completes the question stem. Page 117 has a list of questions that you can ask or can be generated by your students to enhance their awareness of the content they're acquiring.

Domain 2: Analysis to Synthesis

Now that the appetizer has been consumed, it's time for the main dish. The Analysis to Synthesis domain allows the brain to see the whole and the parts and then create a new whole. This domain is about separating and combining knowledge and ideas in order to dive deeply into the parts of the whole and then place those parts back together to form a new whole. You analyze the information and then synthesize it for deeper learning. Learning is not about soaking in knowledge; instead, it's about changing the knowledge into something meaningful for the learner who is processing it.

Use this domain to increase the scope and breadth of the material so as to bring in related material. If students are limiting their topic too much, use these processing strategies. This domain broadens their horizons and gives them more of a sense of what others have already written on the topic. When this domain is used, students can see the bigger picture of the topic. They can see how other big concepts are included in the topic.

Use this domain to develop a topic in greater detail and coherence. Ask students to focus on the details of the main idea. If students are watering down their topic too much, and they're too unfocused and scattered, use the strategies and questions for this domain on page 118.

This domain helps students make sense of the material. You might hear them say, "Oh, now I get it!" This domain allows students to explain to anyone what they learned. Fundamental relationships are enhanced or created between concepts during this processing domain.

The end product of this domain is coherence and eventual richness of understanding that can be explained in the learner's own words. There will be a greater understanding of the parts and whole of the content. New theories might be created, since the learner will be combining the parts into a new whole.

There are several questions on page 118 that teachers and students might ask that could bring about this hourglass of learning. These questions are listed from simple to complex but could easily change, based on the content that completes the question stem.

Domain 3: Application

Now that the food has been digested, it's time to use that food as fuel, to do something productive with that food. Information is great to play Trivial Pursuit with, win game shows, or spit out on a standardized test, but it's what you *do* with information that really counts. The Application domain is about practicing, doing, or using the information that was learned to benefit oneself, one's community, the nation, or the world.

The end product of this domain is evidence that students have mastered the content. Mastery is not just simply reproducing the learning but rather displaying what was learned in a different way than originally given. For more elaborative and effective learning to occur, students need to transform the content to make it more meaningful to themselves so they can apply the information or skills in several ways. For example, a student can learn and memorize the following multiplication fact: $4 \times 5 = 20$. That's great! But so what? Does that student know what that equation really means (4 groups of 5—really addition)? Can that student also solve $5 \times 4 = 20$ and 20 divided by 5 = 4 and 20 divided by 4 = 5? Can the student solve word problems that use that equation? Can the student use that equation in a grocery store while shopping to figure out how much of a product should be purchased? Can that student *use* that equation in several different ways for meaningful, real-world situations?

Part of this step is inviting students to show what they've learned through a variety of products. Students should be transforming the information to show what they learned. We learned that allowing students choice can be very empowering. This is a great opportunity to use a list of products for students to choose from, to bring in multiple intelligences, and to provide real-world ideas of application for the objectives you're teaching.

There are several question stems on page 119 that evaluate whether or not the students can apply what was just learned. Often these questions become the tools for your evaluations. Encouraging students to self-evaluate also enhances this domain. Using rubrics not only helps the teacher to clearly define what is expected from the learning but also explains to students how they'll be assessed in the application of the learning.

Domain 4: Assimilation

Now that some of the food has been used up by doing something with it, the body stores the rest for later use or for it to become a permanent part of the body. Some digested foods become muscle, others fats, some are turned into bone or skin for repair after a cut. Assimilation is the heart of the content, the internalizing of the information personally, or the personal connections with the content or skill. It's the emotional response to the content, the empathizing and putting oneself in another's shoes. It's the key to keeping this world sane. It's the key to personal growth and change. It's the key to eliminating habits and detrimental patterns in the cycle of life. It's the ultimate learning goal.

This domain may not be *fully* reached at the end of a lesson. It takes time, experiences, and maturity to take content from the Awareness domain to this deep Assimilation domain. Students might reach this domain after several Application domains. There are several strategies that you can use to facilitate students in this domain.

This domain utilizes one's perspective and opinion. In this domain, we need to help students respect others' points of view, learn how to support their own, and change their perspective when they see they're wrong. If students are too narrow in their point of view or if they're prejudiced or just incomplete in their perspective, use these processing strategies.

How will you know if your students are processing at this domain with the content that they learned? You might observe some of the following end results of this processing domain: goal setting; journaling or diary writing; emotional responses such as opinions stated strongly, debates, critiques, praise, support, or nonsupport; leaders forming—not following the status quo but doing what is believed to be right; serving others and helping them; and being a role model.

Page 120 contains a list of questions for this domain that helps students arrive at these end results. These question stems are just the beginning of this step. The specific processing strategies in Chapter 5 give you the tools and strategies to help bring all students into this domain of thinking in many lessons.

You officially have the background knowledge to dive deeper into the specific examples of the DEEP. In this chapter, you have explored what processing is, where it occurs in the brain, how the brain works during processing, why processing must be made a priority in the classroom, and the grand finale of putting it all together with the DEEP model.

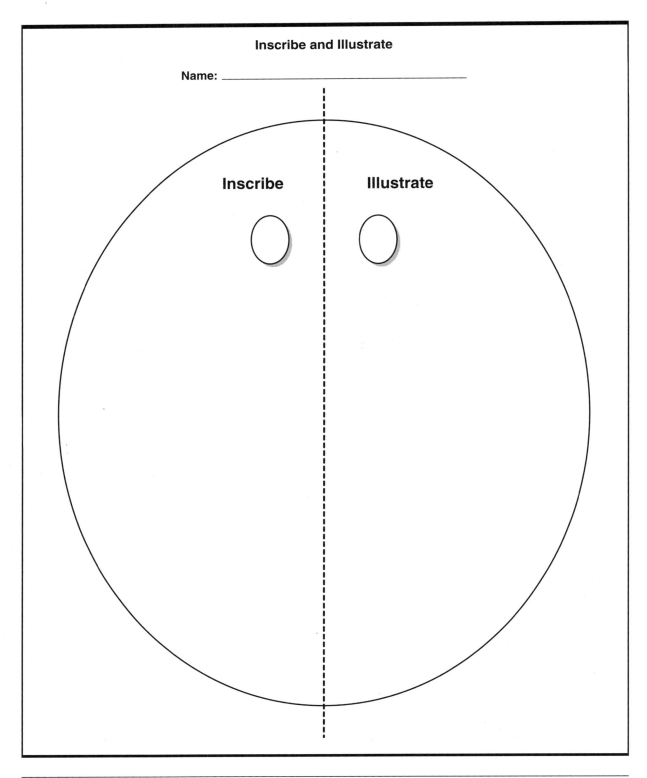

Inscribe and Illustrate

Name: _____

Inscribe   **Illustrate**

TEXT IN THE SPOTLIGHT: PROCESSING THIS BOOK

Name: _____

Book: _Deeper Learning_

Questions That I Have:	
p.	
p.	
p.	
Confusing Sections for Me:	
p.	
p.	
p.	
Personal Connections to Me:	
p.	
p.	
p.	
New Ideas for My Classroom:	
p.	
p.	
p.	
Opinions I Have (agree, disagree, like, dislike, comment, etc.):	
p.	
p.	
p.	
Information to Discuss With Other Educators:	
p.	
p.	
p.	
CREATE:	
p.	
p.	
p.	

(Continued)

(Continued)

TEXT IN THE SPOTLIGHT: STUDENT PAGE

Name: _____

Book: _____

Questions That I Have:	
p.	
p.	
p.	
Confusing Sections for Me:	
p.	
p.	
p.	
Personal Connections to Me:	
p.	
p.	
p.	
New Words for Me:	
p.	
p.	
p.	
Opinions I Have (agree, disagree, like, dislike, comment, etc.):	
p.	
p.	
p.	
Figurative Language:	
p.	
p.	
p.	
CREATE:	
p.	
p.	
p.	

DEEP
Domains for Elaborate and Effective Processing

Domain and Symbol	What Is It?	Variations	End Product
Awareness	The consciousness of what's going on . . . to be cognizant and aware	Retrieving, observing, recognizing, recalling, defining, explaining, identifying, remembering, understanding, describing.	Experience-activated, interest heightened, priming; knowledge and definitions understood; the basic information, sounds and feelings can be described and put in context, new learning; ready for elaboration, detail, and more chunks

Possible Range of Questions

- Who did what, where, and when? What do you know about . . . ?
- Can you define, list, recall, or identify . . . ?
- How would you explain or describe . . . ?
- How did _____ happen?
- Can you explain what is meant by . . . ?
- Are you aware of how you responded to _____ ?
- What background or biases have shaped your awareness?

- How do you know what you know?
- Are you sure . . . ?
- How reliable and valid is . . . ?
- What do you mean?
- What is going on here?
- Do we have enough facts to suggest . . . ?

Processing Activity Titles:

WebMonster	Elaborate and Extrapolate (E & E Time)	Door Pass
The Important Book	Quick Writing Response Tools	Countdown Processing
Stump the Chump	Reporter Goes Big Time	Quality Questioning Strategies
20 Questions	Rap & Chant	

(Continued)

DEEP

Domains for Elaborate and Effective Processing

Domain and Symbol	What Is It?	Variations	End Product
Analysis to Synthesis	Wholes to Parts and Reverse! Separating or combining of knowledge and ideas in order to see the parts from the whole and then to put the parts together to form a new whole	Ordering, synthesizing, summarizing, regrouping, integrating, symbolizing, generalizing, matching, rewording, comparing, contrasting, error correcting, classifying, investigating, abstracting, comprehending, describing, associating, patterning, sequencing, dissecting, dividing, deducting, drawing conclusions, idea to example, reasoning, estimating, assessing, criticizing, decision making, determining fallacies, interpreting, prioritizing, elaborating, organizing, distinguishing, rearranging	Coherence and eventual richness of understanding, more thorough understanding of content in own words; new ideas formed; better wholeness and better understanding of the pieces; the context is better understood and the supporting details too; bigger picture taken apart and put back together differently; aha moments; new theories formed

Possible Range of Questions

- How would you sequence these parts?
- What steps are important in the process of . . . ?
- What are the parts, features, sections, properties, characteristics of ____ ?
- How would you label them to show ____ ?
- How would you organize ____ to show ____ ?
- How is ____ related to/like ____ ?
- How would you support the big idea of ____ ?
- How does this compare/contrast with ____ ?
- Where does this idea/concept fit in a historical context?
- Have you considered . . . ?
- Where does this fit . . . ?

- What solutions are emerging?
- Where do you see gaps or ambiguities?
- How can we fit ____ together with ____ ?
- How can you design, invent, compose, or arrange ____ ?
- What are some alternative solutions and arrangements?
- How would you improve it?
- How did ____ happen?
- Can you explain what is meant by . . . ?
- What changes would you make to solve ____ ? How can these changes improve it?
- Can you formulate a theory?

Title of Activities:

Encode It! Spinner
Super Mooter
ABS: Association by Scavenging
WebQuest

What's the Biggest Idea?
Five and Five
Question Top-Down Webbing
Headlines for Heralding

Smash Pics
HAS Synopsis

DEEP
Domains for Elaborate and Effective Processing

Domain and Symbol	What Is It?	Variations	End Product
Application	Practicing, doing or using what was learned to benefit self, community, nation, or world	Decision making, problem solving, generating and testing hypotheses, adapting, transferring, predicting, synthesizing, visualizing, creating, elaborating, inventing, associating, applying	Evidence that students mastered the content; becomes the evaluation piece; dramatizing, debating, simulating, writing, building, producing art, supplying content for a Web site, creating posters, building models, making a PowerPoint or DVD to share, etc.

Possible Range of Questions

- How can you prove to me that you understand this?
- How does _____ apply to _____?
- How would you use or demonstrate . . . ?
- What approach or technique would you use to . . . ?
- What else could you have done?
- What do you think _____ would have done if _____?

Titles of Activities:

Web-N-Pass

Who's Been There and Done That?

Virtual Interviews

Expert Interviews

Missing Links

Arts Galore!

Connect Four

Independent Contract Choices

Presentations With Pizzazz and Purpose

Choosing Your Task: Structured Choices

Three-Point Summary

Palm Pilot

(Continued)

(Continued)

DEEP

Domains for Elaborate and Effective Processing

Domain and Symbol	What Is It?	Variations	End Product
Assimilation ♥	The heart of the content: internalizing the information personally; personal connections	Absorption, incorporation, digestion, integration, reflection, perspective taking, monitor the process, empathizing, reviewing importance, efficiency, efficacy, emotional response, motivation	Setting goals; journaling or diary writing; emotional responses such as debates, critiques, praise, support, and nonsupport; creating a documentary, being a role model, using a blog, mentoring another learner

Possible Range of Questions

- Do you agree or disagree with _____ and why?
- Do your goals or strategies need to change?
- What makes you say that?
- How would you justify, rate, evaluate, and defend the importance of . . . ?
- Which is better and which is worse?
- How would you prioritize or rank . . . ?
- Which solution is the best and why?
- Does this compete with any values you hold? Which ones? How?
- How did you feel about learning about this?
- What are the most important things that you have learned to date?
- Are there things that you would now do differently if you could repeat the experience, and if so, why? How differently do you see your future role as a learner in light of this learning so far?
- Does this validate or repudiate anything you know?
- How will you take this and grow from it?
- In light of what I have learned so far, what are my learning priorities for the next few weeks? How can I build on what I have already learned? What new knowledge and understanding do I hope to acquire? What new skills do I need to develop? What can I do to ensure that I don't lose sight of these objectives?

Title of Activities:

Processing Notebook
Stop-N-Think
Walking in the Shoes of Another
The Six Thinking Hats

Four-Choice Processing
Media Bias
Create Your Own Rubric to Evaluate
Personal Reflection on Processing

TELL: A Tool for Growth
Goal-Setting Template
Stop-Save-Start
WRITE!

5

Processing Strategies Galore

*DELC Step 6—Processing
the Learning Deeper*

Before-Reading Processing

Ask yourself the following questions:

1. How often do my students process now in a lesson?

   Circle one: rarely   usually   always

2. Which Domain for Elaborate and Effective Processing (DEEP) do I tend to use the most during processing activities in the classroom?

3. Which domain (DEEP) should I branch out to use more?

During-Reading Processing

Use the graphic organizer labeled Favorites of _____ (page 218). While reading through each of these activities, write in the domain's box the name of the activity you like the best from each domain and which upcoming lesson, concept, or skill you could use it with. You will be more committed to using the strategies if you photocopy this graphic organizer, write on it, and place it on your desk to remind yourself to use these strategies and activities.

Graphic organizers are a powerful memory strategy, since they help reinforce the most important information from the reading and store the information near similar known information. Eleven studies have been performed on the benefits of graphic organizers and documented in the *Report of the National Reading Panel* (NRP) (2000). The main advantage of using graphic organizers is improvement of the reader's memory for the content that has been read. Four of the studies showed achievement gains in the content areas too (Armbruster & Anderson, 1991).

After-Reading Processing

Evaluate the 45 processing activities in this chapter by giving them one of the following awards:

1. Most Likely to Use This Week Award: _____

2. Most Excited to Use Soon Award: _____

3. Most Likely to Be Used in the Next Unit Award: _____

4. Most Confusing Activity Award: _____

5. Least Likely to Use Award: _____

You now have the DEEP and directions for when and how to use them. Now we describe the 45 specific processing activities you can use in your classroom. These processing activities get your students actively processing at levels where they can be consistently successful. You can quickly implement these processing activities in your classroom with minimal preparation time because we've included step-by-step instructions, examples of how to use them, preparation and material lists, differentiated ideas, and usually a graphic organizer to support them.

Notice that we explained how to tier up and tier down with each activity. This differentiated section allows you to make it more challenging (tier up) for those students who are ready for it and also to make it less challenging (tier down) for those students who have less background knowledge on the topic or skill at hand.

We've suggested several grade levels for each activity, but we encourage you to read *all* the processing activities. You might have a group of students who need a certain processing activity from a different group of grade levels. We believe that all these processing activities can be used in Grades 4 through 12 classrooms and in all types of training sessions, but we also make grade-level suggestions, since some activities are more geared for the upper grades and adult learners and others are more geared for the intermediate school years.

Keep in mind that you still need to decide how you want to use these activities. You have the following choices with each processing activity. Use them

- Independently, in pairs or small groups (we wrote a recommendation)
- At the beginning of the lesson, during the lesson, or after the lesson (minilesson, reading, video, etc.)
- With social studies, math, science, language arts, foreign language, physical education, art, music, economics, and so on
- By giving the students choices on how to respond or sometimes giving all students the same way to respond

The activities are in the four domains of the DEEP: Awareness, Analysis to Synthesis, Application, and Assimilation.

DOMAIN 1: AWARENESS ACTIVITIES ■

The following processing activities allow students to become more aware of information, surroundings, and other stimuli. Note that the Awareness domain doesn't by itself lead to deeper learning. In actuality, this domain leads students to process simple learning so that successful deeper learning can occur in the other domains.

Activity for Awareness: WebMonster

Objective: Help students make as many connections as possible with your current topic or soon-to-be-taught unit.

Suggested Grades: 4–8

Materials: Large drawing paper for each student, either 11 × 17 inches or flip chart paper or butcher paper, color pens or twist-up colored pencils

Preparation:

- Prepare students for the content with preexposure days, stories, or movies.
- Get them excited about using their built-in human computer—their brain!
- Get a timekeeper for each group and a fast writer.

Time Needed: 13–15 minutes

Grouping Suggestions: Mix up students so they're in fresh groupings of three to four students.

Instructions: This is a three-part activity.

1. State the topic for the groups and challenge them to do a word association by coming up with 10 words in 60 seconds that have some connection to the topic word.

2. Next, have each group delete 3 of the "least relevant" words on their lists and then do a round-robin brainstorming word association on the remaining 7 words, giving them 60 seconds to come up with 10 more words for each of the 7.

3. The paper should now have nearly 70 associations. Now ask the small teams to take 60 seconds and eliminate the 20 most unrelated words. This gives your students a much wider path for the new topic. They now have 50 new subtopics for their learning.

Remember To: Have the students do a quick warm-up physically by walking around and reviewing prior knowledge. Have them warm up mentally by doing a stand-pair-fast read of a book index to their partner for 30 seconds. Remind them that brainstorming means *no* judgments—just quantity. Do plenty of encouraging. Create a fun competition, if that seems to help. If not, back off and throw out a few word samples to keep them going.

Cautions: If their energy sags, don't despair. Get everyone up for a quick 1-minute stretch break or have them circle three tables and touch four walls and then have a seat. Keep the mental and physical energy up.

Differentiation:

Tier Up: Include higher goals per group; give students less time.

Tier Down: Begin with a priming activity before this activity begins to get their brains started; double the time for brainstorming each topic; cut the goals in half.

Example: The topic is photosynthesis. Five groups each come up with 10 words that have some connection (e.g., *plants, sun, green, chemical, survival, light, leaves, oxygen, bacteria, chloroplasts*). Now each group deletes 3 of the least relevant 10 words (now we have left *leaves, oxygen, plants, sun, survival, green, light*). Now the groups do a word association on those remaining 7 words, with only 60 seconds to uncover 10 more words for each of the 7. For just 1 word, the word "leaves," they may come up with *small, big, green, yellow, orange, respiration, food, rake up, fruit,* and *bugs*. Next, students do that with the other 6 words left. They'll have nearly 70 associations. Finally, ask the small teams to take 60 seconds and eliminate the 20 most unrelated words. This gives your students a broader awareness for the new topic. They'll have 50 new subtopics for their learning!

Activity for Awareness: The Important Book

Objective: Students will scrutinize the details of a main idea from a topic being learned and become more aware of the facts involved in a topic.

Suggested Grades: 4–8

Materials: One copy of *The Important Book* and a copy of The Important Book template (page 219) for each student

Preparation:

- Have the book ready to share: *The Important Book* by Margaret Wise Brown (1949) OR
- If you don't want to purchase the book, then use the example below to show the template

Time Needed: 5–7 minutes

Grouping Suggestions: Individual, group share

Instructions:

1. Read aloud *The Important Book* to students. This is a short picture book that explains what is important about the everyday things we see. It's a very simple book but has an incredibly deep structure to it, that is, the most important aspect of an item is mentioned first and repeated again at the end. The other reasons why this item is important are mentioned between the first and last aspect. There are five "other" reasons why this item is important.

2. After learning about a topic, concept, or skill, students are asked to complete The Important Book template about that topic. They have to evaluate what they think is the most important aspect of the topic and then decide on five other aspects that make that item so important.

3. Students can discuss with one another why they chose their particular aspect to be the most important.

Remember To: Read several pages from *The Important Book* so that students understand the format of the book. Discuss with students the idea that choosing the most important information from a text or topic depends on their background knowledge. They need to be able to explain why it's important to them.

Differentiation:

Tier Up:

- Use this format for debates.
- Ask students to support all their statements with details as to why those aspects are so important. Add the word "because" after each statement.
- Ask students to support the most important information with each of the details. In other words, they create a main idea that is the most important information, and the other five details must support it.

Tier Down:
  • Use the template on page 219. The five other aspects about the topic do not necessarily need to support the Most Important Thing.

Example: See Figure 5.1, The Important Book example: Neurons.

Figure 5.1   The Important Book example: Neurons

The Important Book
By: Margaret Wise Brown
Student: _Raul_

The important thing about _neurons_ is that _they transmit electrical and chemical messages._

Write 5 other facts about the above topic:

1. _The electrical impulse starts at the dendrites, flows through the axons, and then sparks the release of the neurotransmitters or chemicals._

2. _We have enough electricity flowing in us to illuminate a 25 watt lightbulb._

3. _Some of the chemicals that are released are dopamine, serotonin, and endorphins._

4. _The neurotransmitters form our states of mind such as focused and alert or sleepy and unfocused._

5. _These states of mind greatly affect how well a student can learn at a given point of time._

But the important thing about _neurons_ is _they transmit electrical and chemical messages._

Activity for Awareness: Stump the Chump

Objective: Student teams will ask questions of other teams in order to enhance their awareness about a topic.

Suggested Grades: 4–10

Materials: Index cards, 10 per small group

Preparation: Make this a fun, not stressful, activity. Consider props or gags to lighten the mood.

Time Needed: 30–45 minutes

Grouping Suggestions: Teams of four to six—you'll need an even number of groups.

Instructions:

1. Students need time to review material already assigned.

2. Groups generate a list of 10 questions from the class or text about material everyone has already been exposed to. Questions should be of moderate difficulty, and the answers should all be short. Encourage students to use the question stems on the DEEP table in Chapter 4 (pages 117–120) to generate questions from each domain. Each group will assign one person to be the Scribe to write these 10 questions on the 10 index cards (one question per card).

3. Students quiz each other in the group to ensure everyone knows the answers to the questions they designed.

4. Teachers ensure that every student has the opportunity to represent his or her group and that each student has the opportunity to cheer the others on. It should be on a rotation basis.

5. Two groups come to the front of the class. The teacher divides the rest of the class in half temporarily so that each group up has its own cheering gallery. Each group directs questions from their list of 10 questions to the leader ("chump") of the other group and tries to "stump" the leader.

6. Groups alternate questions. The group leaders get gallery cheers when they answer correctly. They can get a "lifeline" from their teammates if they wish.

7. When all 10 questions are answered from each group, two new students come up front.

Remember To: You might pick a student to be the emcee so that the two groups keep it moving quickly. Keep it light—it's a fun way to understand the content better as a review.

Differentiation:

Tier Up: Make the questions more complex, no lifelines, or less time to prepare.

Tier Down: Allow more support (chumps can poll the audience if they get stuck and have more lifelines, etc.).

Example: For a unit on drugs and their effects, possible questions to ask: What are three examples of a stimulant? What negative effects does a stimulant have on the body? What are two examples of a depressant? How will a depressant affect your body? How do morphine, heroin, and codeine (narcotics) affect your body?

Activity for Awareness: 20 Questions

Objective: Students will gain a better understanding of the topic.

Suggested Grades: 4–10

Materials: Put the 20 questions on a handout (one for each student).

Preparation: A good priming activity is beneficial. Small groups can browse source materials. Be sure the 20-question list has been modified or adapted especially for the content or topic.

Time Needed: 20 minutes

Grouping Suggestions: Partners

Instructions:

1. Partnerships receive a list of the 20 questions that are designed by you to help students review the topic that is written at the top of the page.

2. Students will receive 60 seconds to write a short, quick answer to the question that the partner reads aloud. The partnerships take turns asking and answering the 20 questions. Encourage partnerships to assist each other and circle the questions they had difficulty answering.

3. After time is up, the students create a new list of five things they need to learn more about and a plan to get the knowledge.

Remember To: Keep the activity light and fast. It would be easy for it to drag. The use of music as background is a good idea.

Differentiation:

Tier Up:

- Ask these students to help you write the 20 questions. Allow them to cross off an easy question and replace it with a more challenging question that they create.

Tier Down:

- Allow the students to work in small groups, give them more time, allow them to use resources, cut the number of questions into five a day over 4 days.
- Create a graphic organizer with 20 boxes so students can easily write quick, short answers to the 20 questions in the boxes (less overwhelming than a bunch of lines).

Example:
Our topic could be anything from haiku, rain forests, the Pythagorean theorem, or global warming to the Korean War. If the topic is the brain, 20 possible questions are as follows (always modify the questions for the topic):

1. What is it? Object or concept?

2. What is it made of?

3. What is its real, elementary nature?

4. What are its parts, various kinds, and facets?

5. What is it like, unlike? (similes and metaphors help in understanding abstractions)

6. How rare or unique is it?

7. What is it a part of? What is that part a part of?

8. Which part of it is unusual or outstanding?

9. In what forms does it appear?

10. Is it typical or atypical of its kind?

11. What is it not? What is it confused with?

12. What is it opposed to?

13. How is it different? What makes it different?

14. Where did it come from? Where was it conceived or developed?

15. Are its origins meaningful now?

16. What makes it spread or multiply or gain adherents?

17. What was the reason behind it? Is the reason still valid or useful? Why? Why not? Is it still needed?

18. What influences it?

19. Does it change?

20. Can it or should it be changed, strengthened, or eliminated?

Activity for Awareness: Elaborate and Extrapolate (E & E Time)

Objective: Students will be able to review, elaborate, and then use vocabulary words in new ways (extrapolate).

Suggested Grades: 4–12

Materials: The Elaborate and Extrapolate Graphic Organizer (E & E Time) (page 220); list of vocabulary words; and the Elaboration Ideas for Vocabulary Words (page 221)

Preparation: Photocopy the Elaborate and Extrapolate Graphic Organizer and the Elaboration Ideas for Vocabulary Words—one of each per student. Post the vocabulary words that you want the students to use for this activity.

Time Needed: 15–20 minutes

Grouping Suggestions: Three to four students per group or partnership (depends on the number of vocabulary words). Each student elaborates on three vocabulary words from the list (for example, having three students per group, you need nine words total).

Instructions:

1. Place students in groups of three or four. Ask them to each choose three words from the list of vocabulary words that you have provided (on the chalkboard, handout, computer, etc.). Each student in the group needs three different words (they can't elaborate on the same word in their groups).

2. Students use the graphic organizer (page 220) to elaborate and extrapolate on each word. Each row on this graphic organizer guides students to a better understanding of their chosen words. In the first box of the row, students list the word and its definition. Explain to the students that a good definition is one that is in the student's own words and written simply for understanding. In the second box of the row, students choose two ways from the Elaboration Ideas for Vocabulary Words (page 221) in which they want to elaborate on the word. They use the provided space (and the back of the page if more room is needed) to show the elaboration choice. Encourage students to use a variety from that list. After these two boxes are filled in, students are ready for the last box of the row—Extrapolation. Extrapolation is the ability to form a new conclusion based on what is known. It's time for the students to use the word in a new way by creating their own sentence using the word. Encourage the students to use the word in at least two different ways in their newly created sentences (suffix change, tense change, different meaning, etc.). The sentence must have enough detail for the reader to know that the writer does understand the word's meaning well, *and* the sentences must reflect how the students think the word will be used in the unit of study or book that is being read.

3. When the graphic organizers are complete, you can do any of the following activities with these words:
   - Students read their sentences aloud, and the other group members need to guess what the word means. The students also teach the other group members the word through the elaboration ideas.
   - Students share their word meanings with the other students. The other students take notes while each student is teaching his or her words. Notes can be taken on another sheet of paper or on the back of the graphic organizer. These notes are used to study for the test or for other activities.
   - Students take the information and create a vocabulary test with the words. The teacher chooses the best vocabulary test to deliver to the whole class.
   - Students share their vocabulary words with their teammates and then they each create another, different sentence using the word.

Differentiation:

Tier Up: Give more challenging vocabulary words. Ask the students to elaborate more and use more challenging elaboration ideas.

Tier Down: Provide more support by helping students with how to elaborate on the word. Cross out one whole row and focus on fewer words. Help these students devise a definition. Ask these students to create just one Extrapolation sentence.

Example:

Word: Extrapolate

Definition: To arrive at conclusions or results by hypothesizing from known facts or observations.

Elaborate on the Word:

1. Synonyms: predict, hypothesize, infer

2. Relate to the real world: extrapolation often occurs in the world of science. Scientists observe what is happening and then create an extrapolation from what they see.

Extrapolation:

1. I extrapolate after my basketball game in order to have a better game next time.

2. In order to think at higher levels with content, we need to extrapolate from the ideas and facts so that new paradigms can be made.

Activity for Awareness: Quick Writing Response Tools

Objective: Students will be able to show quickly if they understood what was taught by sharing answers to questions in kinesthetic ways. This is a quick tool for the teacher to evaluate the accuracy of the students' responses and then correct any misunderstandings. A better awareness is formed of the content being taught.

Suggested Grades: 4–8

Materials: You'll need the following supplies depending on which kinesthetic response you want your students to use:

- Gel boards (see www.gelboard.com)—magnetic gel boards that students can write on with skinny pencils—magnetic response—one per student
- Dry erase boards (purchase from most teacher stores), dry erase markers and erasers too, one per student
- Lap chalkboards (purchase from most teacher stores), chalk and erasers, one per student

Preparation: Have these supplies (depending on which ones you choose to purchase) near the students so they can grab them at any point during your lesson to show you what they know. You can quickly evaluate the level of accuracy in their answers.

Instructions:

1. Gel boards, dry erase boards, or chalkboards—decide which one of these written response tools would work best in your classroom. The pros and cons are listed below to help you with your decision:

   Gel boards: Pros—clean, easy to use, easy to erase (put pressure on the board with your thumb and rub the answer away); Con—could rip or form deep lines if students misuse it

   Dry erase boards: Pros—can use colorful markers; Cons—they smell and create a mess when erasing

   Chalkboards: Pros—easy to write with, no smell; Cons—messy and must have a good eraser

2. After each student has one of the tools readily available, you can use them whenever you want to check the students' understanding to help them gain more accuracy with the information or skill that you're teaching. The students hold up their boards with their responses written on them so you can quickly scan and see who needs additional help and who has mastered the content.

3. Here are some ways to use these response boards:
   - Ask a question, and the students write the answer on the board.
   - Define, describe, or give attributes of a vocabulary word, and students have to write the word that you just described.
   - Teach students a sequence of events, and they have to paraphrase and write that sequence out on the board.
   - Explain a diagram to the students, and they draw and label the diagram on the boards.
   - Ask them a question, and they write "agree" or "disagree" (or "yes/no" or "true/false") on the board.

Remember To: Follow up with those students who have incorrect information on their boards. This opportunity to check understanding is so valuable and can correct misunderstandings quickly and help students gain accuracy immediately.

Differentiation:

Tier Up:

- Give students a couple of choices as to how to respond to the questions.
- Once students have shown mastery, give them an assignment that begins where each student is in his or her understanding. Don't make them keep practicing something when they already know it well and consistently.

Tier Down:

Allow students to grab a lifeline to help them write a response on their boards.

Example: See Figure 5.2, Quick Writing Response Tools example: Middle school students Addison and Sydney Sanislow practicing multiplication on gel boards.

Figure 5.2 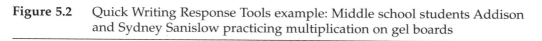 Quick Writing Response Tools example: Middle school students Addison and Sydney Sanislow practicing multiplication on gel boards

Activity for Awareness: Reporter Goes Big Time

Objective: Students will become aware of what they know and what they don't know by participating in a minisimulation.

Suggested Grades: 4–12

Materials: Content background (text, handouts, web options, etc.). Ask students to create or bring in accessories, props, or costumes for the two roles, since they won't know which role they're doing it for. Half the class gets "reporter" hats or name tags. The other half (the "experts") get some type of disguise accessory (rubber nose, scarf, glasses, books to stand on, or special coat). The experts have to research and take on a nontraditional point of view.

Preparation: This activity works best when students can get into the roles of reporter and expert. You need to ask the students to brainstorm characteristics of good reporters and experts (how do they act, facial expressions, words that come out of their mouths, etc.).

Time Needed: 18–20 minutes

Grouping Suggestions: Partners

Instructions:

1. Once students are partnered up, one becomes the reporter and one becomes the expert.

2. Each gets 8 minutes to prepare.

3. Reporter creates 10 questions about the topic just learned, and expert prepares answers to likely potential questions and key sound bites.

4. Students may sit or stand and prepare their outfits for their particular roles.

5. For 5–10 minutes, the reporter interviews the expert by asking him or her the 10 questions.

6. The expert answers as best he or she can by looking at the notes he or she prepared.

7. Teacher gives the partnership time to sit and debrief.

8. Partners jointly answer a brief questionnaire to debrief the process.

9. Students stand and share with the class what happened and what they learned.

Remember To: Put some stakes in the process, like points or grades to help the students put their hearts into it. Have students turn in a written summary at the end of their debriefing.

Cautions: Some students may think it's a bit childish to role-play. You'll want to make it safe for them to have fun and get into the roles.

It's working when . . . students show that they're having fun; the reporters are asking tough questions and the experts are actually doing well.

Differentiation:

Tier Up: Students work with another partnership and rotate questions and answers; the questions should be written at a higher level or the students should be given less time to prepare their questions and possible answers.

Tier Down: Allow the reporter and expert to help each other with the answering of the questions. Assist the reporters with question generation and assist the experts with note taking.

Example:

Reporter:	Dr. Travelot, I heard that you just got back from Darfur. Where is it and what's going on? Tell me what you saw.
Expert:	The armed conflict is in the Darfur region of western Sudan. It's mainly between the Janjaweed, a militia group, and farmers of the region. The Sudanese government has provided arms to support the Janjaweed and is targeting other ethnic groups. It's overwhelming. It rips your heart out. Children, lost, everywhere, and other children are recruited and have guns.
Reporter:	What's driving the conflict and what can be done about it?
Expert:	It's a combination of environmental mistakes and political corruption. Some call it a civil war, others, genocide. It's definitely worse than a civil war.
Reporter:	In your opinion, is this a problem, a serious problem, or an emergency and great international crisis?
Expert:	Estimates of the number of deaths in the conflict have ranged from a low of 50,000 to as many as 450,000, and as many as 2.5 million are thought to have been displaced.
Reporter:	Could you share with our audience more about the people of Darfur?
Expert:	There are many ethnicities and political or military groups. The Janjaweed is a militia group recruited from the tribes of camel-herding Arabs, and the farmers are the non-Baggara people, as are the Fur, Zaghawa, and Massaleit ethnic groups in Darfur.
Reporter:	What are the locals saying has to be done?
Expert:	It depends on who you ask.

Activity for Awareness: Rap & Chant

Objective: Help students put needed content in a rap, song, or chant to improve the memory of simple content.

Suggested Grades: 4–8

Materials:

- Karaoke music (no words, just instruments), a list of simple songs that your students might know the tune to (e.g., "Row, Row, Row Your Boat," "Jingle Bells")
- Have a variety of musical instruments available to help students create their rhythm (e.g., drums, keyboards, recorders, microphones, maracas, guitars).

Time Needed: 20–30 minutes

Grouping Suggestions: Partners

Instructions:

1. Partner the students up and then ask them to list 10 facts about the content they just learned.

2. Take these 10 facts and incorporate them into a rap, song, or chant.

3. Feel free to use any musical instrument or song rhythm that you feel comfortable with. The song must be appropriate for school.

4. After students have written their songs, raps, or chants, ask them to be ready to perform them the next day. Remind them to try not to use their written notes but to know their material by memory.

Remember To: Keep this low-key and fun. It's not about being under pressure to impress their peers. It's about having fun with it and remembering the 10 facts.

Differentiation:

Tier Up: Ask them to include more facts and more rhymes.

Tier Down: Reduce the number of facts that they're working with; give these students a partner with high background knowledge in the area.

Example: Addition and subtraction code word songs: some students have a challenging time during math problem solving knowing which words mean to add, subtract, multiply, or divide. The songs in Figure 5.3 were created to help them remember the subtraction, addition, multiplication, and division code words— words that tell them to add, subtract, multiply, or divide while solving word problems. The division words became an acrostic rather than a song.

Figure 5.3   Rap & Chant example: Math problem solving

CODE WORD RAP

Addition Code Word Rap (2 beats) These words tell you to add (clap with each syllable).

In all (clap, clap), altogether (clap, clap), combined (clap, clap), together (clap, clap),

Let's add (clap, clap), let's add (clap, clap), let's add (clap, clap, clap, clap).

Total (clap, clap), & spend (clap, clap), & spent (clap, clap), & plus (clap, clap),

Let's add (clap, clap), let's add (clap, clap), let's add (clap, clap, clap, clap).

Joined (clap, clap), & both (clap, clap), also (clap, clap), AND more (clap, clap),

The sum (clap, clap), the sum (clap, clap), the sum (clap, clap, clap, clap).

Subtraction Code Word Rap ("Frère Jacques" Tune) These words tell you to subtract.

Left, less, minus

Left, less, minus

Difference, change, profit

Difference, change, profit

off, not, more

off, not, more

Subtract, subtract, subtract

Subtract, subtract, subtract

Multiplication M-U-L-T-O Song (To the Tune of B-I-N-G-O) These words tell you to multiply.

There was a product, times and twice

And Multo was his namo

M U L T O, M U L T O, M U L T O

And Multo was his namo

Each, per, every, apiece, and one

BEFORE the question

M U L T O, M U L T O, M U L T O

And Multo was his namo

Division (SHEQ) Acrostic These words tell you to divide.

Separate

Half

Equal

Quotient

"Each, per, every, apiece & one,"

IN the question sentence.

Activity for Awareness: Door Pass

Objective: Students will quickly respond to a prompt from the teacher after the lesson. This is a closure that enhances the memory of the lesson that was taught that day. Students' awareness levels are heightened after this activity.

Suggested Grades: 4–Adult

Materials: The Door Pass reproducible figure has four door passes (page 222). Cut them apart from one another and give each student one; pencils/pens for each student.

Time Needed: 2–3 minutes

Grouping Suggestions: Individual

Instructions:

1. After a chunk of learning is complete (this could be during the lesson or at the end of the lesson), ask the students to reflect on what they learned and then respond in a particular way on the door pass (¼ piece of paper shaped like a door).

2. There are so many ways students can respond on this small sheet of paper. Remember to have the responses reflect the objective from that lesson and also give students choices of complexity of the questions.

3. Place the choices on the chalkboard so all students can see and choose. Once they have completed the written response, ask the students to hand their door passes to you as they exit the door to go to their next class or next subject.

Remember To: Have many of these door passes ready to go. Closures need to be a part of every lesson. Door passes are excellent, quick ways to have students respond to the learning that day. They are also great ways to check understanding. We always make sure to be at the door to wish them well for the day. This is a very positive way to end the class period.

Differentiation:

Tier Up: Give the students more challenging questions to answer, for example, "If you could teach today's lesson, what would you do differently?"

Tier Down: Use easier, simple learning questions. Ask the students to write down three new facts they learned today or to draw a picture of what they learned. Ask students what they already knew from today's lesson and what was new information.

Example: See Figure 5.4, Door Pass example: Greenhouse Effect.

Figure 5.4   Door Pass example: Greenhouse Effect

Name: Amanda   **Date:** 5-20

Door Pass

Greenhouse Effect
(Summary)

Energy from the sun passes through the Earth's atmosphere and is changed to heat. This heat gets trapped because of a buildup of pollutants (carbon dioxide) in our Earth's atmosphere. This could cause temperatures on Earth to rise.

Activity for Awareness: Countdown Processing

Objective: Students will review the content that was just taught with quick responses that are written in four different categories chosen by the teacher. Their awareness levels are enhanced after this activity.

Suggested Grades: 4–Adult

Materials: Photocopy Countdown Processing (page 223) for each student OR the Make Your Own Countdown Processing reproducible (page 224).

Time Needed: 3–5 minutes

Grouping Suggestions: Partnership or individual

Instructions:

1. After the learning occurs, give each student a copy of Countdown Processing. Ask them to write down the topic at the top of the page. Then give them processing time to complete the boxes. This activity has many possibilities.

2. You can use the figure we created in Countdown Processing or create your own by filling in the Make Your Own Countdown Processing reproducible (page 224). You could ask students to choose three out of the four squares to complete or have a partner complete two and the other student complete the other two.

Remember To: Mix the following ideas with whatever numbers you want to use (4, 3, 2, or 1), or better yet, let the students choose what goes into each box. Let them create their own Countdown Processing sheet by using the Make Your Own Countdown Processing reproducible. See Figure 5.5 for an example of this type.

Differentiation:

Tier Up: Place these ways to process in the boxes—they're more complex:

- Create analysis and application type questions
- Give pros
- Give cons
- Compare it to something
- Contrast it to something
- Give an opinion about it
- Create test questions
- Create evaluation and synthesis type questions
- Give arguments for it
- Give arguments against it

Tier Down:

- Define it in your own words
- Give characteristics of it
- Give examples of it
- Give nonexamples of it
- Draw a diagram and label it
- Create knowledge and comprehension type questions

Example: See Figure 5.5, Make Your Own Countdown Processing example: Albert Einstein, and Figure 5.6, Countdown Processing example: Energy.

Example: The Parts of a Cell

Box 1: Write the Most Valuable Piece of Information that you learned about cells (MVPI).

Box 2: Compare a plant cell to a body cell.

Box 3: If you could change the cell's structure and components, how would you change them and why? List three ways.

Box 4: List four new vocabulary words that you learned from today's lesson.

Figure 5.5   Make Your Own Countdown Processing example: Albert Einstein

**Make Your Own
Countdown Processing**
Topic: Albert Einstein

4 Inventions by Einstein	3 Roles He Had
1) Struture of the Cosmos 2) The Bomb 3) space travel 4) electronics	1) Musician 2) Scientist 3) Dreamer
2 Unusual Facts	1 MVPI
1) He found an uncashed check in a book ($1,500). 2) His brain remains in a jar and is studied by neuroscientists.	1) He was friends with President Franklin D. Roosevelt (constructed uranium bomb).

Figure 5.6   Countdown Processing example: Energy

Countdown Processing
Topic: Energy

4 New Words That I Learned	3 New Facts That I Learned
1) Pivot Mill – blades of a windmill face in the direction of the wind. 2) Crude Oil – petroleum 3) Refinery – Crude oil is separated by several steps. 4) Potential Energy–Stored but waiting to be used	1) Foods we eat supply us with potential chemical energy measured in calories. 2) Most energy comes from the sun. 3) Plants grow because they convert sunlight into chemical energy.
2 Questions That I Have	1 Most Valuable Piece of Information
1) How did Einstein develop $E = mc^2$? 2) Will Earth ever run out of energy?	Energy comes from so many different forms: sun, wind, falling water, volcanoes, plants & animals. Without energy, there is no life

Activity for Awareness: Quality Questioning Strategies

Objective: Students will be able to generate and answer a variety of higher-level questions that help them to become more aware of the content and skills being learned.

Suggested Grades: 4–Adult

Materials:

- Photocopy From Easy to Challenging Questions (page 225) for each student.
- Photocopy Quads (page 226) for each student.

Time Needed: 5–10 minutes, depending on which strategy is chosen

Grouping Suggestions: Independent, then partners

Instructions:

1. From Easy to Challenging Questions: Encourage students to create challenging, open-ended questions rather than easy, one-word recall questions by using From Easy to Challenging Questions (page 225). Ask students to answer the following question: "What do you fill a pool with?" The students will all say "water." That was an easy question with a one-word answer. How can they change this question so it becomes more challenging and open-ended with several answers? Ask them, "What would you like to fill your pool with?" Encourage students to write several easy questions and then transform them into challenging questions about the content they just learned. Then they can switch challenging questions with a partner so they answer each other's questions.

2. The Big Four: Give students the following four question starters and ask them to create six questions using those four question starters to structure the questions from the content that was just learned: "how," "what if," "why," and "should." After they've formed their questions, have them switch with a friend to answer. *Example:* Should students be forced to eat fruits and vegetables during school lunchtime? Why are fruits and vegetables good for the brain? What if fruits were junk food and junk food were fruits? How do antioxidants attack free radicals?

3. Quads: Place students in groups of five. Give each student a Quads reproducible (page 226). After reading a book, listening to a minilesson, or viewing a video, students create four higher-level questions about the content that they learned. Each question is written in a different box on this reproducible. Author #1 is the student who wrote the questions. Once the questions are filled out in each box and Author #1 writes his or her name in each box, the student cuts each square out and gives four other students a different question square. When all students in the group do this, each student in that group has four questions to answer.

Each student begins to answer all four questions and signs his or her name on the Author #2 line (see Figure 5.7). After all the questions have been answered, the questions and their answers are returned to Author #1 for grading and feedback to Author #2.

Figure 5.7   Quads example: Pueblo homes

Author #1: _Spencer_

Question:

How are Pueblo homes different than your home?

Answer:

A Pueblo home is in the desert and made of clay. It is several stories high and built upon cliffs.

Author #2: _Katie_

Differentiation:

Tier Up: Give these students more challenging question stems to create their questions. Some students might not need question starters or question stems. They can ask each other their challenging questions. Ask them to create questions from the Analysis to Synthesis, Application, and Assimilation DEEP domains.

Tier Down: These students will most likely need the question starters or stems to create their questions for these activities. Encourage them to ask questions at the Awareness and Analysis to Synthesis DEEP domains. Group them so they're generating and answering questions that are in line with their background knowledge level.

Examples: See Figure 5.7, Quads example: Pueblo homes.

DOMAIN 2: ANALYSIS TO SYNTHESIS ACTIVITIES ■

The Analysis to Synthesis domain has students analyze and synthesize the information they have in order for deeper learning to occur. Many times the act of analyzing information leads to synthesizing it—taking parts of information and then reorganizing them into something else, something different. Yet there are times when students will only analyze information or only synthesize information. The activities below are a combination of the three: analyzing, synthesizing, and both combined.

Activity for Analysis to Synthesis: Encode It! Spinner

Objective: Students will be able to process for the long term by being engaged in a spinner activity that allows for a variety of ways to encode content. Encode It! Spinner is a kinesthetic activity that allows students to discuss in seven different ways what they just learned. The potential discussions brought about by this game range from analyzing the topic to synthesizing the topic.

Suggested Grades: 4–8

Time Needed: 4–6 minutes

Grouping Suggestions: Groups of three to four students

Materials: Photocopy the Encode It! Spinner (page 227) and glue it onto cardstock paper. Create enough so that each group can have one. Laminate each spinner if you plan to write on them with a Vis-à-Vis marker. Place a spinner brad in the middle of each spinner. If you can't find these spinner brads in a teacher store, just use a pencil or pen and a paper clip (see Figure 5.8).

Instructions:

1. After students have learned about a particular chunk of information, group them and give each group one spinner. After you look at their preassessments on the topic *or* after you observe them in the lesson, place the students in groups with similar background knowledge or in heterogeneous groups, depending on your purpose.

2. Have each student spin the spinner immediately and remember what he or she has spun. After all students have spun the spinner, they should reflect on how they're going to respond. The person who spun first responds first. After each student has been given a chance to respond, discussion can take place concerning anybody's comments. This gives all students a chance to share and process what they learned.

Remember To: Allow students to *all* spin first, then reflect, and then share their answers. Every brain needs time to retrieve quality information.

Differentiation:

Tier Up: Have students combine two spins so their choice is more complex. Give students a timed deadline for the response (30 seconds versus 60 seconds). Have students respond immediately so others in the group can hear the processing (i.e., thinking out loud) going on in the brain.

Tier Down: Students get to work with a buddy to create a collaborated answer. Students work their way around the group doing the spin, then they get time (3–4 minutes) to work out their answer and present it to the group. Allow some

Figure 5.8 Encode It! Spinner

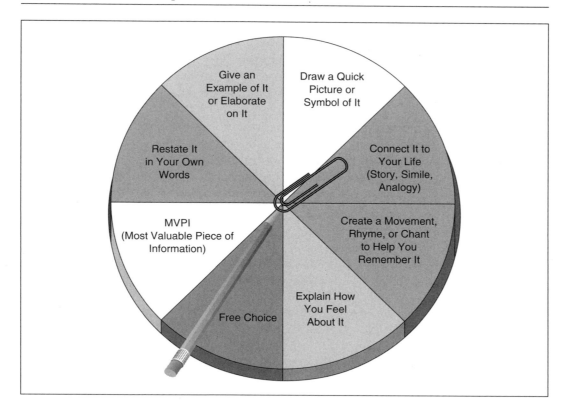

students to walk over to a tier-up group and observe for 10 minutes to pick up ideas and then go back and try them.

Examples:

Topic: Lightning Is Electricity!

- Tell students to connect the topic to their life: describe how they have experienced or learned about this concept or topic. How does it relate to their personal life? Have them tell stories that they've heard.
  Example: Lightning. "My grandmother saw lightning hit her tree in the front yard."
- Use it in a simile. A simile is a comparison using "like" or "as."
  Example: "Lightning is as bright as the sun but comes in shocking streaks."
- Explain how they feel about it.
  Example: "I like lightning since it's so beautiful to watch. I don't have fears about it because it has never done anything to me."
- Free choice: Have students choose anything on the spinner or create their own way of remembering it.
- MVPI: The Most Valuable Piece of Information: Ask students to state a fact about it or what they learned that was new to them.
  Example: "I didn't know that lightning really starts from the ground and goes up."

- Have them give an example or elaborate on it.
  Example: "I saw lightning from my window at night on Tuesday. Lightning is so powerful that it causes most forest fires."
- Have them restate it in their own words.
  Example: "Lightning is an electrical charge between the earth and a cloud or clouds. Electrons move quickly and then stop. This causes the flash. Lightning can cause fires and power outages. Make sure to follow the lightning safety rules when a storm comes."
- Have students draw a quick picture or symbol of it. (Student draws a picture of lightning extending from the ground up.)
- Tell students to create a movement, rhyme, or chant to help them remember it. (Student stands up and chants, "Lightning is electrifying!")

Activity for Analysis to Synthesis: Super Mooter

Objective: Increase the scope of learning by discovering how wide and varied the content is in the chosen topic.

Suggested Grades: 4–12

Materials: Computer, Internet access

Time Needed: 12–15 minutes

Grouping Suggestions: Put students in pairs, or at the most, groups of three

Instructions:

1. Take 60 seconds to brainstorm key words for the topic with your students.
2. Vote on the top three key words.
3. Enter each key word into a "Mooter search" at www.mooter.com.
4. Note all the clusters offered on the topic. Pick the three most relevant.
5. Mooter those outlier topics again.
6. Organize new topics into either an outline, a new table of contents, or a graphic organizer.

Remember To: Keep time deadlines sharp.

Example: Along with your students, select the phrase "global warming" and go to www.mooter.com to see what you get for ideas. Put quotes around the phrase so the two words are kept together in the search. After the first click, it should look like this:

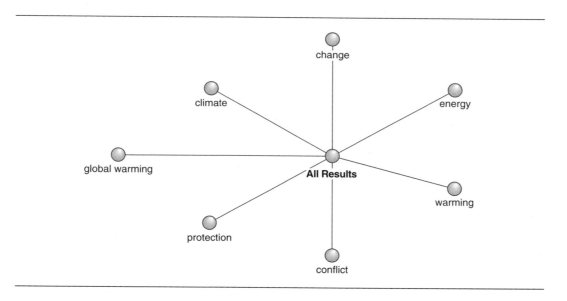

Because Mooter is a dynamic search process, your search will come up different. Mooter is always changing, based on the number of relevant options available. This is a graphic organizer with the following subtopics: change, energy, climate, protection, conflict, warming, and global warming. That's a good start; it gives you seven general topics. But go wider. Now click on "next clusters" to get even more groupings, so you get past the original broad topic, and Mooter that one. It'll look like this:

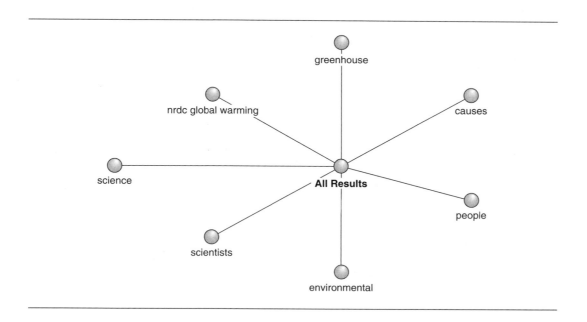

Not a bad cluster group. So your search is getting more useful. But click on "next clusters" again and see if you can get even more ideas.

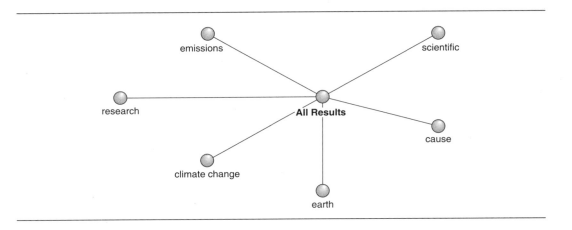

Now you have a wider, better assortment of ideas. The cool thing is that you can click on each one of these groupings and find articles and resources that have been written about them. None of these are one-shot exceptions.

Once students have these choices, they can create a new outline or mind map with a much more expansive idea base. You went from one concept (global warming) to about 15 ways or directions to organize your thinking. To come up with all of these Mooter ideas, you would have to already have quite a bit of background on the global warming issue. But this process allows students to understand the bigger, wider picture first before they start digging in for the details. It's fast and effective. The whole point of doing this process is that it can help jump-start students who are stuck for ideas. It's perfect for the wide, broad brushstroke of content.

Differentiation:

Tier Up: Work with tighter time deadlines; challenge them to get a quantity of minitopics (perhaps 20) for further breakdowns.

Tier Down: Working in pairs, give them more time for the assignment and prep them with more background knowledge first.

Activity for Analysis to Synthesis: ABS—Association by Scavenging

Objective: Use objects in the classroom as prompts for ideas to expand the breadth of a topic.

Suggested Grades: 4–8

Materials: Music (teacher plays it), paper and pens for students, graphic organizer (page 228)

Preparation:

- Talk to students about how their brain works with environmental prompts. They see an ice cream store and think of their last ice cream, who they were with, and the weather. Things in the environment trigger their brains. For this topic, notice all the nouns in the classroom.

- Reproduce the ABS Think Sheet (page 228) for each student.

Time Needed: 10–12 minutes

Grouping Suggestions: Whole group

Instructions:

1. Begin with a topic linked to your curriculum of study. Students write in the topic at the top of the ABS Think Sheet (page 228).

2. All students stand up, take a pencil and the ABS Think Sheet.

3. Students have 20 seconds to write down on the ABS Think Sheet one item they can physically touch from where they're standing.

4. Music begins again; repeat the last instruction in a new part of the room.

5. After five times, students go back to their original seats and pair up. By this time, each student should have five objects written down that they touched.

6. With a partner, their new goal is to combine the objects they touched, then narrow down their word list to one useful association they can make with the topic.

7. Now write the topic and association (object) in the Association Box to keep the brain focused on the objective.

8. Now create questions about how these two objects are related to one another. See the example below for ideas on how to write the questions. Write these questions down in the section called Questions for the Associations.

9. Finally, of the questions that the students wrote, which ones do they actually want to find the answers to? Students should list them and explain how they plan to find out the answers (Internet, interview, book, magazine, encyclopedia, etc.).

10. Give students time to do the research.

11. Create an ABS showcase to share what they learned about the questions in the Questions for the Associations. The sky is the limit on how the showcase is created (talk show, one-on-one interview, PowerPoint, etc.).

Remember To: Provide plenty of examples to jump-start their brains. For example, if the topic is global warming, students can see the air conditioner or heater in the class and write down the associations it creates in their minds about energy consumption, emissions, or alternative energy. Use upbeat music that students really get into. Monitor the students' word lists so they stay productive.

Cautions: If students are slow to associate after the first one or two chances, pair them up. Make sure they know the goal of the activity.

It's working when . . . Students come up with many crazy associations and have fun.

Differentiation:

Tier Up: Increase the goals of the activity; work alone.

Tier Down: Use Google to pair up the two words ("tornado" and "chair" give thousands of associations).

Example: See Figure 5.9, ABS Think Sheet example: Tornadoes.

Figure 5.9   ABS Think Sheet example: Tornadoes

ABS Think Sheet

Topic: _Tornadoes_

Objects That Are Touched:

#1 _table_

#2 _chair_

#3 _rug_

#4 _window_

#5 _pencil sharpener_

Partner's Name: _Sam_

Partner's Objects:

#6 _pencil_

#7 _paper_

#8 _stapler_

#9 _eraser_

#10 _water bottle_

Chosen Object From Both Lists: _#2 - chair_

Association Box

Tornado :	_Chair_
(Topic)	(Object or Association)

Questions for the Associations:

1. How far have chairs been tossed during a tornado?

2. Is it safe to hide under a heavy chair?

3. What is the chair's safety level while bolted to the floor?

*4. What if the chair changed into a gust of warm air? What would it take for this gust of warm air to form a tornado?

5. What are all of the possibilities of what would happen to a chair in a tornado?

6.

7.

8.

9.

*Star the questions that you want to personally research and find the answer to. Each student should place his or her initials next to the question that is to be researched.

Activity for Analysis to Synthesis: WebQuest

Objective: Students will use an inquiry approach method for research in which the information the students interact with comes from resources on the Internet. They will use information from Kathy Schrock's Web site, http://kathyschrock .net/webquests/index.htm.

Suggested Grades: 6–Adult

Materials: Computer, Internet sites, WebQuest graphic organizer (page 229)

Preparation: You can create a WebQuest for your students, borrow from the Internet from the listed sites below, or ask your students to use the template to create their own WebQuests with a question that they have about a certain topic. The Instructions section guides you through these steps. You could also "borrow" the many WebQuests for your grade level that have been posted on Kathy Schrock's Web site for your use. That's why the teachers have posted their ideas.

Time Needed: 1–3 days of research

Grouping Suggestions: Partners to small groups of four

Instructions:

1. Use the Web Quest graphic organizer (page 229) to create the critical components for your WebQuest.

    • The Task: A clear description of what is expected.
    • The Background: Should build background knowledge, interest, and what is to occur during the WebQuest.
    • The Process: Step-by-step directions of the process students will go through to complete the task.
    • The Sources: A list of Web pages and other resources that you have located to help your students accomplish the task.
    • Evaluation: Rubrics designed by you (students can help too) to assess the task and process.
    • Conclusion—Closure to the entire process and task and an opportunity to review what was learned.

2. Use the following Web sites to help you:

    http://kathyschrock.net/webquests/index.htm
    http://webquest.org
    http://www.alicechristie.org/edtech/wq/matrix
    http://www.west-bend.k12.wi.us/webquest/
    http://www.milforded.org/teachers_rooms/wq.asp
    http://bestwebquests.com
    http://school.discoveryeducation.com/schrockguide/museum/webquest.html
    http://school.discoveryeducation.com/schrockguide/math.html

Remember To:

- Monitor students' Internet searches by making sure they stay with the Web sites that are part of your WebQuest.
- Teachers should become familiar with online resources in their content area—be the expert of where the best Web sites are for your content.
- Teachers should organize the Internet resources into categories like databases, reference materials, and links.

Differentiation:

Tier Up: Make more in-depth Web sites available for this group (more complex content); more in-depth research questions.

Tier Down: Less complex questions for research; have students partner up with a student with more background knowledge; give them more time and fewer choices of Web sites—could be overwhelming the more choices that are available.

Example: See the following Web site: http://school.discoveryeducation.com/schrockguide/museum/webquest.html

---

Activity for Analysis to Synthesis: What's the Biggest Idea?

Objective: Take words and labels and connect them to bigger themes or concepts.

Suggested Grades: 4–8

Materials: Post-it notes, 3 × 5-inch cards, markers

Preparation: Explain to students that words and labels can all be connected to bigger ideas, concepts, or themes in life. We want to store words and labels into these bigger categories or neural networks in our brains for easier retrieval. Association is a key ingredient to a powerful memory.

Time Needed: 5–8 minutes

Grouping Suggestions: Partners or trios

Instructions:

1. Students receive a list of words from their unit of study. This activity can be used before, during, or after the unit is taught. The finished product looks like a web of words categorized by big picture labels.

2. Ask students to write these words on 3 × 5-inch cards with markers. Students start sorting the words by similarity or within related chunks.

There should always be at least two words per chunk. After sorting all the terms, students need to label the groups with a category word. They will write on Post-it notes the big idea or category that all the words in each chunk fall into. In other words, each chunk will have a Post-it note above the words to represent the big idea of all those words.

3. To label these chunks, students need to find the commonalities between the words that are grouped together. The common threads among these words become the big ideas for the categories and are written on Post-it notes.

4. Once the big ideas are completed, students need to create a name for the web, which is the biggest idea. The main idea or biggest idea of the whole web should be created once students see all the words and their categories. Write the biggest idea on colored construction paper and cut it into the shape of an oval.

Remember To:

- Encourage students to discuss their groupings or categories with all members of their group. There is no right or wrong answer. They need to respect all opinions. Because everyone has different background knowledge, students will have different ideas of which categories to create and what the bigger picture is.
- Take pictures of the web before the unit begins so they have something to compare their thoughts with after the unit. In other words, create a web before learning and create a web after the learning—they will look different because of the learning that took place. Great comparisons can be made with these pictures of the before-learning web.

Differentiation:

Tier Up:

- Ask students to create their own words related to the unit versus you giving them the list of words to categorize.
- Ask students to support in writing why they created the groups, categories, and bigger picture.

Tier Down:

- Give students a glossary of the words that they're categorizing so they can look up the meanings of the words.
- Be there to ask them guiding questions to help them create the categories.
- Group them with a student who has strong background knowledge of these words.

Example: See Figure 5.10, What's the Biggest Idea? example: The Memories of Skiing.

Figure 5.10   What's the Biggest Idea? example: The Memories of Skiing

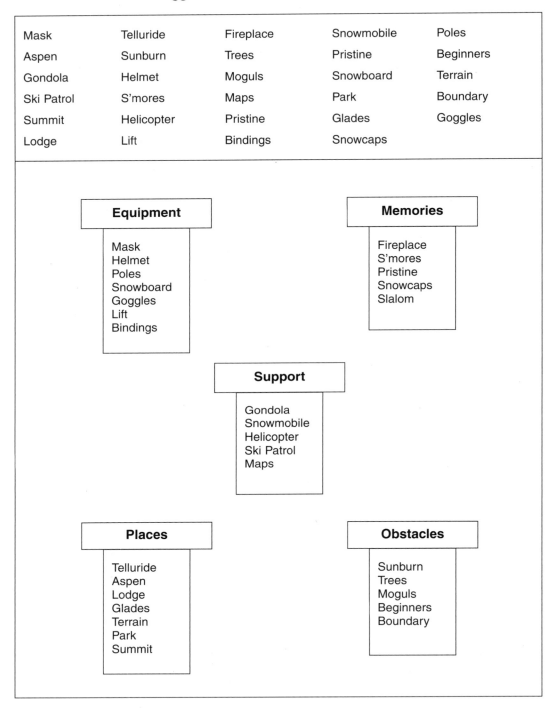

Biggest Idea: The Memories of Skiing

Mask	Telluride	Fireplace	Snowmobile	Poles
Aspen	Sunburn	Trees	Pristine	Beginners
Gondola	Helmet	Moguls	Snowboard	Terrain
Ski Patrol	S'mores	Maps	Park	Boundary
Summit	Helicopter	Pristine	Glades	Goggles
Lodge	Lift	Bindings	Snowcaps	

Equipment

Mask
Helmet
Poles
Snowboard
Goggles
Lift
Bindings

Memories

Fireplace
S'mores
Pristine
Snowcaps
Slalom

Support

Gondola
Snowmobile
Helicopter
Ski Patrol
Maps

Places

Telluride
Aspen
Lodge
Glades
Terrain
Park
Summit

Obstacles

Sunburn
Trees
Moguls
Beginners
Boundary

Activity for Analysis to Synthesis: Five and Five

Objective: Find more content on students' topics by researching what else has been done so far by other authors. The goal is to get new content from five new books and five new magazines or journals.

Suggested Grades: 6–12

Materials: Library access, computer, Internet access, magazines

Preparation: As you should with any activity, walk through every step in your mind.

Time Needed: 60–90 minutes

Grouping Suggestions: Best when done in student pairs

Instructions:

1. The first key is to plan a way for students to get vested in the topic. This can be done in many ways, including a good story, personal experience, or a cliff-hanger.

2. Then provide clear models of the finished product. What should their end product look like? Show and post some examples.

3. Ask students to brainstorm with a partner five source books and five journals or magazines that might have information about their project topic. We recommend that they have access to the Internet or the library. Give them time to look through these sources and create other subtopics. Each subtopic could become a whole project in which they choose to present their new knowledge.

Remember To: Keep them engaged by posting or announcing the results of this project on a group basis.

Cautions: It's easy for students to get discouraged, because this activity requires 10 total chunks of information. Be a cheerleader and give feedback to keep the students excited.

It's working when . . . Each find excites your students!

Differentiation:

Tier Up: Instead of five and five, you might make it a seven and seven for new sources.

Tier Down: Work in pairs; give more time for the assignment; prep them with more background knowledge first.

Example:

Students might begin with just a brief goal on paper. It might look like this:

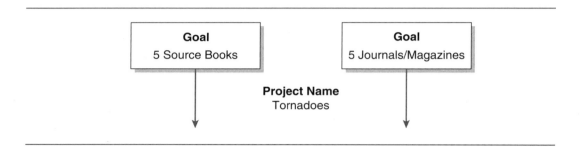

Once students know what they're looking for, their search might turn up sources like this:

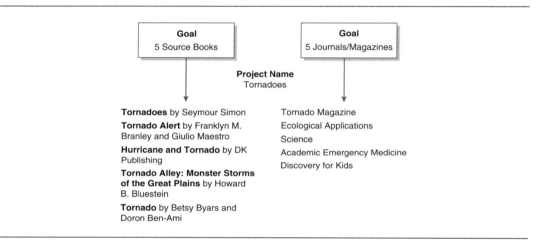

Then students have as a follow-up goal to brainstorm a wider range of subtopics for their main, original topic. With these books and journals, students discover that a lot more is out there than they originally thought. Typically, you see transformations and improvements from original brainstorming that started like this:

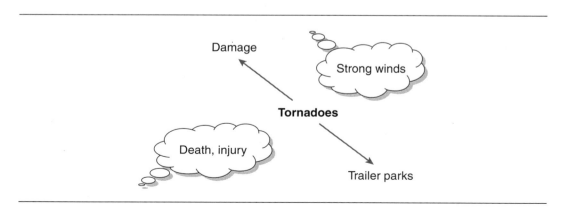

Ultimately, students develop a wider, more professional landscape of subtopics that looks more like this:

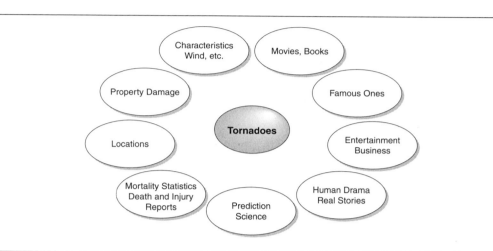

Once they get to this new landscape, they can better prepare their topic for a paper or a presentation.

Activity for Analysis to Synthesis: Question Top-Down Webbing

Objective: Answer the question but support it with details; dive deeply into the questions that are asked and support the objective.

Suggested Grades: 9–12

Materials: One large piece of construction paper (light colored) for each student

Preparation: Prime the students' brains about what they know about the topic.

Time Needed: 10–15 minutes

Grouping Suggestions: Make sure students practice this with you and a partner before doing this independently.

Instructions:

1. Tell the group of students what the topic is. While they're reading about it, listening and taking notes on your lesson, or viewing a video, make sure they have at least three purpose questions before acquiring the information.

2. Students then write these questions at the top of the piece of construction paper that is positioned horizontally. Create boxes around each question. Make sure they leave enough space between these questions. You want the questions to stand out from other text that will be written below them.

3. Students are to find the answer or answers to that question while acquiring the information. They write these answers in a box directly below the question. Make sure they include lines with arrows showing that the answers go along with the particular question (so that a web is forming from top to bottom—arrows are all pointing downward).

4. Most answers have many details to support them. In the third layer of boxes (further down the page, closer to the bottom of the page), students support the answers with more detailed answers below them. Again, they should draw lines from the answer to the detailed answers with the arrow pointing downward and place each detail in its own shaped box (create a different shape for the details).

Remember To: Invite students to use twist-up crayons, skinny markers, or colored pencils to enhance the memory of the content. One idea is to color code each question so it's clear which answers support the questions. Highlight the boxes that the words are written in.

Differentiation:

Tier Up:

- Allow students to create their own set of questions to answer in the weblike formation. They may need to search other resources in order to answer their questions.
- Ask students to create another layer of details—a fourth row of details to the answers from the third row. This is another layer of support.

Tier Down:

- Ask students to work on this web with a partner rather than independently.
- Support the students by creating the web for them so they know where to place the information.
- Give students less complex resources to research their questions.
- Give them more time to complete the web.

Example: See Figure 5.11, Question Top-Down Webbing example: Tundra and Taiga.

Figure 5.11 Question Top-Down Webbing example: Tundra and Taiga

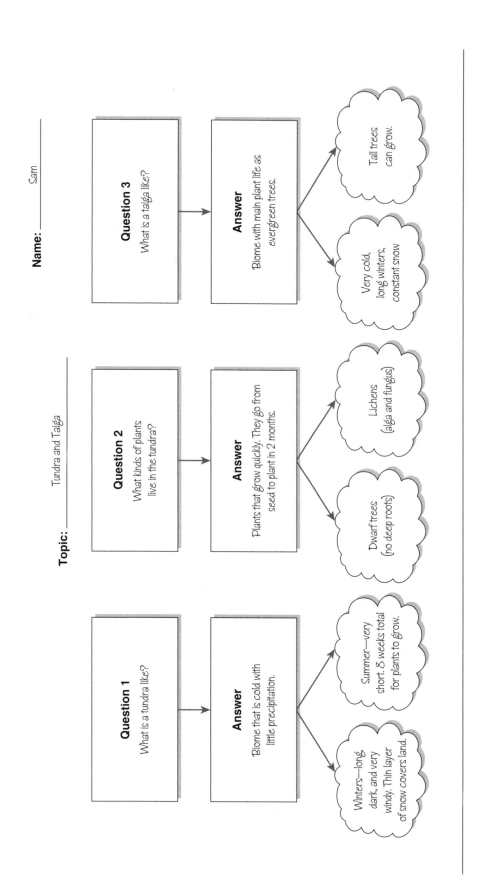

Name: _____ Sam

Topic: _____ Tundra and Taiga

Question 1
What is a tundra like?

Answer
Biome that is cold with little precipitation.

Winters—long, dark, and very windy. Thin layer of snow covers land.

Summer—very short. 8 weeks total for plants to grow.

Question 2
What kinds of plants live in the tundra?

Answer
Plants that grow quickly. They go from seed to plant in 2 months.

Dwarf trees (no deep roots)

Lichens (alga and fungus)

Question 3
What is a taiga like?

Answer
Biome with main plant life as evergreen trees.

Very cold, long winters, constant snow

Tall trees can grow.

Activity for Analysis to Synthesis: Headlines for Heralding

Objective: Create a better understanding of the material by summarizing the learning into condensed headlines.

Suggested Grades: 4–12

Materials: Word processor, paper or pen, Headlines for Heralding (page 230)—one per student

Preparation: Collect local or national newspapers for about a week. Have those ready to show students what the headlines do. Students should have already done much of their background learning on their topic. Talk to them about how newspapers have to come up with hundreds of headlines a day and thousands per year.

- Give all students one of the newspapers and have them read a few articles and the headlines that go with them.
- Let students share out loud what the headlines did for the articles and how they represented the content.

Time Needed: 35–40 minutes

Grouping Suggestions: Independent or partners

Instructions:

1. Give students a reading passage of information about your content. This could be a content area reading book that almost every subject has for each student or one that you purchase as a single topic from *National Geographic*. It could be a newspaper article or Web site article.

2. Explain how a paragraph has a topic sentence and supporting sentences to elaborate on that topic sentence.

3. Explain how each paragraph could be labeled as a headline based on the topic sentence. The topic sentence contains the main idea of the whole paragraph. You can take the main idea, or topic sentence, and condense it down to a short phrase, like a headline. Remember, a headline explains the big picture of the paragraph.

4. Have students read the first paragraph, write a one-sentence summary about the paragraph, and then create a headline for it. The headline is just a short phrase, not a complete sentence, that explains the big picture of the paragraph or one-sentence summary that you just wrote for that paragraph (teacher support).

5. Have students read the second paragraph, write a one-sentence summary about it, and then create a headline for it (partner support).

6. Have students read the remaining paragraphs and create headlines for each one of them (one-sentence summary too). After headlines have been created for each of the paragraphs, have students create a *big* headline for the whole passage with a partner after they write a paragraph-long summary about the whole passage. Share these headlines with the whole group to see the variety. Possibly have a vote for the best headline.

Remember To: Make sure students already know how to write summary paragraphs. Allow time for them to make connections between the newspaper's headlines and the summary sentence. Remind them to start with quantity and then edit the headlines to get quality.

Cautions: To keep things going, you may have some of your more verbal or linguistic students act as editors who walk around jump-starting the work of others.

It's working when . . . Students love their headlines, want to share them with others, or even use word plays.

Differentiation:

Tier Up: Give more complex reading materials to those who are ready. Ask them to create summaries after every two to three paragraphs instead of every paragraph. Ask students to write a summary of the whole article after creating the headline.

Tier Down: If the one-sentence summary is stumping them, ask them to just create a headline for each paragraph.

Example: See Figure 5.12, Headlines for Heralding example: The Earth's Sun.

Figure 5.12   Headlines for Heralding example: The Earth's Sun.

Headlines for Heralding

Paragraph #1
One-Sentence Summary: _Billions of stars in the universe, but Sun is closest star to Earth._

Headline: _The Amazing Star_

Paragraph #2
One-Sentence Summary: _Sun is the largest thing in our solar system._

Headline: _Big Ball of Fire_

Paragraph #3
One-Sentence Summary: _Sun is made up of 4 layers; but mostly hydrogen._

Headline: _Heated Layers of the Sun_

Paragraph #4
One-Sentence Summary: _There are 2 types of energy from the Sun: heat, light_

Headline: _The Sun's Energies_

Figure 5.12 (Continued)

Paragraph #5
One-Sentence Summary: <u>One form of light from the Sun is radiation.</u>

Headline: <u>Ultraviolet Rays Attack Again</u>

One BIG headline to herald:

The <u>Earth's</u> Sun

Activity for Analysis to Synthesis: Smash Pics

Objective: Get to the core of content through pictures and questions.

Suggested Grades: 9–12

Materials: Large drawing paper for each student, either 11 × 17-inch, flip charts, or butcher paper, colored pens, and graphic organizer Smash Pics (page 231)

Time Needed: Two class periods

Grouping Suggestions: Groups of eight for the jigsaw, but then working with a partner

Instructions:

1. Brainstorm with a large group of eight students to get a list of key topic words. Have all students write all the words that are brainstormed on the top half of their Smash Pics graphic organizer (page 231).

2. Vote on the key topic words to determine the top three of greatest importance. Give each student a Post-it note to vote on *one*. One student totals these up, hopefully coming up with three top words. After the three words are announced, all students write these three words in the correct place on the graphic organizer.

3. On their own, have each student draw pictures of each key word or concept of the problem or situation under study. Use specific pictures of concrete words (classroom, V-2 rocket, paper, treaty, molecule) and symbols for abstract terms ("crowded," "democratic"). Graphic representations tap into the visual part of the brain, so the more pictures a learner draws, the more it triggers even more visuals for learning and content interest.

4. Next, from these groups of eight students, place them into productive partnerships. Have them work with a partner to "mash" the illustrated concepts into four pieces—using *one* of the four following categories for thinking and

understanding: description, process, priority placement, and story. You need one category per partnership from that group of eight students.

5. Have students work with a partner to answer the questions generated from the four categories.

Sample Topic: A history class teacher wants his students to better understand the role that German V-2 rockets played in world history.

1. *Description Questions:* Have students create and answer as many questions as they can about what they're learning. These questions and answers might include the types, steps, parts, descriptions, players, people, locations, dates, objects, actions, and results.

   Examples:

   What was the V-2? (Answer: First called the A-4, it was a single-stage rocket fueled by alcohol and liquid oxygen that stood 46.1 feet high, had a thrust of 56,000 pounds, and traveled 3,500 miles per hour. It was the first human-made device to go out of our atmosphere.)

   Who was the inventor? (Answer: German engineer Werner von Braun was a key player in its development.)

   What was it used for? (Answer: After many successful test rockets were built from 1933 to 1944, Hitler used them to bomb Paris and London.)

2. *Process Questions:* Have students create and answer as many questions as they can about the problems, challenges, and difficulties faced. What were the proposed solutions, and how did they work?

   Problem: Germany was struggling in World War II.

   Hitler's solution: Use V-2 weapons to bomb London.

   Problem: The pacifist inventor von Braun was arrested by the German SS and the Gestapo for crimes against the state because he persisted in talking about building rockets that would go into orbit around the Earth. How could America get the V-2?

   Solution: Inventor von Braun and many of his team escaped Nazi Germany and surrendered to the U.S. military. Many of his almost 100 German V-2 rockets were dismantled and brought to the United States. The U.S. Army undertook the task of assembling the rockets at White Sands, New Mexico.

   Problem: The U.S. military ran out of German V-2s.

   Solution: The government developed a missile program of its own.

3. *Priority Placement Questions:* Describe the topic in its context in history, in its field, and in its level of importance throughout all time.

   Example: The recruitment of von Braun and his team from Germany, the onset of the Cold War, and the eventual development and use of these rockets launched the United States into the nuclear race, the space age, and eventually the landing on the moon. The V-2 program accomplishments include the first direct measurement of atmospheric pressure above 18 miles, the first high-altitude photos of Earth, the first detection and measurement of the Lyman-alpha radiation ultraviolet solar spectrum, solar X-rays, and ionospheric electron density versus height. This was the birth of both space-based astronomy and the U.S. Navy's space program. When it became evident that the supply of V-2 rockets would be exhausted, the United States proceeded to develop its own rocket.

4. *Story Questions:* Discover how the authors, politicians, the media, and so on have chosen to downplay, illuminate, highlight, and modify this event or story. What are the movies, books, legends, and stories we're left with? The legend of the V-2 rocket has been well established in the media. Werner von Braun (1912–1977) was one of the most important rocket developers and champions of space exploration during the period between the 1930s and the 1970s. He was consulted for many of the early science fiction space movies and was portrayed in several movies. He coauthored several books, including *Across the Space Frontier* in 1952. His place is history appears to be ensured.

Remember To: Keep students focused on the exact nature of the questions or they'll get sidetracked. Give time allotments in short intervals.

Cautions: The drawing can stump some students, so you can ask them to do a 2-minute tracing activity of a picture, hand, or object to get the brain in the drawing mode.

It's working when . . . Students start talking about the topic to each other and showing new interest in it.

Differentiation:

Tier Up: Do a two-stage process, with the first stage being drawing from memory with no Internet, raising the quantity of questions you expect per category to five each, tie in personal interest issues, have students work alone and post their work on the walls and then critique each other's.

Tier Down: Limit the questions, work in pairs the whole time, allow for access to resources, and give extra time for each of the four chunks.

Activity for Analysis to Synthesis: HAS Synopsis

Objective: Make an abstract topic more concrete by creating an H diagram, analogy, and simile with the abstract term. When students compare and contrast, they find common and uncommon details of concepts.

Suggested Grades: 4–8

Materials:

- Prepare an abstract term that students will use for the activity.
- Photocopy the reproducible HAS Synopsis (page 232) for each student or partnership.
- A thesaurus might be helpful.

Time Needed: 5–8 minutes

Grouping Suggestions: Partners

Instructions:

1. Explain to students that comparing and contrasting, similes and metaphors, and analogies are strategies that make the abstract term more concrete and help the brain understand abstract terms better.

2. Give them an abstract word (you can give the same word to all students or distribute a variety of abstract terms that are related to your lesson) and the description of the word. This is a definition but should be much easier to understand than the exact words from the dictionary.

3. Ask them to use the H diagram to compare and contrast the focus word with one of the three words listed in the top section. They put the differences in the vertical sections of the H and then write the characteristics of how the word is different from the other word under each term in the vertical legs. Then they should write what these two words have in common in the center horizontal bar of the H. It's just like a Venn diagram but has more room to write the similarities.

4. When the H diagram is finished, ask the students to compare that abstract term with a different concrete word by creating an analogy with that term. The abstract term should be different from the one used in the H diagram.

5. To use the analogy graphic organizer, students place the abstract term on either of the first two blank lines. Make sure they include a written relationship between the words. You might need to teach students how to write analogies ("blank is to blank as blank is to blank"). You might also need to list some of the relationships that can be used to create an analogy—for example, cause-effect; big picture-small picture; part-whole; synonyms; antonyms; class membership; change; quantity-size.

6. After the analogy is complete, ask students to create a simile with the abstract word and explain why it is like that word. They fill in the blanks like so: "[abstract word] is like [create a new concrete word that has not been used yet] because . . ."

7. It's important that students get an opportunity to share these. The more students are exposed to others' comparisons, the more the abstract word can become clearer to each student.

Remember To: Encourage students to choose three different concrete words to compare the one abstract term with. These terms can be ridiculous (totally unrelated to the abstract word), or they can be more serious.

Differentiation:

Tier Up:

- Encourage students to create more analogies instead of doing the simile.
- Give these students very abstract, complex words to use for this activity.
- Do the activity independently instead of with a partner.

Tier Down:

- Allow these students to use a thesaurus if they need to think of a similar word to compare it with.
- Allow these students to draw pictures of the abstract word before doing this activity. It might help prompt better comparing.
- Some students might have difficulty creating the analogy. If so, allow them to do more similes and skip the analogy.
- Allow these students to use the same word in each section. Allow them to use the word from the H diagram in each of the sections versus trying to come up with three different terms or ways of comparing this abstract word.

Example: See Figure 5.13, HAS Synopsis example: Processing.

Figure 5.13   HAS Synopsis example: Processing

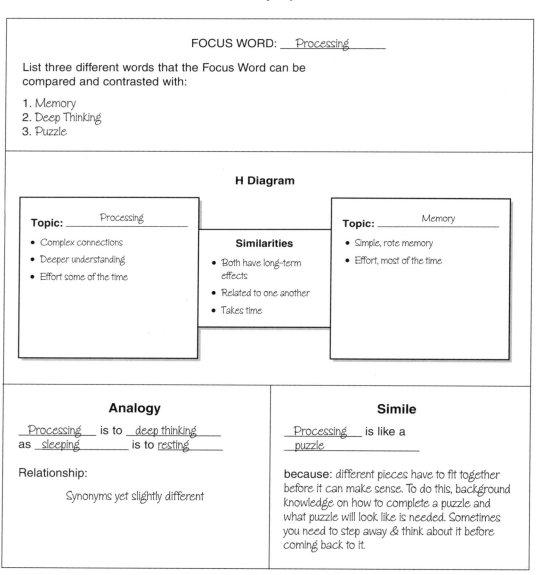

HAS Synopsis

FOCUS WORD: ___Processing___

List three different words that the Focus Word can be compared and contrasted with:

1. Memory
2. Deep Thinking
3. Puzzle

H Diagram

Topic: ___Processing___

- Complex connections
- Deeper understanding
- Effort some of the time

Similarities

- Both have long-term effects
- Related to one another
- Takes time

Topic: ___Memory___

- Simple, rote memory
- Effort, most of the time

Analogy

___Processing___ is to ___deep thinking___ as ___sleeping___ is to ___resting___

Relationship:

Synonyms yet slightly different

Simile

___Processing___ is like a ___puzzle___

because: different pieces have to fit together before it can make sense. To do this, background knowledge on how to complete a puzzle and what puzzle will look like is needed. Sometimes you need to step away & think about it before coming back to it.

DOMAIN 3: APPLICATION ACTIVITIES ∎

The application domain really gets your students thinking deeply about how to apply the information to benefit themselves, their community, their nation, and the world. This domain can use the information from the first two domains to make this an even deeper experience. The following variety of application activities are very engaging and extremely deep.

Activity for Application: Web-N-Pass

Objective: Students will be able to brainstorm several solutions to a question or problem through the perspectives of their local environment and the world.

Suggested Grades: 4–8

Materials: Graphic organizer called Web-N-Pass (pages 233–236). Copy the number of webs that you need to brainstorm solutions.

Preparation:

- Prepare your students' minds by explaining that the same problem can occur throughout the world, but depending on the location of the problem, different solutions are needed.
- Discuss at great length the problem they will be brainstorming solutions for. This could take a couple of class periods. The problems could range from hallway behavior to global warming issues. Choose a problem that goes along with your curriculum.

Time Needed: 15–20 minutes on Day 1; 20–30 minutes on Day 2

Grouping Suggestions: This depends on how many graphic organizers you have per group. For example, if you have four different Web-N-Pass pages, you should have four students in a group. If you have three different Web-N-Pass pages, you should have three students per group.

Instructions:

Day 1

1. Place students in groups of four (or whatever number you choose—see above).

2. Give each student in each group a Web-N-Pass graphic organizer (pages 233–236).

   Student #1—Web starter says (in the middle of the circle): Solutions for My Personal Realm.

   Student #2—Web starter says: Solutions for My Town or State.

   Student #3—Web starter says: Solutions for My Nation.

   Student #4—Web starter says: Solutions for the World.

3. Each student in a group starts with one of the above web starters. After the students write an idea, they pass the web to the next person in the group. (It's a good idea to ask students to write their initials next to their idea just in case further explanation is needed.) This continues until no student can think of any more solutions in any of those four areas.

4. Students get back the original web they started with. They take those webs and meet with other students from other groups that started with the same web. This forms four larger groups. In these larger groups, students get into groups of three and create a master list of solutions, with no repeats. They check off their sheets to make sure all ideas are included on the master sheet. The comparing occurs until there is one master list of solutions to a problem for a particular location (depending on the one that group was assigned to).

5. The teacher collects these master lists for each of the four Web-N-Pass pages that he or she originally created.

Day 2

6. The teacher creates "rather than" statements based on the master list of solutions. For example, using the master list of solutions from the Web-N-Pass about solutions for students' personal realm, the teacher chooses several statements to ask the students to compare. If the problem is not enough recycling, the solution statement might be "Would you rather create a Web site about how to recycle simply for your community *or* go into four or five neighbors' homes and set up recycling bin organizers for them?" Students respond to the teacher's "rather than" questions on the paper at the bottom of the page by explaining which one they would prefer. The teacher could create about three "rather than" statements for each of the categories for the Web-N-Pass.

Follow-Up

Ask students to set a goal to do two of the items they said they would rather do and commit by writing them out. Have a due date for the students.

Differentiation:

Tier Up: Give these students the Web-N-Pass for the national and international levels. Challenge them with more complex solutions. Support them with information about the problem at the national and international levels.

Tier Down: Encourage these students to focus on the Web-N-Pass for the personal realm or local and state level. Ask them to create only two goals if they feel overwhelmed with three goals.

Example: See Figure 5.14, Web-N-Pass example: Lyme Disease.

Figure 5.14 Web-N-Pass example: Lyme Disease

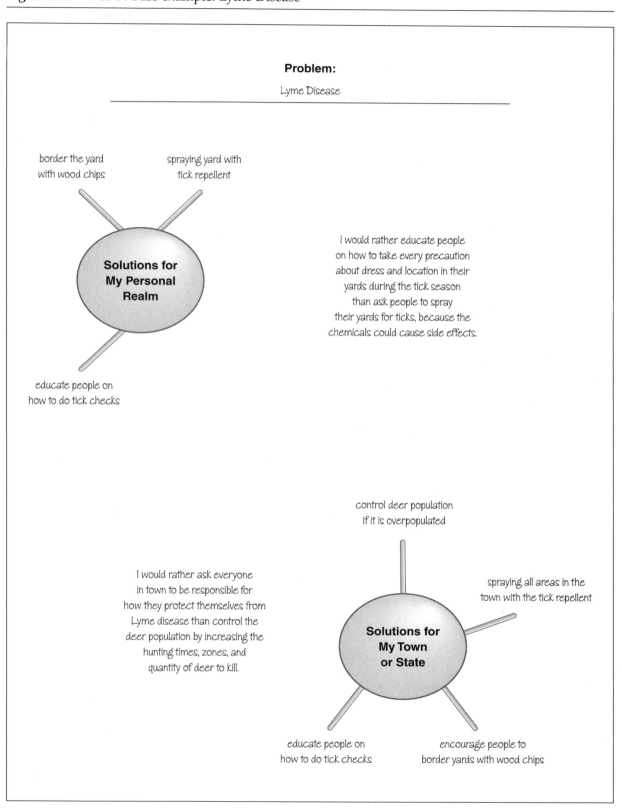

(Continued)

Figure 5.14 (Continued)

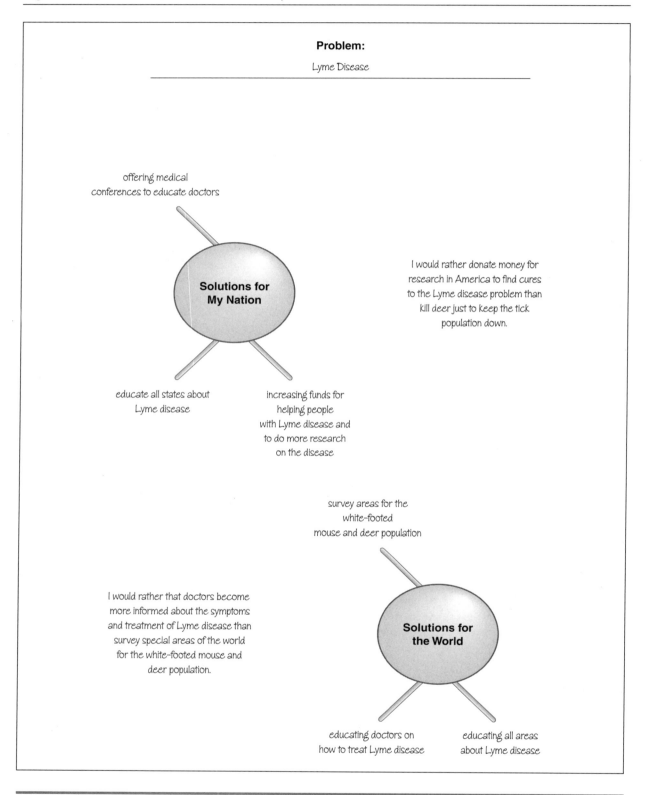

Activity for Application: Who's Been There and Done That?

Objective: Students will expand their horizons by research on what writings and movies have been done on the same topic.

Suggested Grades: 4–12

Materials: Computer, Internet connection, a copy of Who's Been There and Done That? Partner Support Sheet (page 237) and a copy of Who's Been There and Done That? Individual Student Support Sheet (page 238).

Preparation: Define the topic at hand. Explain that many other people (some of them with great minds) have already researched this topic. Student goals are to find out what others have discovered.

Time needed: 12–15 minutes; best when done as a priming activity a week before the actual unit begins

Grouping Suggestions: Pairs

Instructions:

1. Pair students up and give each pair one Who's Been There and Done That? Partner Support Sheet (page 237) graphic organizer to complete together. They write their names and define the topic in the designated spots on the graphic organizer.

2. They begin Google searches with their topic and the media. If their topic is the Civil War, they type in "Civil War+films" or "Civil War+best seller" to find media already produced on the topic.

3. Give students 3 minutes to come up with a video or movie media list and 3 minutes for a book or article list.

4. After the 6 minutes of searching, students pair up with another pair to compare and combine their lists.

5. All students pick two media sources for them to personally explore for further ideas.

6. Students get a week to locate and browse their media sources for more ideas and themes. Give each student the Who's Been There and Done That? Individual Student Support Sheet (page 238) graphic organizer. Each student individually completes this graphic organizer.

7. Students report to the class their results, and all classmates benefit.

Remember To: Keep time deadlines sharp, or students will wander off course.

Cautions: Monitor the Web surfing and let students start with an initial list of ideas or topics so they can see the results of their efforts.

It's working when . . . Students can see their before-and-after subject knowledge expand fivefold.

Differentiation:

Tier Up: Challenge these students to choose more complex movies and books to use in their research. Challenge them to use a variety of resources. Give them less time for the assignment; have them work alone; give them a different end product; for example, students produce their own movie or PowerPoint short subject or they produce a product to show to other students as a guide to the learning.

Tier Down: Have students work in pairs; give them more time for the assignment; prepare them with more background knowledge first.

Example:

1. If their topic is the Civil War, they will find movies such as *Cold Mountain, The Outlaw Josey Wales, North and South, Gods and Generals, The Red Badge of Courage, Andersonville, Glory, Gettysburg, Ride With the Devil,* and the Ken Burns special *The Civil War.*

2. They might come up with books such as *The Civil War Trilogy, The Killer Angels, Battle Cry of Freedom, The Gettysburg Campaign, A Stillness at Appomattox, Gettysburg: The Second Day, Civil War Memoirs of Captain William J. Seymour,* and *Civil War Memories of Two Rebel Sisters.*

3. After the 6 minutes of searching and pairing up, the two students might add 25% to 50% more options.

4. Students might pick two movies to rent from Blockbuster or Netflix such as *Glory* and *Gods and Generals.* Students can work in pairs and divide up the movies. They may come up with other ideas for studying such as racism and democracy, dignity, brotherhood, and honor. *Glory* is an amazing film for insights on the Civil War, and *Gods and Generals* is an accurate portrayal of the times.

5. During the week that students locate and browse their media sources for ideas, they'll come up with multiple new themes, and the next challenge is to sort out and narrow down the human element themes.

6. Students can choose a theme to study more and report on about the Civil War. They might pick courage or patriotism. They can report on their study to the class with a one-page paper or PowerPoint presentation.

Activity for Application: Virtual Interviews

Objective: Gather firsthand or best available evidence for a topic that can lead to solutions to a problem.

Suggested Grades: 6–12

Materials: Internet access.

Preparation: There was an old TV show (1953–1957) called *You Are There* (Fonda & Russell, 1953), where reenactments were done of key events in history. The actors were interviewed as if they were alive today. This was an amazing way to get the inside scoop on a topic. Your students will research to find out who the experts are in the field and talk to them.

Time Needed: 2–3 weeks, 10 minutes per day

Grouping Suggestions: Independent or partners

Instructions:

1. Get students excited about those who have witnessed history in the making.
2. Students work in pairs to create a list of current experts on the topic.
3. Compile a list of potential experts in the field by using university professors, scientists, authors, and so on.
4. Students get permission from the experts to ask them questions.
5. Students send their list of questions to the experts.
6. They compile their results and integrate them into a project or present them to the class.

Remember To: Keep their spirits up; sometimes chasing experts leads down blind alleys and unresponsive "heroes."

Cautions: This should be done online. Remember, for safety reasons, kids should never agree to meet with an outside expert unless accompanied by an adult.

It's working when . . . Kids actually get a response from an expert. They'll need to send many inquiries to get a few interviews. It might be a 20-to-1 ratio of tries to hits.

Differentiation:

Tier Up: Students can have higher goals, get less time, or work alone.

Tier Down: Allow students to find printed interviews online to use; allow them to break down the task into smaller chunks; put three in their group, with one acting as a consultant who seeks help from other groups and relays it back to his or her own group.

Example:

1. Get students interested in a topic such as the Iraq War. Some students might have family serving in the war. That may need to be addressed first. Other topics may be better for students under age 12 who have a parent in Iraq.

2. Students work in pairs to create a list of current experts on the topic. This search turns up and eventually includes (but may not be limited to) the Council on Foreign Relations, former generals Norman Schwarzkopf and Colin Powell, the Israeli Think Tank, political writers for the *New York Times* and the *Washington Post*, the Center for Foreign Policy, and the U.S. Senate Committee on Foreign Relations.

3. Students and teachers should compile a list of potential experts in the field by using university professors, scientists, authors, and so on. This list might include those who have written on the war and done serious homework and journalism. That might include authors William R. Polk, Peter W. Galbraith, Thomas E. Ricks, Ahmed S. Hashim, and James Baker and colleagues, authors of the Iraq Study Group Report.

4. Students send their list of questions to the experts and some may get responses. They should include local political figures (local newspapers or local professors of history or foreign studies).

5. If they get no responses, they compile quotes from published articles.

6. Students compile their results and present them. For example, students might present the findings to the class from the Iraq Study Report.

Activity for Application: Expert Interviews

Objective: Individually develop depth and then share it so all can benefit.

Suggested Grades: 6–12

Materials: Index cards (one for each student), flip chart paper (one per group of three or four), teacher-created We Must Know reproducible (based on unit objectives), teacher-created Rubric of Expectations

Time Needed: Teacher prep time is about 1 hour to subdivide units into microtopics. Once the activity starts, it'll take 1–3 hours of homework time and about 1–2 hours of class time.

Grouping Suggestions: Independent and then share with group

Instructions:

1. Teacher subdivides the unit into microtopics based on meaning, length, or complexity. The number of microtopics is equal to the total number of students in class.

2. Each microtopic is written on a piece of paper or index card and placed in a large bowl. Teacher guides this activity.

3. A drawing determines who gets which topic. After the drawing, students get 2–3 minutes to make any trades they want with other students for their topic OR allow them to choose, reminding them that every student must have a different topic. Compromising is very important with this choice.

4. Students get a week to individually learn their topic well. The teacher provides a template for "must know" format that includes who, what, why, where, when, how, meaning, process, results, implications, and so on. Teachers need to create a template or graphic organizers with the components that they expect students to gather during this search. In fact, place all the required pieces on a rubric so they know they'll be evaluated based on meeting the requirements for the assignment.

5. Students work in small teams to assemble their knowledge on a graphic organizer and determine their gaps.

6. When complete, in a smaller class, each student could stand and give a 60-second overview of his or her topic. In a larger class, students can report and send their overview to the classroom Web site or create a one- to two-page summary paper.

7. Teams seek out the experts in the class to get their knowledge completed on the What We Must Know reproducible the teacher creates based on what students need to know for the unit test. Teachers could create two to four questions per topic and place them on this reproducible. Each student would be in charge of finding these answers by interviewing the experts in the classroom on these questions. The goal is to complete the What We Must Know reproducible, which is graded for accuracy and then used as a study guide for the test.

Remember To: Use your judgment to decide how students want to seek out others' expertise. Some may want to talk to or interview the classroom expert; others may simply want to get an executive summary posted online.

Cautions: Unless you stay excited about the wonder of the little pieces to the big picture, the students may lose interest.

It's working when . . . Students really get into collecting the data from others.

Differentiation:

Tier Up: Ask these students to help you create the expectations for the rubric and decide what the experts need to research. They can also help create the two to four questions for the What We Must Know reproducible.

Tier Down: Allow these students to have partners for the interviewing process OR with the completion of the interviewing in order to complete What We Must Know.

Example: The U.S. Constitution is the topic at hand. The following are possible subtopics in which students can become experts: the preamble, legislative branch (Congress and House of Representatives), judicial branch, executive branch, separation of powers pros and cons (checks and balances), Senate, vice president, elections, impeachment, forbidden powers and powers denied to states, military powers, Amendments (Part I and Part II), taxes, and the founding fathers.

Activity for Application: Missing Links

Objective: Make connections between the content and students' personal life. The goal is to find the missing links between the content and themselves.

Suggested Grades: 4–10

Materials: Three sheets of 8½ × 11-inch paper per person

Preparation: Think about the topic and divide it into four major areas. For example, if the topic was history, the four topics might be (1) locations, (2) people, (3) what values or causes were fought over—religious, land, hunger, and so on, and (4) importance or results.

Time Needed: 15–20 minutes

Grouping Suggestions: Whole group, partners, or small groups

Instructions:

1. Lead students through a guided class assignment. First, they'll divide a piece of paper into four equal sections—squares are fine.

2. Give different titles to each of the four boxes; for example, People, Activities, Things, and Values.

3. In the People box, students list all the people that are important to them: parents, friends, siblings, and even celebrities. The next box is for activities such as going to movies, holiday travel, surfing, partying, and church. The next box is for things such as a car, iPod, cell phone, MP3 player, and clothes. The final box is for values such as having fun, being healthy, honesty, fairness, and faith. Ask students to fill in at least 10 items for each box. The idea is that the more items listed, the greater the likelihood of finding a personal connection to the content.

4. With another piece of paper, have students divide it into four sections. The teacher has already preselected the more relevant categories that allow the students to make connections.

5. Now ask students to make connections. Explain that the connections might not be obvious. Putting both pieces of paper next to each other, on a third paper they list as many connections as they can see.

6. Allow students to share their connections out loud after 10 minutes. This helps the class hear about others' work and serves to encourage them.

Remember To: It's very important to role-model the insights and joys of connections. Provide an example or two so that they can see the connections you've made. For example, what freedoms do you enjoy every day as a result of a battle that was fought?

Cautions: The key to this activity is your choice of connecting possibilities that you share with them for their second sheet of paper. The better your choices, the better the likelihood of students finding connections to make meaning.

It's working when . . . Students show new interest in history (or whatever the topic is) based on finding new meanings in it and their connections to it.

Differentiation:

Tier Up: Students work in pairs, not a foursome; the questions have to be short-answer questions and relate to topics the teacher has preselected; the students get less time to prepare, or the students take an assignment home to prepare really solid questions.

Tier Down: Allow the two experts in the same foursome to cooperate and help each other out on the answering process; give the reporters more time to prepare the questions.

Example:
Here's what the students might start out with on a piece of paper.

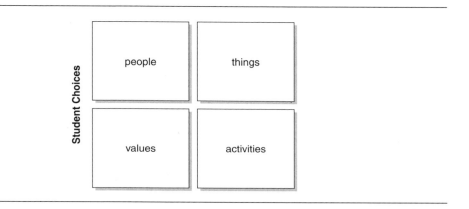

The students fill it out, and it might look like this for some of them:

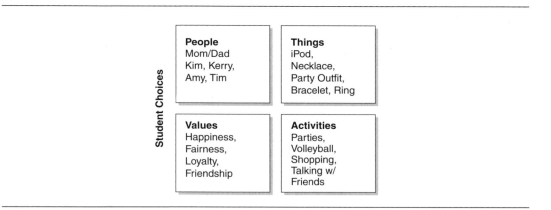

The idea behind this activity is for students to learn to make connections beyond themselves with the world. Next, teachers can share their own quadrants, which, on a unit about the environment, might have some of these choices:

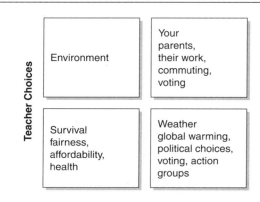

The possible connections students can make are many. Students might link up their parents driving their car as a way to connect to the environment. The jewelry that a girl wears may come from third world producers who exploit the environment. Students need coaching on this, but the bottom line is that they become much more aware of how their world affects the bigger world and vice versa.

Activity for Application: Arts Galore!

Objective: Individually develop depth and wisdom and then share it so all can benefit.

Suggested Grades: 6–Adult

Materials: Paper, clay, colored markers or paint, several musical instruments (piano, drum, shakers, or other instruments)

Time Needed: Teacher prep time is about 1 hour. Activity time is 1–3 hours.

Grouping Suggestions: Small groups of two to four students

Instructions:

1. Place students into small groups of two to four.

2. Give all students a choice of working with either a sculpting medium such as clay, a theater performance such as a commercial, a musical instrument, or flip chart paper and markers. The choices are a tactile, auditory, or visual medium.

Remember To: Help them brainstorm first the pluses and minuses of each medium before they make the small group decision about which one they'll use.

Cautions: Unless you stay excited about creativity of the moment, the students may lose some interest.

It's working when . . . Students really get into the flow of their work and want extra time for their art form.

Differentiation:

Tier Up: Ask these students more questions to help them decide to do a more complex project pertaining to the topic. You might need to give them ideas. For example, a relief map is more complex than a drawing of landforms.

Tier Down: Allow these students to have the use of "roving artists" (student class experts) or your help for the art-making process, *or*, with the completion of the art, they can do a handbook on what we now know.

Example: The U.S. Constitution is the topic at hand. The following activities are possible: (a) reenact the signing of the Constitution, (b) do a rap that describes the process from start to finish, (c) create a sculpture of the Pennsylvania State building where the Declaration of Independence is housed, and (d) create a drawing or painting of the actual signing of the Constitution with all the signers present.

Activity for Application: Connect Four

Objective: Students will be able to make personal connections with the topic at hand in four different ways: personal life or local community, national, international, other resources.

Suggested Grades: 9–12

Materials: Copy of the Connect Four (page 239) reproducible for each student

Time Needed: 5–8 minutes

Grouping Suggestions: Independent first, then share with partner

Instructions:

1. After studying, reading, or discussing the topic at hand, ask students to connect the topic to all or some of the four areas on the Connect Four reproducible.

2. Students should think how the topic connects with
   - The student's personal life or world (family, friends, town, school, state, etc.)
   - The student's repertoire of media that he or she has been exposed to (novels, nonfiction, Internet sites, journals, movies, etc.)
   - The student's nation (other states, current events in the country, etc.)
   - Other countries or nations of the world (peace, war, politics, religion, culture, traditions, etc.)

3. When finished, ask students to share with one another how the topic was connected to those four areas.

Remember To:

- Help students brainstorm the nation and world ideas with current event articles. You could list several events that might help them create the connections.
- Show them the example of how to make the connections (Supply and Demand, Figure 5.15).

Differentiation:

Tier Up:

- Give the students a choice to elaborate on the last two connections: nation and world. Ask them to use current event newspaper articles to support their connections.

Tier Down:

- Ask students to focus on one of the connections instead of all four. The first two connections are less complex: personal life and media.
- These students might need a Venn diagram or H diagram to help them compare the topic with their personal life or other texts. Provide the graphic organizer if needed.

Example: See Figure 5.15, Connect Four example: Supply and Demand.

Figure 5.15   Connect Four example: Supply and Demand

Connect Four

Topic: _Supply and Demand_

Personal Life **(family, friends, town, school, state)** Limited time to do things with friends due to increased demands of work, family	**Media** **(books, Internet sites, videos, movies,** **TV shows, journals, magazines)** Satellite radio Delivering newspaper subscriptions
Nation **(other states, current events)** Concern for environment drives demand for "sustainable" resources and process Presidential race, many candidates, high interest in outcome	**Other Countries/World** **(peace, war, politics, religion,** **culture, traditions)** Growth of China's economy impacts demands for energy War in Middle East and price of gas

Activity for Application: Independent Contract Choices

Objective: Students will be able to create their ideal way of expressing what they learned at the end of the learning unit or lesson. They get to create their own product, design what content will be part of it, create their own rubric, and decide how they plan to share what they learned.

Suggested Grades: 4–12

Materials:

- Give each student the list of products (pages 240–241).
- Give each student a copy of the Product Rubric (page 242).
- Give each student a Product Planning Page Research Project (pages 243–244).

Time Needed: Several days

Grouping Suggestions: Independent or partner

Instructions:

1. Tell students they have the opportunity to create their ideal way of expressing what they learned at the end of the learning unit or lesson. They get to create their own product, design what content will be part of it, create their own rubric, and decide how they plan to share what they learned.

2. Students should use the list of products, Product Rubric, and Product Planning Page Research Project to plan their product.

3. Students should write their plans on the Product Planning Page Research Project.

Remember To: Go over all students' plans before they start the project. It's important that you help them think through the details before they start. Have a conference with each student and sign their plans before they begin.

Differentiation:

Tier Up: Challenge these students to choose a difficult product and a unique way to present it.

Tier Down: You might need to help these students complete their rubric and gather the content. You could partner them up with another student to lighten the load.

Activity for Application: Presentations With Pizzazz and Purpose

Objective: Students will learn the characteristics of a good presentation, create a presentation, and then perform it. Students will be able to evaluate themselves and others while presentations are delivered with the categories from the Presentation Rubric (pages 245–246).

Suggested Grades: 6–12

Materials: One copy of the Presentation Rubric (pages 245–246) for each student

Preparation: Make sure that all students can explain what each category looks like and sounds like during a presentation.

Time Needed: 3–4 minutes

Grouping Suggestions: Teacher uses the Presentation Rubric to evaluate students' presentations, *but also* other students evaluate each other.

Instructions:

1. Model a minipresentation in which the components on the rubric are exaggerated. Have fun and be creative with your presentation. Make the topic about something personal in your life—let the students get to know you better. The focus is not on the content but on your delivery of the content.

2. While you're presenting, tell them to check off each category when they see or hear it and rate within that category at the specified level (needs improvement, good, or excellent).

3. After the presentation, debrief the class, asking them how your presentation met the requirements of the categories of the rubric. Create a list of examples and categorize them in a T-chart labeled Sounded Like and Looked Like. Obviously, some items like gestures won't have a "sounded like" example.

4. Explain to the students what they need to implement in their presentation that is coming up. They need to make sure that each category can be seen or heard or both.

Remember To: Go over each category on the rubric so students know exactly how to present. Practice each category with minisimulations or skits.

Differentiation:

Tier Up: Add some items to the rubric (depending on the student). For example, some students might be expected to present objects pertaining to the topic.

Tier Down: You may need to eliminate certain categories such as facial expressions, gestures, or eye contact with some students who have fears of public speaking.

Activity for Application: Choosing Your Task—Structured Choices

Objective: Students will evaluate their understanding of a topic based on one of the following categories: (a) not quite sure of today's learning, (b) starting to understand today's learning, or (c) completely understand today's learning. Then they will choose a task that goes along with their understanding.

Materials: Graphic organizer Choosing Your Task: Structured Choices (page 247).

Preparation: Remind students how important it is that they understand themselves as learners.

Time Needed: 3–5 minutes to evaluate self; time to complete the choice of product

Grouping Suggestions: Independent

Instructions:

1. After a unit of study or lesson, give students the Choosing Your Task: Structured Choices graphic organizer (page 247) and ask them to evaluate how well they understand the concept or concepts taught by placing themselves in one of the following categories:
   - Not quite sure of today's learning—Task 1 Choices
   - Starting to understand today's learning and feel comfortable practicing it—Task 2 Choices
   - Completely understand today's learning and can teach it to another student—Task 3 Choices

2. After students have evaluated themselves, they may choose from two choices that you have written in each of the tasks. A Task 1 product choice is much easier to complete because it focuses on the basics of the content (for example, a crossword puzzle). A Task 2 product choice might have product choices that are semicomplex (for example, conducting an interview). A Task 3 choice is the most complex, since these students understand the learning well (for example, creating a play with the content). You will see a whole list of product ideas in this chapter in the Independent Contract Choices activity.

3. Students choose one of the choices from the task that they believe they best fit into.

Remember To: Ask students to help you create a rubric for each of the product choices. They need to know exactly what is required of them.

Differentiation:

Tier Up: Task 3

Tier Down: Task 1

Activity for Application: Three-Point Summary

Objective: Students will be able to respond to three questions that will help them devise a plan of application.

Suggested Grades: 4–8

Materials: Transparency of the Three-Point Summary (Figure 5.16), writing paper for the students

Figure 5.16   Three-Point Summary

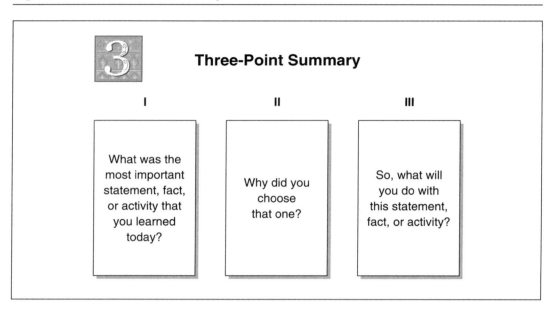

Time Needed: 3–5 minutes

Grouping Suggestions: Independent first, then small group share and repair

Instructions:

1. After students have acquired information from a lesson, reading, or video, ask them to process it by using the Three-Point Summary (Figure 5.16), which you've placed on the overhead projector.

2. Ask students to write out their responses to each of the following questions on paper:
   - What was the most important statement, fact, or activity that you learned today?
   - Why did you choose that one?
   - What will you do with this statement, fact, or activity?

Remember To: Encourage students to give detailed answers. Remind them that not all students will judge the same information to be the most important. What a student deems important depends on the student's background knowledge and experience.

Differentiation:

Tier Up:

- Extend the third question by asking how this would affect others positively and negatively.
- Ask these students to elaborate on step-by-step ways they will apply the information.

Tier Down:

- If these students have a challenging time writing their thoughts, allow them to share their answers verbally, but insist that they answer each question. They can then have a partner do the same.

Example:

(The student is verbally responding to another participant. Another idea is to have the students respond to the answers on their gel boards—see Awareness Activities in this chapter for more information on gel boards.)

- What was the most important statement, fact, or activity you learned today?
  Participant in a training on the topic of differentiation: "The most important fact that I learned today was that differentiation is a must in today's classrooms."
- Why did you choose that one?
  Participant in a training: "I chose this statement because I was very skeptical of the word 'differentiation,' since so many terms are thrown out to us educators and they stay for a while and then leave. Differentiation will never leave—it's a topic that all teachers will face for eternity. No two brains learn the same way, so a variety of strategies will need to be used to meet and reach students."
- What will you do with this statement, fact, or activity?
  Participant in a training: "I will try several of the differentiated strategies that I learned from the training today. I will try the Six Thinking Hats, Choosing Your Task: Structured Choices, and Choice Reflection."

Activity for Application: Palm Pilot

Objective: Students will be able to write down a solution they have to a problem that is occurring in their classroom, town, country, or world. Each student will ask at least three other students to swap their opinions of the solutions to the problem. Each student will have several solutions to the problem and then will choose one of them to write a problem/solution response.

Suggested Grades: 4–8

Materials:

- Palm Pilot for each student (page 248 or 249)—one per student There are two Palm Pilots per page. Cut them apart from one another. Copy enough so each student gets one Palm Pilot.
- Create a transparency of the Palm Pilot reproducible so that you can explain its parts.

Time Needed: 5–8 minutes

Grouping Suggestions: Independent and then partners sharing ideas (at least three different partner sharings per child)

Instructions:

1. After the learning occurs and it's time to process the information, give each child a copy of the Palm Pilot reproducible (page 248 or 249). Use a transparency of it to explain it to the students.

2. Ask students to write a solution to a problem that has been discussed in the classroom. They should write that problem at the top of the Palm Pilot. Give them 1–2 minutes to do this. Remind them to be very detailed with their answers.

3. When all students are finished writing on the top half, tell them to fold their Palm Pilots in half so that the bottom half (Other Solutions) is facing them. They place this bottom half in the palm of their hand, take a pencil with them, and then write down three other students' solutions to the problem. In other words, they need to meet three different friends, exchange solution ideas, and write down what the other three students have written in the Other Solutions section. Encourage discussion about their solutions.

4. This is called Palm Pilot because they're writing what they learned in the palm of their hand—not their real palm, but the paper in their palm. The Palm Pilot guides them to creating a solution to a problem.

5. After they've gathered three different solutions to the problem, ask them to write on a clean sheet of paper: "The best solution to the problem is . . . because . . ."

Remember To: Use the Palm Pilot in a variety of ways, not just for problem solving. Have each student create an open-ended question to ask three other students. The open-ended question is written in the top half of the Palm Pilot (changing the Problem section to Open-Ended Question), and the answers that the three students give are written on the bottom half (changing the Other Solutions section to Answers From Students). This activity creates great discussion and analysis of different answers to the same question. You could use it as a review or closure to a lesson.

Differentiation:

Tier Up: This could be structured so that students have to think globally but act locally. Students have to develop a plan for implementation of the actions.

Tier Down: Allow students to work in pairs so they have some support. They need to cooperate and agree on the issue they choose.

Example: See Figure 5.17, Palm Pilot problem example: The National Debt, and Figure 5.18, Palm Pilot topic example: Earth's Parts.

Figure 5.17   Palm Pilot problem example: The National Debt

Figure 5.18   Palm Pilot topic example: Earth's Parts

Palm Pilot

Problem: _The National Debt._

A solution to this problem is:
Must balance the federal
budget like a household budget.
You can't spend more than
you have coming in.
Develop a research committee
to get the facts.

Other Solutions:
1) _Create fliers with information_
about the debt and distribute to
the community.
2) _Invite speakers to towns to_
present the problems with
specific solutions: tax increases
and unnecessary spending.
3) _Present information to_
newspapers, state leaders, etc.
about our bankrupt nation.

Palm Pilot

Topic: _Earth's Parts_

I learned the following:
We live on the outside layer of
the earth. This layer is called
the crust.

Other students learned:
• _The mantle layer is made of_
hot rock.
• _The inner core is the center_
of the earth.
• _Scientists use various tools to_
measure these layers.

DOMAIN 4: ASSIMILATION ACTIVITIES ■

The aha moment has arrived: the assimilation domain. Not every lesson brings students to this domain. In fact, it could take quite some time in life's journey for this goal to be achieved. The goal for the following activities is to get students to really "feel" the content, to make the content a part of them so they form opinions. This is the heart of learning.

Activity for Assimilation: Processing Notebook

Objective: Process chunks of information during note-taking time so that greater understanding and assimilation of the concept is accomplished.

Suggested Grades: 9–12

Materials:

- Each student should have a spiral notebook or three-ring binder.
- Photocopy Choice Reflection (page 24) for each student and glue it to the inside cover of the notebook. This strategy is ongoing throughout the school year and can be used with any content.
- Option: colored pencils or thin twist-up crayons. Don't use markers, since they'll bleed through the paper.

Time Needed: Each opportunity for processing on the left-hand side of the notebook could take about 3–5 minutes.

Figure 5.19   Processing Notebook

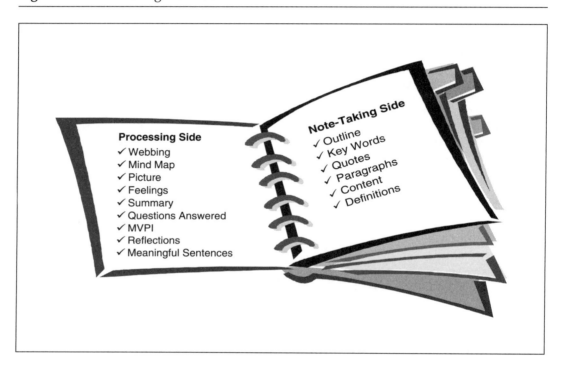

Grouping Suggestions: Individual or partner

Instructions:

1. Students take notes from your lesson on the right-hand side of their notebook in pencil if possible. These notes can be in any form that you choose (outline, web, sentences, or writing the information down any way). This right-hand side is the content that you want them to learn. Show students Figure 5.19 for a visual or example of this.

2. After teaching for about 7–10 minutes (or viewing a video or reading a chunk from a book), stop and allow the students to choose how they want

to process what they just learned on the left-hand side of the notebook. They could choose the Choice Reflection page (page 24) that is glued to the inside cover of their notebooks, or you could give them a different way to process the content, such as a mind map.

3. Once they've chosen, they document their processing on the left-hand side of the notebook so they can refer back to the notes. We encourage students to use colored pencils or twist-up crayons while they're writing what they processed, since color enhances memory.

4. The teacher continues to teach the next chunk of information after students complete that processing (3–4 minutes). Then after the next chunk is completed, students again choose how to process that last chunk of information. They write down their thinking on the left-hand side again under the first processing. This procedure continues until the lesson is complete. Students could write or discuss a closure that summarizes all the chunks together in their notebooks.

Remember To: Remind students to be creative with their processing or reflection on the notes. Encourage them to choose a variety of ways to process rather than use the same ways over and over. Ask students to share how and what they processed with a partner so they can learn from one another.

Encourage students to study from these notebooks for their tests or quizzes. Remind them that learning comes from the processing of content.

Differentiation:

Tier Up:

- Encourage these students to choose their processing opportunities from the section labeled Synthesizing It All that is located at the bottom of the Choice Reflection page (page 24). These processing responses are more challenging than the other two categories.
- Encourage them to use content from previous notes in their processing opportunities (connect the content across the curriculums).

Tier Down:

- Just before these students are given quiet time to write on the left side of their notebooks, ask them to share which way they plan to process to give others ideas.
- Allow pairs of students to create their processing response together, but both students write what was learned in their notebooks.
- Encourage these students to choose processing opportunities from the Forming the Basics section at the top of the Choice Reflection sheet, since these responses are easier.

Example: See Figure 5.20 , Processing Notebook example: Teaching With the Brain in Mind.

Figure 5.20   Processing Notebook example: Teaching With the Brain in Mind

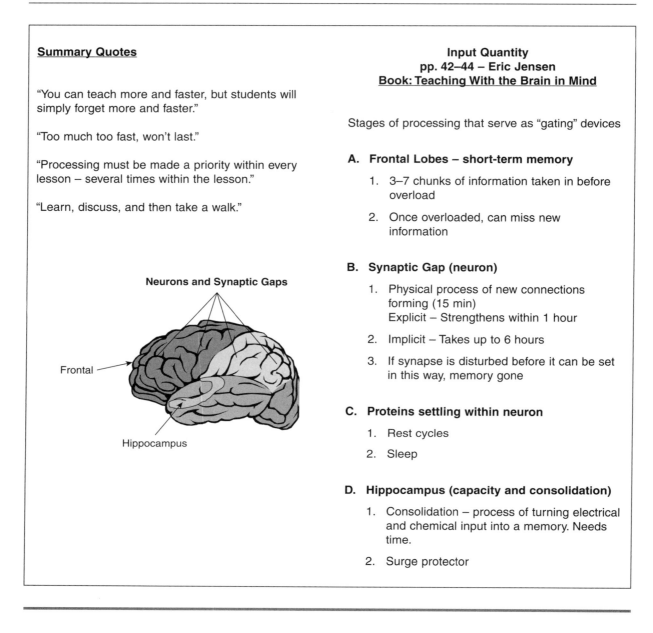

Summary Quotes

"You can teach more and faster, but students will simply forget more and faster."

"Too much too fast, won't last."

"Processing must be made a priority within every lesson – several times within the lesson."

"Learn, discuss, and then take a walk."

Neurons and Synaptic Gaps

Frontal

Hippocampus

Input Quantity
pp. 42–44 – Eric Jensen
Book: Teaching With the Brain in Mind

Stages of processing that serve as "gating" devices

A. **Frontal Lobes – short-term memory**

   1. 3–7 chunks of information taken in before overload

   2. Once overloaded, can miss new information

B. **Synaptic Gap (neuron)**

   1. Physical process of new connections forming (15 min)
      Explicit – Strengthens within 1 hour

   2. Implicit – Takes up to 6 hours

   3. If synapse is disturbed before it can be set in this way, memory gone

C. **Proteins settling within neuron**

   1. Rest cycles

   2. Sleep

D. **Hippocampus (capacity and consolidation)**

   1. Consolidation – process of turning electrical and chemical input into a memory. Needs time.

   2. Surge protector

Activity for Assimilation: Stop-N-Think

Objective: Process chunks of information while acquiring information (note taking, video, or reading text) so that greater understanding of the concept is made.

Suggested Grades: 4–8

Materials: One copy of Stop-N-Think (page 250) for each student

Preparation: Create questions for each tiered group depending on what you're teaching (questions from a book, questions about a video, and questions about notes taken).

Time Needed: Each opportunity for processing could take 3–5 minutes.

Grouping Suggestions: Individual or partner

Instructions:

1. Teach students how to use the Stop-N-Think by having them process with the reproducible in front of them.

   Chunk 1: Teach students the purpose of Stop-N-Think:

   - The brain can only pay attention for so long before it needs to stop and think about what was just said, heard, or seen. When the teacher is finished teaching why Stop-N-Think is so important, then students get to respond to this section or chunk of learning in a particular way (noted below) in Stop #1.
   - Learning doesn't come in the lecture or video of the content. Learning comes in the processing of the content, in the thinking of what was just learned. Thinking can be in the form of personal reflection through writing, drawing, webbing, or discussing what was learned. After each chunk of content, students have the opportunity to write, draw, or web what they just learned in a particular box.
   - When the lesson has been completed, students have the opportunity to process all the pieces from the lesson by examining each chunk and tying them all together. The last box in the Stop-N-Think is the summary box of what students learned.

   Teachers ask students to respond to what they just learned by answering the question, "In your own words, why is Stop-N-Think such an important strategy for improving our learning?" Students write their answer in Stop #1 on the Stop-N-Think reproducible.

   When all students have written their responses, have them share with a partner what they wrote. If they like what their partner wrote, they can add that comment to their box in another color of ink or pencil.

   Chunk 2: Show the students a video about their next concept. For example, if you're going to teach a lesson about biomes, show a video about them. Make sure you share the purpose questions about what students are about to view before viewing it. There should always be a purpose question before reading or viewing a video; otherwise, the brain might be more challenged to decipher what the most important information may be. View the video in advance so that you know where to stop the video so that students can respond to the purpose question about the chunk they just saw. Play the video for about 6–10 minutes. Turn off the video and ask students to respond in Stop #2 with an answer for the purpose question that you posed before the video was turned on (e.g., "What four biomes will we be studying in this unit? Give a characteristic of each.").

   Chunk 3: For example, say to students, "Read Chapter 4 called Monerans and Viruses in your science books. Read from pages 48 to 50 to answer the following questions in Stop #3." List the questions on the chalkboard. Encourage students to choose one of the questions to respond to.

The idea is to let students experience learning in chunks and then processing in chunks before learning more. The brain has the opportunity to remember information better when each chunk is processed and partially consolidated. This process also allows for the teacher to check for understanding after each small chunk rather than waiting until the end of the class and trying to figure out which step wasn't mastered.

2. Invite students to write in Stop #4 a summary of how Stop-N-Think can benefit the learner. Notice that you don't have to complete all five stops. In fact, in some lessons you'll only use two, and in other lessons you might create more boxes on the back of the reproducible.

Remember To:

- You can use this strategy after chunks of lecture, reading, discussions, and video observations.
- Encourage a variety of responses such as complete sentences, webbing, drawing pictures, brainstorming words and their concepts, and so on.
- Give students choices they can respond to.

Differentiation:

Tier Up:

- Give a variety of questions for students to answer for each stop and point out the more challenging questions to answer.
- Ask them to write a more elaborate summary of all the chunks.

Tier Down:

- Give a variety of questions for students to answer for each stop and point out the less complex questions to answer.
- Allow students to collaborate on the formation of their answers.
- If writing is challenging for the students, invite them to web or draw their learning.

Example: See Figure 5.21, Stop-N-Think example: Water—Shaping Earth's Surface.

Figure 5.21   Stop-N-Think example: Water—Shaping Earth's Surface

---

Stop-N-Think

Name: _Ryan_   Date: _8/29_

Circle One: (Book,) Lecture, Video, Other _Water: Shaping Earth's Surface_

Stop #1

Forces change the Earth's surface through water (frozen or liquid), volcanoes, and earthquakes.

Stop #2
Water can change earth by carving out canyons, valleys, and holes. Ocean waves and powerful rivers strike against rocks and soil, changing their shape (weathering). Erosion occurs when water picks up the loose rocks.

Stop #3
Levees are like dams but are made out of earth, rocks, stones, or sand. They stop water flow after heavy rainfalls. 

Stop #4
Building dams and flood control channels are 2 ways of decreasing the chances of flooding.

Synthesis of the Stops:
Water changes the Earth's surface in many different ways such as creating canyons, valleys, and holes. Levees and dams are built to control the direction and power of the water.

Activity for Assimilation: Walking in the Shoes of Another

Objective: Students will put themselves in someone else's shoes so that they can appreciate and understand someone else's perspective (not necessarily change their perspective but respect another's perspective).

Suggested Grades: 4–Adult

Materials: One copy of Walking in the Shoes of Another (page 251) for each student

Preparation: Share your perspective and a friend's perspective on any topic. Explain how you don't necessarily agree, but you understand why that person has that perspective, and it is respected. Explain the importance of this attitude.

Time Needed: 8–10 minutes

Grouping Suggestions: Partners with different perspectives on an issue

Instructions:

1. After sharing the above scenario under Preparation/Materials, ask students to help you brainstorm why appreciating another's perspective might be important in this world. What are the pros of respecting another's

perspective? What are the cons? What would our world look like if we didn't appreciate or value others' perspectives? What would our world look like if everyone appreciated everyone's perspectives all the time?

2. Decide on a topic you're currently studying that has several perspectives (stem cell research, war versus peace, governmental issues, scientific issues, policies in school, rules in the home, literature, etc.). Ask students to research it to gain a perspective on the topic. Make sure they can support their perspective with facts. Students should write their perspective down on the left-hand side of the Walking in the Shoes of Another sheet. Once the perspective has been thoroughly thought through and written out, ask students to partner up with somebody who has a different perspective.

3. Once partnered up, partners should interview one another. Interviewer 1 asks the following questions while actively listening—no writing yet, just listening well with eyes and body language.
   • What is your perspective on this topic?
   • How can you support it?
   • Where did you get this information?
   • What might change your mind?

4. Then Interviewer 1 takes a moment to recollect what was said and asks more clarifying questions while writing his or her partner's perspective on the right-hand side of the figure.

5. Now the students switch roles. The other student asks the same four questions in order to understand his or her partner's point of view.

6. When this interviewing and documentation stage is complete, the students take a moment to reflect on each other's perspective. They write their thoughts in the section that begins "After the interview, put yourself in your partner's shoes. Explain what you understand, appreciate, or respect about your partner's perspective."

7. Finally, each student has an opportunity to change his or her point of view after this discussion with the partner. Have them write any changes in thinking in the section that begins "After considering both perspectives, what is your perspective now?"

Remember To:

• Do a human graph in order for all the students to know where they stand on the topic at hand. Create a line with masking tape that is about 20 feet long. Place a paper plate on the beginning and end of the line. Tell students that if they agree that the United States should withdraw its troops from Iraq immediately, they should stand over here (extreme left-hand side of the line on the floor behind the paper plate). If they disagree that the United States should pull its troops out immediately, they should stand on the other side of the line behind the other paper plate. Do this so a bar graph is created with the students.
• Teach students what actively listening looks like and sounds like.
• Remind them what it looks like to respect someone else's perspective.

Differentiation:

Tier Up:

- Allow students with greater background knowledge to pair up and challenge one another.
- Play devil's advocate with students while they're thinking up their perspective. Really make them think.
- Allow these students to debate and challenge one another more than with only those four suggested questions.

Tier Down:

- Allow students with similar background knowledge to partner up so each understands what the other is talking about.
- Support these students in the gathering of research. Ask them very often, "Does this fact really support your opinion?" You might need to supply them with explicit facts.

Example: See Figure 5.22, Walking in the Shoes of Another example: Renting versus Owning.

Figure 5.22 Walking in the Shoes of Another example: Renting versus Owning

Walking in the Shoes of Another

My Name: Jim	Partner's Name: Dolores
Topic: Renting or Owning a Home	Topic: Renting vs. Owning
My Point of View or Perspective: Renting a home is a smarter decision since you have more flexibility and less responsibility.	His/Her Point of View or Perspective: Owning a home will always be my choice. Renting is a waste of money – nothing to show for it.
Why I have this perspective: (support with facts) • Convenient and no maintenance • No taxes or no deposit (usually) • Not as permanent; could move easily.	Why do you have this perspective? (Support with facts) Equity in a house is an investment. More control of my environment. Owning payments are sometimes cheaper than rent.
I received this information from: (sources) • Experience • My parents	Where did you receive your information? (sources) • My money manager • My parents
The following fact or idea might change my perspective: If there was not a down payment on the house.	Is there a fact or idea that could change your perspective? If so, list it here. no
After the interview, put yourself in your partner's shoes. Explain what you understand, appreciate, or respect about your partner's perspective. Respond on the back of this page.	
After considering both perspectives, what is your perspective now? Write on the back of this page.	

Activity for Assimilation: The Six Thinking Hats

Objective: Focus on several different types of thinking, but one at a time, in order to gain a larger perspective on a particular topic, question, or problem. Feelings, opinions, and deep perspectives are challenged during this activity.

Suggested Grades: 4–12

Materials: Six paper hats for groups of students, transparency of Six Thinking Hats (Figure 5.23)

Time Needed: 7–10 minutes

Grouping Suggestions: Groups of six, then eventually individual

Instructions:

1. The Six Thinking Hats are like color printing: each color is printed separately, but in the end, they all come together. The hats are tools to help focus thinking and examine other points of view. They are physical symbols that trigger specific roles to play that enable our thinking to break out of normal patterns. Putting on a hat is a deliberate process, because each hat activates a particular type of thinking. You can put on or take off one of the hats, but you can't have two hats on at the same time. When you put on a hat, you must think like the hat. In other words, when you're wearing a hat, you must use only the type of thinking indicated by that hat color. Always refer to the hats by their color, not their function. You can ask someone else to put on a hat or take one off.

The Six Thinking Hats comes from Edward DeBono, author of *The Six Thinking Hats*. We have adapted the idea to fit into the classroom.

Figure 5.23   Six Thinking Hats

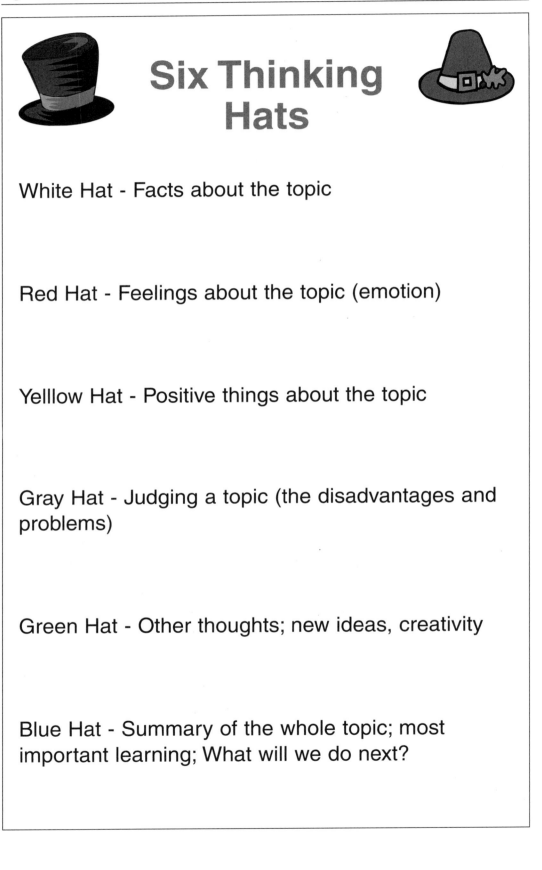

Six Thinking Hats

White Hat - Facts about the topic

Red Hat - Feelings about the topic (emotion)

Yelllow Hat - Positive things about the topic

Gray Hat - Judging a topic (the disadvantages and problems)

Green Hat - Other thoughts; new ideas, creativity

Blue Hat - Summary of the whole topic; most important learning; What will we do next?

2. What are the benefits of the hats?
   - They simplify thinking by allowing students to deal with one thought at a time because the human brain works best when people focus in on one task or idea at a time (rather than multitask).
   - They allow us to switch our thinking or ask others to switch their thinking without anybody being offended.
   - They lead to more creative thinking and higher-level thinking.
   - They focus and improve communication, problem solving, and decision making.

3. Use Figure 5.23 as a transparency to teach the students what the Six Thinking Hats are:

   White Hat: You brainstorm the facts that you know about _____.

   Red Hat: You explain your feelings about _____.

   Yellow Hat: You explain the pros or bright side of _____.

   Gray Hat: You explain the cons or the problems that could occur with _____.

   Green Hat: You create a what if? question about the topic.

   Blue Hat: You summarize what you learned about _____.

4. There are several ways to use the hats:
   - Use them to shorten and focus meetings, to solve problems, to discuss a topic, to ask and answer questions, and to experiment with ideas.
   - They can activate prior knowledge. See Activating prior knowledge using the Six Thinking Hats (Figure 5.24) to structure the conversations that students have about the topic at hand. They can write about it or discuss it. One student is responsible for discussing the question that goes along with the hat color. Others can participate in the discussion as well.
   - Students can review any content by answering questions based on the Six Thinking Hats. Place students in groups of six and let them choose which hat they want to represent. Whoever has the white hat must respond to the white hat question. When that student is finished responding verbally to the whole group, he or she says, "Open floor," and anybody can respond to the white hat question. Teachers must give a time limit for each hat (blue hat person is the timekeeper). We usually give two to three minutes per hat. There is no particular order for hats. So if the red hat is next, that student who represents the red hat explains how he or she feels about the topic at hand. This continues until all the hats have been discussed. The blue hat is the hat that wraps it all up. It's the best one to end with, since students summarize the learning or explain the next steps after the learning.
   - Use the hats informally, like for short discussions. Example: "I know that the hallway fight disrupted the learning, so let's take a few minutes to put on our red hats and talk about how we feel about what just happened."
   - Use the hats formally, such as for tests, lessons, or faculty meetings.
   - Use the hats privately in order to think through your thoughts about a topic or decision that needs to be made.

Figure 5.24   Activating prior knowledge using the Six Thinking Hats

	White Hat	What do you know about _____?
	Red Hat	How do you feel about _____?
	Yellow Hat	What are the benefits of understanding _____?
	Gray Hat	What problems might be attached to _____?
	Green Hat	What if _____ did not exist? How would life on Earth be different?
	Blue Hat	What do you think is the most important idea about _____ that all humans need to understand?

Differentiation:

Tier Up:

- Assign students the green or blue hats to deeply process and discuss, since they're more challenging than the other hats.
- When doing a jigsaw, allow these students to attend a similar-ability focus group on one hat. They'll become the experts on their hat, and then they'll get into a different group with other hats (one expert from each hat meeting together) in order to help all students gain a broader perspective on the topic.

Tier Down:

- Assign students the white or red hat to get a grasp on the topic first.
- Allow these students to be in a mixed-ability group of students to gain a bigger perspective on the topic.

Remember To:

- Use the Six Thinking Hats daily for needed discussions. For example, the teacher might tell two fighting students, "Put on your red hats and tell me how you feel about what he did to you. How would you feel if that happened to you? Now put on your white hats. What exactly happened—I want only the facts. Then put on the blue hats and tell me what you could do the next time."
- Use the Six Thinking Hats in faculty meetings to solve problems or to brainstorm ideas to improve learning.

Example:

The teacher hands out the following six thinking questions about the American Revolution on paper so students respond independently to the questions by writing the answers down. The teacher has left plenty of space between the questions so there is room to write others' responses as well.

1. What are 10 facts you know about the American Revolution?

2. If you were a Loyalist, how do you think you felt before the war, during the war, and after the war? If you were a Patriot, how do you think you felt before the war, during the war, and after the war?

3. What were the pros to being a Loyalist? Patriot?

4. What were the cons to being a Loyalist? Patriot?

5. What if the Loyalists had won this war? How would life be different now?

6. Write a summary about the American Revolution (remember to include who did what, where, when, why, and how).

After students answer these questions independently, they are given a partner, who they share their responses with and add to their answers if needed.

Activity for Assimilation: Four-Choice Processing

Objective: Students will be able to make a topic more meaningful by exploring the topic with different types of thinking. Awareness, Analysis to Synthesis, Application, and Assimilation are all represented in this graphic organizer.

Suggested Grades: 4–Adult

Materials: Copy of Four-Choice Processing graphic organizer (page 93) for each student

Time Needed: 4–7 minutes

Grouping Suggestions: Independent first, then share in small groups

Instructions:

1. Give all students the Four-Choice Processing graphic organizer (page 93).

2. Give students a topic to explore. This topic can be your unit topic or a more specific topic. You can give students all the same topic to explore or give a variety of topics related to each another.

3. Students choose one question to answer from each of the boxes under Choices and place the answers in the empty box in the top half of the figure that corresponds to their first box. For example, for Box 1, a particular student chooses to summarize the topic, while another student might choose to define it in his or her own words. Students are basically answering four questions from their designated boxes about the topic at hand (one question per box).

4. When students complete their processing, ask them to share their responses with other students.

Remember To: Encourage students to answer each question in great detail and write neatly.

Differentiation:

Tier Up:

- Give students the option to write more on another sheet of paper—they don't have to use only the questions in the boxes if they want to elaborate.
- Encourage them to create another box, a fifth box, with questions that they would like to answer about the topic.

Tier Down:

- Give these students fewer choices—these four or five questions in each box could overwhelm them. You could eliminate the more challenging questions from each box or choose a question for them if they want.
- Allow them to just answer questions from Box 1 and Box 2—they're simpler questions that focus on the basics of the topic.

Example: See Figure 5.25, Four-Choice Processing example: Differentiation. (This example was written by a teacher.)

Figure 5.25 Four-Choice Processing example: Differentiation

Four-Choice Processing

Topic: _Differentiation_

1. Differentiation is a philosophy of teaching students with a variety of strategies in order to maximime their learning so they can taste success.	**2.** Examples: Tiering; providing choices of products; providing a variety of leveled books for students to read.
3. I feel excited about this word because it means that teachers won't give up on students.	**4.** All schools need to be trained intensely on the topic, and then try out the strategies. Teachers need support from principals, colleagues, and instructional specialists.

Choices

Box 1 - Choose One	Box 2 - Choose One
How would you describe it? How would you define it? Which words are related to it? How could you illustrate it? How would you summarize it?	What are some examples of it? What are the pros and cons of it? How would you categorize, classify, or group it? What would you compare it with and why?
Box 3 - Choose One	**Box 4 - Choose One**
How do you feel about it? How does it compare with your life and what you know? Do you agree or disagree with it and why?	How would you improve it? Can you develop a new use for it? What if it didn't exist—how would life be different? What solutions can you devise for it?

Activity for Assimilation: Media Bias

Objective: Discover how different media report on the same subject.

Suggested Grades: 4–Adult

Materials: Paper for notes (or laptops) and name tags for reporters

Preparation: The teacher talks about news bias, special interests, and alleged journalistic integrity and identifies 10 different media sources. Each source has a bias in the news. The student's job is to identify the bias and use that bias to interpret a news story. For example, if the science unit is on climate changes around the world in the last 40 years, the teacher might identify the media sources as the following:

Exxon Oil Company public relations

National Petroleum News magazine

RV Trade Digest

Disney/*ABC News*

Former vice president Al Gore

Solar Energy News

Fox News reporter Bill O'Reilly

Senator Hillary Rodham Clinton

Ford Motor Company public relations

White House press secretary

Time Needed: Two 45-minute segments

Instructions:

1. Students are put in pairs and given (or they choose) the media source they'll analyze and use for their report.

2. Students are given time to research their media source and to learn how that source would report news on that topic.

3. Students are given instructions to review the topic again, this time from the point of view of the media source they're analyzing.

4. Students write out notes that reflect their "position" based on their media source.

5. Students also research potential opposing views about that same topic.

6. They each present their material in a larger group and get feedback from their peers.

7. The group gives feedback to each pair on their discovery of the biases in the media.

Remember To: Give the student pairs a model of how to analyze the bias from their media source. Give plenty of examples to ensure understanding. Give each group a time deadline for preparation and 3–6 minutes maximum for the presentations.

Cautions: Students often have difficulty getting out of their own personal views. Stress the importance of being in the media's mind-set.

It's working when . . . Students have some ahas.

Differentiation:

Tier Up: Give less time, have stricter guidelines for each of the presentations, or have students prepare a PowerPoint presentation.

Tier Down: Provide more examples for each passage and more peer review time.

Example: Typical types of media bias students can look for: ethnic or racial bias (racism, nationalism), corporate bias (favors corporate interests), class bias (favoring the rich or any other class or class divisions), political bias, religious bias (a preference of one religious viewpoint over others), sensationalism (bias in favor of the exceptional, grotesque, or bizarre over the ordinary), or an exaggerated minority influence in an attempt to be "fair" or to find something worth reporting. Topics like climate change might be exaggerated by some media and downplayed by others (corporate bias). The cost of making economic changes might be reported in a class-bias way (the rich can afford it). The impact of the changes might be reported in ways that affect social or economic classes disproportionately. The whole activity is designed to alert students to the many types of media bias and to the many perspectives on each issue.

Activity for Assimilation: Create Your Own Rubric to Evaluate

Objective: Students will create their own rubric for evaluating their own work or another student's, or for the teacher to use on students' work.

Suggested Grades: 9–12

Materials: RubiStar (http://rubistar.4teachers.org/index.php) is a free online tool that teachers and students can use to generate rubrics. Create your own rubric with your high expectations or have students create one.

Time Needed: 10–15 minutes

Grouping Suggestions: Independent or partners

Instructions:

1. Tell students how important it is to evaluate work (to know what quality work is, to set high expectations and then meet them, to know what is expected of them for an assignment, and for what is quality work and what is not, etc.).

2. Tell students they will have the opportunity to create the expectations for a certain project or assignment that is coming up. It's important that the rubric be created before the assignment starts. Begin with the end in mind so you know what is expected.

3. Students can create their own rubric for this assignment by using the Product Rubric (page 242) or by going to the RubiStar Web site to create the expectations: http://rubistar.4teachers.org/index.php.

4. After creating the rubric, students need to get feedback from another student and then from the teacher. Once all is set on the rubric, students can start the assignment or project. Students need to continually check the rubric to make sure they're doing what's expected.

Remember To: Show students a project or assignment from last year and the rubric that went with it. Ask students to evaluate whether or not last year's students met the expectations. Ask the students to evaluate the work using the rubric that was created for it. Ask them what the pros and cons are for creating a rubric.

Differentiation:

Tier Up: Ask these students to have more requirements on their rubric.

Tier Down: A partner can help create the rubric.

Example: See pages 245–246 for an example of a Presentation Rubric.

Activity for Assimilation: Personal Reflection on Processing

Objective: Students will use this rubric to reflect on the quality of their processing.

Suggested Grades: 4–12

Materials: Copy of the Personal Reflection on Processing rubric (page 252) for each student

Preparation: Explain to the students that every now and then we need to reflect deeply on how we're doing in lifelong skill areas. The Personal Reflection on Processing rubric will assist them in becoming better processors and creating a goal for future processing opportunities.

Time Needed: 5–8 minutes

Grouping Suggestions: Independent and then shared with teacher, or if students choose, to share with another peer

Instructions:

1. Distribute copies of the Personal Reflection on Processing rubric (page 252) to your students after allowing them time to process and respond to the content just learned. It could be after any of the processing specific examples in this chapter or after one that you created.

2. Ask students to complete each question by checking the box they feel best describes the processing activity they just completed. They should answer the following questions:
   - How would you rate your background knowledge on this topic or skill before the lesson?
   - Check all the ways you processed this topic or skill during the lesson.
   - Check all the ways you deepened your understanding of this topic or skill.
   - How do you know that your work or processing is accurate?
   - What was the most valuable, interesting, or surprising aspect of what you learned?

- Ask yourself, "Now that I've processed what I've learned, I think I need to do one of the following . . ."
- Ask yourself, "Next time I process, I'd like to . . ."

Remember To: Teachers should share a processing goal they've made for themselves. Encourage students to post this goal in a notebook for quick referencing or reminding. Explain to them how important goal setting is. Some possible processing goals are the following:

- To think deeply before responding
- To write out my thinking before responding
- To draw or web my thinking before responding
- To compare the content to something I already know about
- To ask others to challenge my perspectives more
- To personalize the processing more
- To ask others questions before I respond
- To encourage the partner that I'm working with

Differentiation:

Tier Up:

- Ask students to write more descriptive sentences after each question rather than just check off one of the choices. Ask them to elaborate on their answer.
- Encourage them to add more choices for each question.

Tier Down:

- Give these students more time to complete this activity.
- Allow them to receive feedback from a peer who just processed with them.

Example: See Figure 5.26, Personal Reflection on Processing example: Liquids, Solids, Gasses.

Figure 5.26   Personal Reflection on Processing example: Liquids, Solids, Gasses

---

Personal Reflection on Processing

Topic or Skill: _Liquids, Solids, Gasses_

1. How would you rate background knowledge on this topic or skill before the lesson?
   - ☐ I knew a lot
   - ☑ I knew a little
   - ☐ I didn't know much

2. Check all the ways that you processed this topic or skill during the lesson.
   - ☐ Discussed it with one person
   - ☑ Discussed it with several people
   - ☑ Wrote about it
   - ☑ Webbed it
   - ☐ Played a game about it
   - ☑ Created a product about it

(Continued)

Figure 5.26 (Continued)

3. Check all of the ways that you deepened your understanding of this topic or skill.
   - ☑ Read a book
   - ☐ Read a journal or magazine article
   - ☑ Searched and read on the internet
   - ☑ Reviewed notes from teacher
   - ☐ Viewed a video or DVD
   - ☐ Read the newspaper
   - ☐ Discussed with others (peers, family, teacher, expert)
   - ☑ Other: __Experiment__

4. How do you know that your work/processing is accurate?
   - ☑ Peer editing (product)
   - ☐ Compared it with something
   - ☑ Teacher checked work
   - ☐ Did additional research
   - ☐ Used the following resource: _____

5. What was the most valuable/interesting/surprising aspect of what you learned? __You can actually draw pictures of the molecules to represent whether or not it is a liquid, solid, or gas.__

6. Now that I have processed what I've learned, I think I need to do one of the following:
   - ☐ Ask more questions about the concept in order to improve my understanding.
   - ☐ Continue at the pace I'm going.
   - ☑ Extend my learning because I understand it and want to learn more.
   - ☐ Other:_____

7. Next time I process, I would like to: (GOAL)
   __Ask my group members more questions when I get confused.__

Activity for Assimilation: TELL—A Tool for Growth

Objective: Students will reflect internally about

What they should be thankful for

How they would evaluate their life based on what they just learned

What they learned from the lesson

What their plan of action is

Suggested Grades: 4–9

Materials: Photocopy the TELL reproducible (page 253)—one per student. Place these sheets inside the covers of your students' notebooks. Students will be able to respond to a day's or a lesson's learning by completing the TELL templates in their notebooks or learning logs (student notebooks used to summarize daily learning). TELL responses also enable students to write about their feelings and disturbances.

Time Needed: 4–7 minutes

Grouping Suggestions: Independent

Instructions: After a lesson or a day of learning, ask students to respond in their learning logs as follows:

T = Thankful for

- Describe all the things you were thankful for during the lesson or through-out the day.
- Who was helpful?
- Was there a good book involved?
- Did an author touch you somehow?
- Did another student or teacher give you feedback?
- Did you learn an amazing fact today?

E = Evaluate

- How well do you understand the information?
- How well did you do on _____?
- What questions do you still have?
- What do you need more help with?

L = Learned

- What did you learn?
- Did you learn a new social skill?
- New words?
- New connections?
- Any aha moments?
- List facts or list sequence of skill learned.

L = List your plan of action now

- New goals based on the day?
- Any apologies need to be made?
- How can you deal with that student or teacher differently tomorrow?
- What further learning do you want to explore now?

Remember To: Give students the freedom to skip some components of TELL when they need to. Remind them that what is written in their learning logs is only seen by you, the teacher.

Differentiation:

Tier Up: Encourage more elaborate plans.

Tier Down: Encourage these students to draw what was learned every now and then if it's easier.

Example:

Topic: My Behavior Today

T = Thankful for: I'm thankful that Mrs. Nickelsen is not yelling at me for what I did. I'm thankful that she is remaining calm and neutral. I'm thankful for this opportunity to get away from the other kids so I can think about what just happened. I'm thankful for this Quiet Spot.

E = Evaluate: I did not do the right thing by passing the note about Alyson. I did it for attention and to tease her. It was not a true statement and was not nice. I was just joking.

L = Learned: I learned that passing notes, especially false notes, can cause a lot of harm. I also learned not to trust my friends who told Alyson what I wrote.

L = List my plan of action

1. I plan to apologize to Alyson personally.

2. I plan to apologize to the students who read the note too.

3. Because I disrupted Mrs. Nickelsen, I need to apologize to her as well.

Activity for Assimilation: Goal-Setting Template

Objective: Students will set a specific goal for improvement and complete the Goal-Setting Template in order to have a plan of action.

Suggested Grades: 4–Adult

Materials: Copy of Goal-Setting Plan (page 254) for each student

Preparation: Remind students how important goals are. Goals give us energy to overcome bad habits, to excel, and to grow in ways we never thought of before.

Time Needed: 10–15 minutes

Grouping Suggestions: Independent and then partner for peer feedback (if not too personal)

Instructions:

1. Every month each student should have a goal to improve in some area that affects the learning of the curriculum or life skills. These goals could fall into any of the following categories:
   - Behavior (participation, outlook, treating others respectfully, helpfulness, responses, etc.)
   - Academic (word choice in writing, rereading when not understanding, remembering the details, check work thoroughly before turning it in, etc.)
   - Management of life (organization, supplies readily available, being on time, overcommitting, etc.)
   - Lifelong goals (more sleep, better nutrition, less soda, no smoking, no drugs or alcohol, etc.)

2. Have students fill out the Goal-Setting Plan (page 254)
   - Goal: should be very specific and measurable
   - Benefits of Accomplishing This Goal: students should write the benefits out so they can keep in mind the positives for accomplishing the goal.
   - Strategy: students should list at least four strategies that will help them achieve this big goal.
   - Action Plan: these are things that students can write on their planner or to-do sheet. Students might research something and schedule a trip to the library.
   - Result: during the month or later, students evaluate themselves on how well the strategy and action plan worked.
   - The Next Steps After Evaluation: Students need to decide if they need this goal for another month or need to change goals based on the achievement and evaluation of this goal.

Remember To: Share your goals with your students. It makes a difference when they see you doing it. We post ours and share our evaluation of the goals too.

Differentiation:

Tier Up: Challenge these students—ask them to tier up their goals.

Tier Down: These students might need a daily evaluation sheet to check how they're doing daily rather than just periodically.

Example: See Figure 5.27, Goal-Setting Plan example: Health & Wellness.

Figure 5.27 Goal-Setting Plan example: Health & Wellness

Goal-Setting Plan for the Topic of __Health & Wellness__

Author of Plan: __Dolores Helm__

Dates __8/1__ **to** __8/30__

Goal:

To eat 7-9 fruits and vegetables every day.

Benefits of Accomplishing This Goal:

- Lose weight
- Feel better
- More antioxidants

STRATEGY	ACTION PLAN *Write these in your planner	RESULT
1. Breakfast – 2 fruits (juice + fruit)	Purchase 100% orange juice and a variety of fruits.	
2. Snacks – easy to eat	Purchase bananas, grapes, or apples for this snack.	
3. Salad for lunch	Purchase spinach leaves, cherry tomatoes, and cucumbers.	
4. Two vegetables at supper	Purchase asparagus, green beans, peas, and broccoli.	

The Next Steps After Evaluation:

Activity for Assimilation: Stop-Save-Start

Objective: Students will be able to evaluate or reflect on what they plan to "stop" doing in their lives based on the topic, what they plan to "save" or continue to do, and what they plan to "start" doing in their lives based on the topic.

Suggested Grades: 4–Adult

Materials: Copy of the Stop-Save-Start reproducible (page 255) for each student

Time Needed: 4–6 minutes

Grouping Suggestions: Individual

Instructions:

1. After you teach the lesson, ask the students to personally reflect on what they plan to stop doing, what they're going to keep doing, and what they're going to start doing based on what they learned. This activity is good when you're focusing on the application of what was learned.

2. Benefits: The Stop section promotes what could be changed in that student's life. The Save section is an affirmation that the student is doing something right and making efforts. The Start section promotes a growth plan or goal to implement something that the student learned. All responses should be written in complete sentences in paragraph form.

3. This activity is often used to set goals based on what broad concept was learned (problem-solving situations in the classroom, writing skill, reading skill, government, environmental, character analysis, etc.).

Remember To: Remind students that paragraphs have topic sentences and then details that support that topic sentence. Use this activity after faculty meetings and after professional developments.

Differentiation:

Tier Up: Ask students to think broadly and then specifically.

Tier Down: If these students have difficulty writing a paragraph, accept sentences.

Example: See Figure 5.28, Stop-Save-Start example: Recycling, and Figure 5.29, Stop-Save-Start example: Math Word Problems Solved.

Special thanks to Rachel Billmeyer, trainer and author of *Strategies to Engage the Mind of the Learner* (2003, p. 235), for giving us permission to use this activity.

Figure 5.28   Stop-Save-Start example: Recycling

Name: Maria   Topic: Recycling

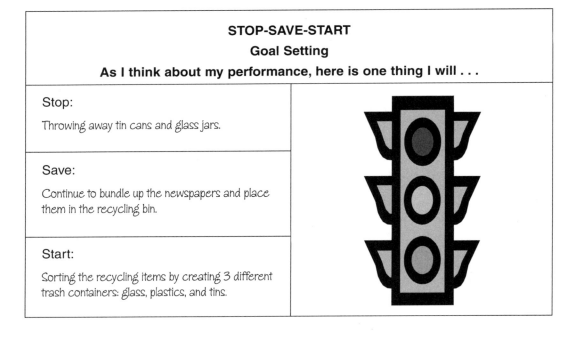

| **STOP-SAVE-START** |
| **Goal Setting** |
| **As I think about my performance, here is one thing I will . . .** |

Stop:

Throwing away tin cans and glass jars.

Save:

Continue to bundle up the newspapers and place them in the recycling bin.

Start:

Sorting the recycling items by creating 3 different trash containers: glass, plastics, and tins.

Figure 5.29   Stop-Save-Start example: Math Word Problems Solved

Name: Maria   Topic: Math Word Problems Solved

| **STOP-SAVE-START** |
| **Goal Setting** |
| **As I think about my performance, here is one thing I will . . .** |

Stop:

Working the math computations in my head since I'm making too many little mistakes because I'm rushing and not able to check work that is not written down.

Save:

I do a great job using a variety of strategies to solve my word problems. I usually choose the best, easiest strategy to solve the word problem.

Start:

I want to start checking to see if my answer makes sense. I need to reread the question statement within the word problem to see if my answer is a logical conclusion.

Activity for Assimilation: WRITE!

Objective: Creatively write from a unique perspective in order to get a point across. WRITE is an acronym for

W= Writer's role

R = Reader

I = Include product

T = Topic or time

E = Emotion

All these components are thought through before writing. The motivational levels of students are very high with this activity.

Suggested Grades: 4–12

Materials: Paper and pencil

Preparation: Post the acronym WRITE so all students can see it; prepare WRITE choice strips so students can document their choices before they write.

Time Needed: 30–60 minutes

Grouping Suggestions: Independent or partners

Instructions:

1. Teach students what the acronym WRITE stands for:

   W= Writer's Role (What role will the writer take: reporter, observer, eyewitness, stomach, brain, desk, *anything* or *anybody* that complements the rest of the acronym?)

   R = Reader (Who will be reading this piece of writing? Teacher, parent, students, dog, rocks, community, skin, president, etc.)

   I = Include Product (What is the best way to present this writing? Friendly letter, diary, poem, article, brochure, newspaper, PowerPoint, etc. See list of products in the Independent Contract Choices activity in this chapter.)

   T = Topic or Time (Who or what is the subject of this writing? Is it a time period or a topic? Civil War, 20th century, Native Americans, Black History Month, etc.)

   E = Emotion (What emotion will the writer take on in this writing? Happy, argumentative, disgusted, joyful, pleasant, alarmed, curious, etc.) Students will brainstorm words to use for how the writer feels.

2. After explicitly teaching the students what WRITE stands for, show them some of the following examples to help them understand their choices for this activity:

   W= Writer's Role—George Washington

   R = Reader—His wife, Mrs. Washington

I = Include Product—Friendly letter

T = Topic or Time—About life during the American Revolution

E = Emotion—Sad, he misses her, things not going well

W= Writer's Role—Junk food

R = Reader—Adolescent brain

I = Include Product—Brochure

T = Topic or Time—About how bad junk food is for your brain

E = Emotion—Told-you-so attitude; Ha-ha-ha-ha! Rub-in-your-face emotion

W= Writer's Role—Harriet Tubman

R = Reader—Herself and generations to come

I = Include Product—Diary

T = Topic or Time—Life in the Underground Railroad

E = Emotion—Mixed: Happy that so many have helped; sad that some didn't make it; scared about being caught or knocking on wrong house

W= Writer's Role—Democrat or Republican candidate

R = Reader—Voters in Texas

I = Include Product—Speech (four paragraphs)

T = Topic or Time—2008 election

E = Emotion—Pleading for vote; persuasive; bragging

3. Once students have seen these examples, give them each a WRITE slip so they can decide how they'll organize their WRITE activity. They staple this slip to the top corner of their product.

   a. They choose all components of WRITE.
   b. They choose WRIE (teacher gives them the topic and time).
   c. They choose I (teacher chooses the rest).
   d. Any other assortment

Differentiation

Tier Up: They choose all the components of WRITE and create challenging choices.

Tier Down: Teacher might need to help these students brainstorm some of their choices of WRITE. Help these students choose an easier product to write with. Help them with the research needed to write the contents.

WRITE Strip

Name:

W = Writer's Role: _____

R = Reader: _____

I = Include Product: _____

T = Topic or Time: _____

E = Emotion: _____

CONCLUSION ■

This chapter has given 45 examples of how to process content and skills. As you have seen, most of these activities are fairly simple and can be done with minimal preparation. None of these examples require much money or time. But their simplicity should not be confused with their value. Too much of the current learning in schools is too shallow. There's plenty of "sit and git" (on a good day) or, more often, "yap and nap" when things aren't working well. These 45 processing activities are sure to dive those brains into deeper thinking across the curriculum.

However, readers like yourself might feel a bit overwhelmed with all of these processing activities. Relax; it's common. You need just a few more pieces of the learning puzzle. We started with the why of deeper learning and the reasons why more processing is very important. Now we've shared the how, which gives you the practical steps for deeper learning. What's left is the when and which of the strategies to use. In the next chapter, we reveal how to pick which strategy and when you should use it.

Favorites of _____

AWARENESS	ANALYSIS TO SYNTHESIS
Activity:	**Activity:**
Lesson to Use With:	**Lesson to Use With:**

APPLICATION	ASSIMILATION
Activity:	**Activity:**
Lesson to Use With:	**Lesson to Use With:**

THE IMPORTANT BOOK

By: Margaret Wise Brown

Student: _____

The important thing about _____ is that

_____

_____

Write five other facts about the above topic:

1. _____

_____

2. _____

_____

3. _____

_____

4. _____

_____

5. _____

_____

But the important thing about _____ is

_____

_____

ELABORATE AND EXTRAPOLATE GRAPHIC ORGANIZER

E & E TIME—Elaborate and Extrapolate Time

Word: Definition:	Elaborate on the Word (Elaboration List) 1. 2.	Extrapolate 1. 2.
Word: Definition:	Elaborate on the Word (Elaboration List) 1. 2.	Extrapolate 1. 2.
Word: Definition:	Elaborate on the Word (Elaboration List) 1. 2.	Extrapolate 1. 2.

ELABORATION IDEAS FOR VOCABULARY WORDS

Give an example of the word

Give a nonexample of the word

Create clues about attributes of the word

Create a question about the word—answer it

Create a simile or metaphor using the word

Give synonyms for the word

Give antonyms for the word

Draw a quick picture of the word

Explain how the word relates to your life

Create an analogy with the word

Give additional information about the word (more facts)

Paraphrase what the word means

Explain how this word relates to the world currently

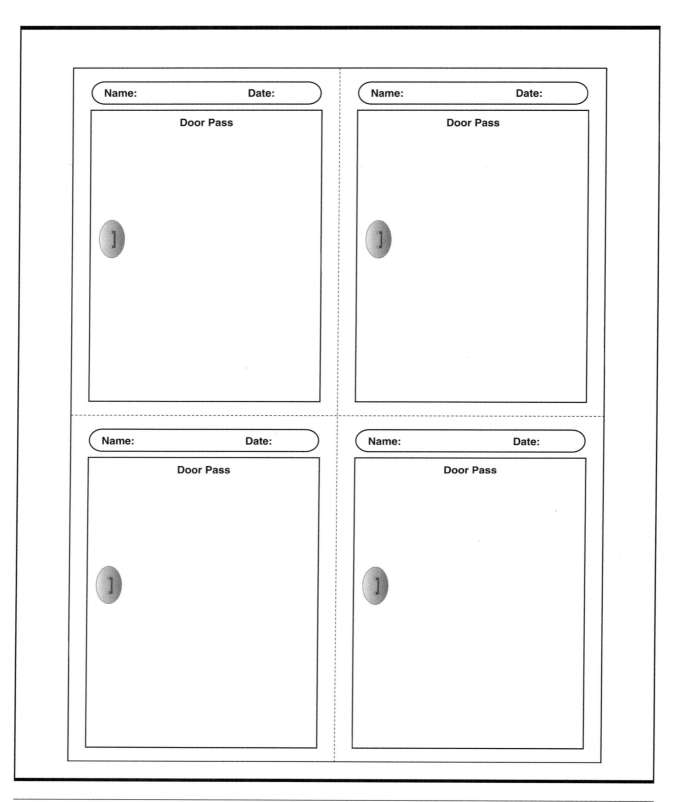

COUNTDOWN PROCESSING

Topic: _____

4 New Words That I Learned	**3** New Facts That I Learned
2 Questions That I Have	**1** Most Valuable Piece of Information

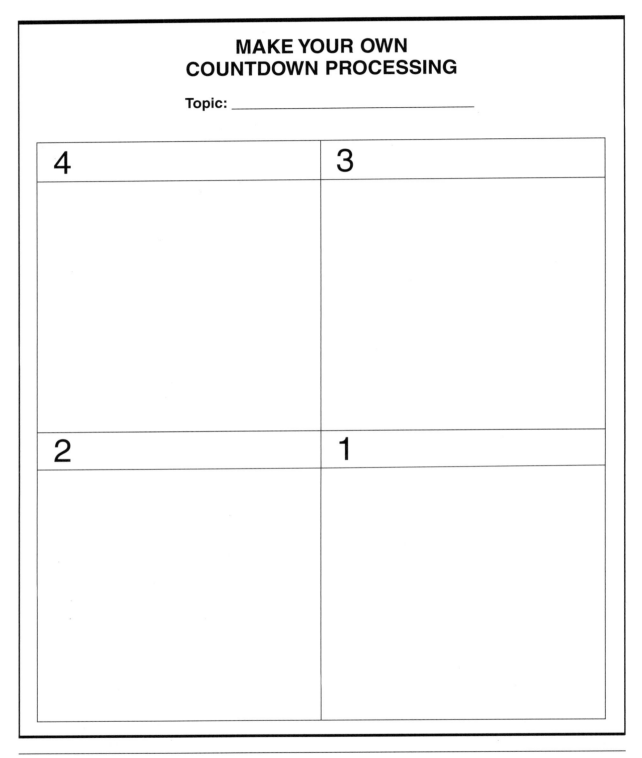

MAKE YOUR OWN
COUNTDOWN PROCESSING

Topic: _____

4	3

2	1

FROM EASY TO CHALLENGING QUESTIONS

Easy Questions	Challenging Questions
1. Answer:	1. Answer:
2. Answer:	2. Answer:
3. Answer:	3. Answer:

QUADS

Author #1: _____	Author #1: _____
Question:	Question:
Answer:	Answer:
Author #2: _____	Author #2: _____
Author #1: _____	Author #1: _____
Question:	Question:
Answer:	Answer:
Author #2: _____	Author #2: _____

Encode It! Spinner

It = _____

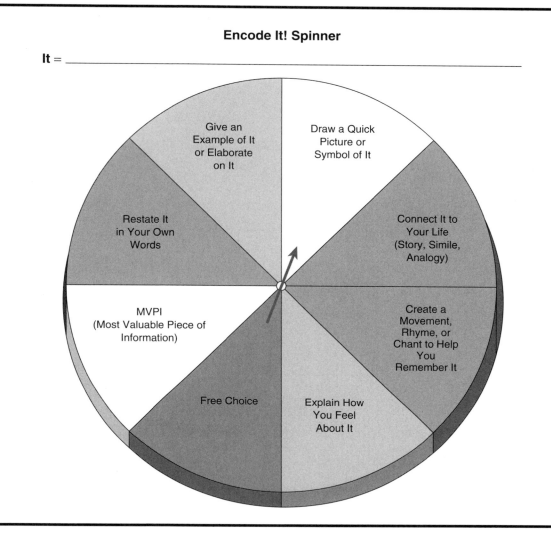

ABS THINK SHEET

Topic: _____

Objects That Are Touched:

#1 _____

#2 _____

#3 _____

#4 _____

#5 _____

Partner's Name: _____

Partner's Objects:

#6 _____

#7 _____

#8 _____

#9 _____

#10 _____

Chosen Object: _____

Association Box

_____ : _____

    (Topic)   (Object or Association)

Questions for the Associations:

1.

2.

3.

4.

5.

6.

7.

8.

9.

*Star the questions that you want to personally research and find the answer to. Each student should place his or her initials next to the question that is to be researched.

WebQuest Topic: _____

The Task	
The Background	
The Process	
The Resources	Print resources from library: Web resources:
Conclusion	
Evaluation	See attached rubric

HEADLINES FOR HERALDING

Paragraph #1

One-Sentence Summary: _____

_____

Headline: _____

Paragraph #2

One-Sentence Summary: _____

_____

Headline: _____

Paragraph #3

One-Sentence Summary: _____

_____

Headline: _____

Paragraph #4

One-Sentence Summary: _____

_____

Headline: _____

Paragraph #5

One-Sentence Summary: _____

_____

Headline: _____

One BIG headline to herald:

SMASH PICS

Situation/Problem/Concept:

Brainstormed Key Topic Words:

Picture Caption:	Picture Caption:	Picture Caption:

Circle a Category to Explore: Description, Process, Priority Placement, Story

Questions Created:

Answers:

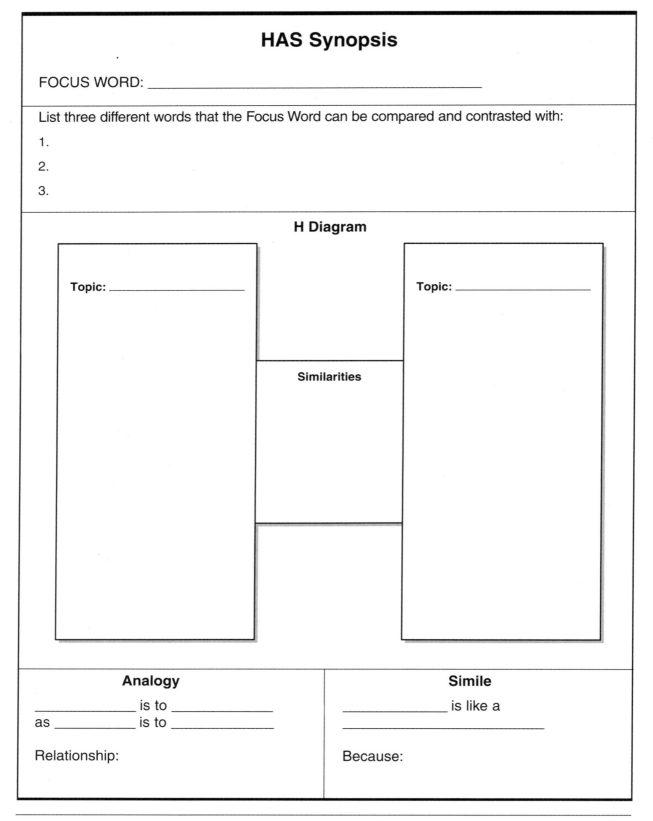

HAS Synopsis

FOCUS WORD: _____

List three different words that the Focus Word can be compared and contrasted with:

1.

2.

3.

H Diagram

Topic: _____

Topic: _____

Similarities

Analogy

_____ is to _____

as _____ is to _____

Relationship:

Simile

_____ is like a

_____

Because:

Web-N-Pass

Problem

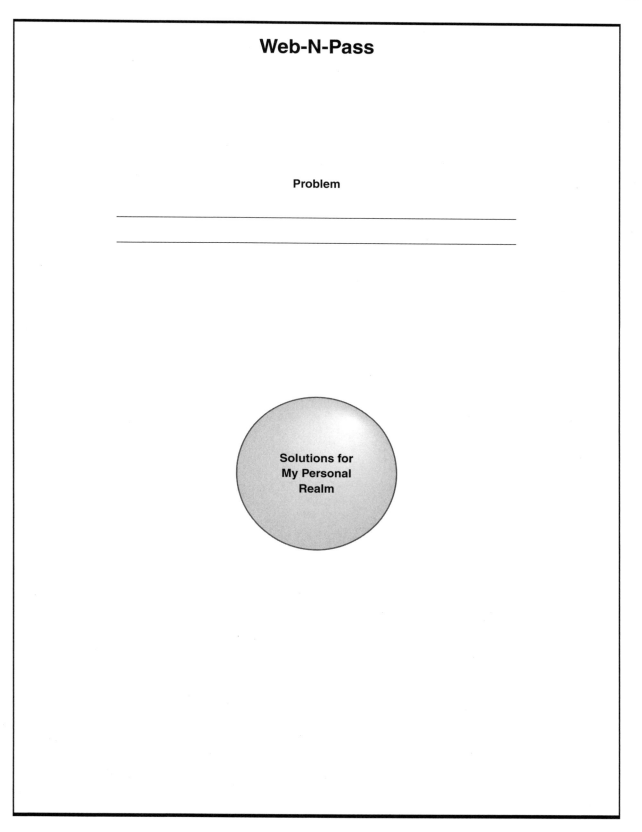

Solutions for
My Personal
Realm

(Continued)

(Continued)

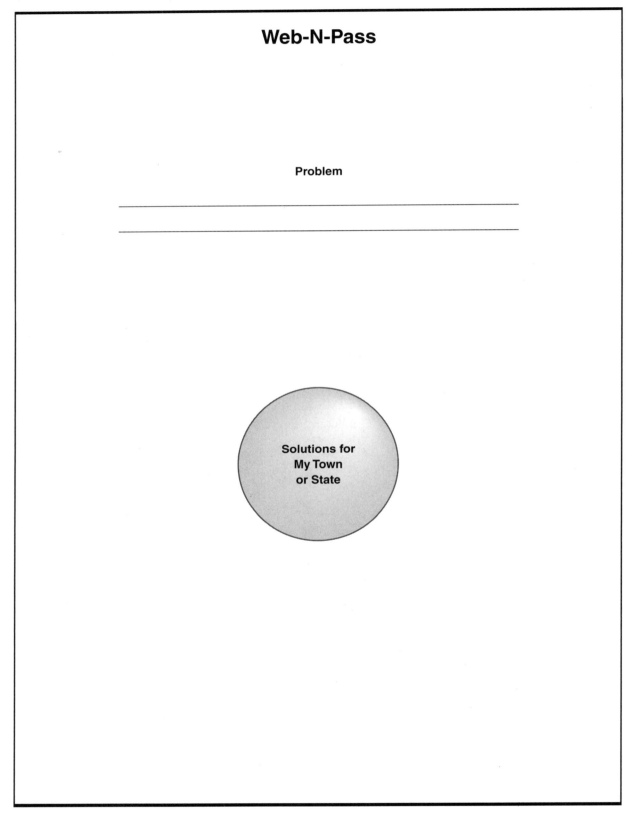

Web-N-Pass

Problem

Solutions for My Town or State

Web-N-Pass

Problem

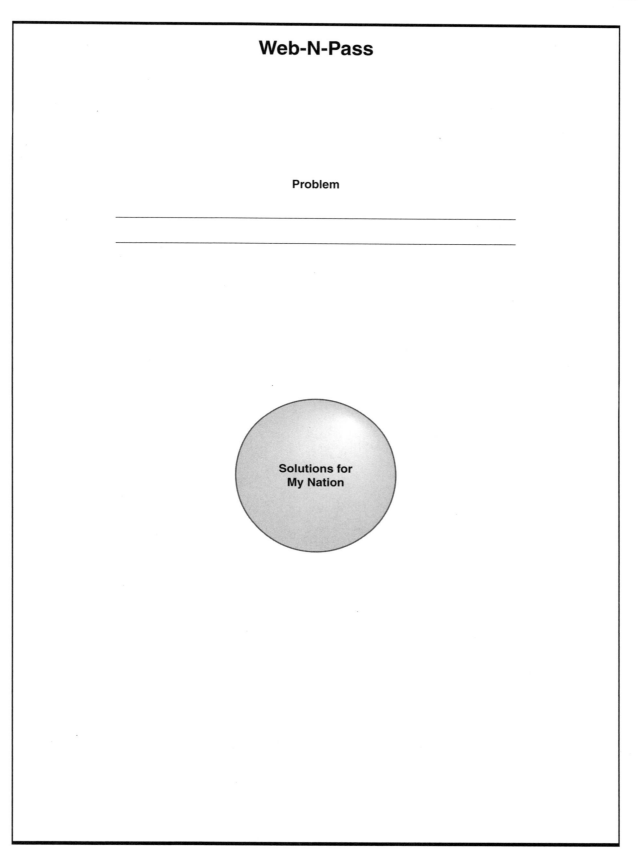

Solutions for
My Nation

(Continued)

(Continued)

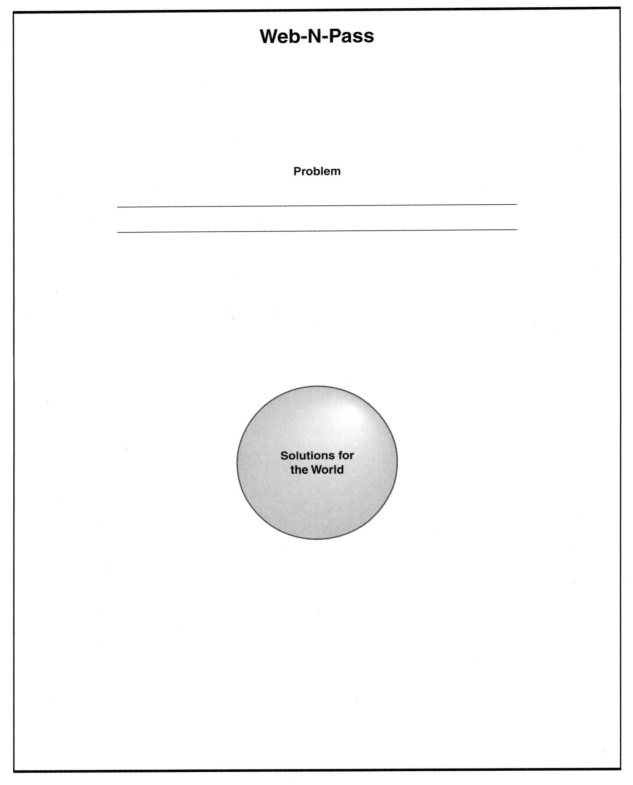

Web-N-Pass

Problem

Solutions for the World

WHO'S BEEN THERE AND DONE THAT?

PARTNER SUPPORT SHEET

Student Name: _____ (1)
Student Name: _____ (2)

☐ Explain the Topic: _____

_____

_____

_____

☐ Google It! _____ and _____
                     (Topic)   (Media—movie or book)

☐ List what you find:

Film/Movie List	Book/Article List
_____	_____
_____	_____
_____	_____
_____	_____
_____	_____
_____	_____
_____	_____
_____	_____
_____	_____

☐ Join up with another partnership and write their names here:
_____ & _____

☐ Compare lists of films/movies and books/articles. Which movies and books would you like to add to your list?

_____   _____

_____   _____

☐ Student #1: List 2 media sources to explore in further detail from your list above.
_____ & _____

☐ Student #2: List 2 media sources to explore in further detail from your list above.
_____ & _____

WHO'S BEEN THERE AND DONE THAT?

INDIVIDUAL STUDENT SUPPORT SHEET

Name: _____

Topic: _____

Media Source #1: _____

List all the ways this media source has explored this topic:

Media Source #2: _____

List all the ways this media source has explored this topic:

CONNECT FOUR

Topic: _____

Personal Life **(family, friends, town,** **school, state)**	**Media** **(books, Internet sites, videos,** **movies, TV shows, journals,** **magazines)**
Nation **(other states, current events)**	**Other Countries/World** **(peace, war, politics, religion,** **culture, traditions)**

776-0821

PRODUCTS

Artistic Products
Prototype
Mobile
Diorama
Pamphlet/Brochure
Puzzle
Timeline With Photos
Charts/Graphs/Diagrams
Game Boards
Photo Album
Poster/Mural/Collage
Pop-Up Book
Cartoon/Comic Strip
Puppets/Papier-Mâché
    Sculptures
Construct a Model
Storyboard
Postcard
Museum Exhibit
Lego Prop
Advertisement
Sandwich Board
Book Jacket
Billboard
Scale Drawing
Window Display

Ways to Present Products
Speech
Debate
Storytelling
Audiotape Creation
Videotape Creation
Share a Survey
Computer Program
    (PowerPoint, KidPix,
    Inspiration, etc.)
Map to Teach From
Transparencies
Physical Props
Role-Play, Simulations, Plays
Pantomiming
Creative Movements
Experiment/Invention/Demonstration
Melodrama
Interview
Campaign
Panel Discussion
Meeting Format

Song-Related Products
Rap/Song/Jingle
Poetry (Many Types)
Choral Read
Playing Instruments
Karaoke
Limerick
Create an Opera
Ode
Singing Telegram
Ballad
Epistle

PRODUCTS

Writing Products

Fact File

Essay

Research Paper

Biography/Autobiography/Memoir

Magazine or Newspaper Article

Creative Writing

Riddles

Crossword Puzzle

Journal/Diary

Summary

Writing a Dialogue

Letter to Editor or Friend

Fable/Fairy Tale/Tall Tale

Syllabus

Web Site Creation

Epitaph

Flipbook

Glossary

Illustrated Story

Last Will and Testament

Maximize Learning

Memo

Myth

Prologue or Epilogue

Vita or Résumé

E-mail

Anecdote

PRODUCT RUBRIC

Product: _____ Name: _____ Date: _____

Criteria	0 No Attempt	1 Some Attempt	2 Proficient	3 Excellent	Comments
Requirements for Product					
1.					
2.					
3.					
4.					
Content Expressed Through Product					
1.					
2.					
3.					
4.					
Mechanics					
1. Spelling					
2. Sentence & Paragraph Formation					
3. Grammar					
4. Neatness, Color, Detail					
Presentation					
1. Organized					
2. Eye Contact					
3. Voice Loud and Clear					
4.					
TOTAL POINTS					

PRODUCT PLANNING PAGE
RESEARCH PROJECT

Name: _____

1. Topic of Interest:	2. What do you already know about this topic?

3. What do you want to know about this topic? Create at least 3 questions that you want to answer with this research.

4. Check all the ways that you will acquire your information in order to answer these questions and perform the research.
   □ Books
   □ Internet
   □ Resource books (dictionary, thesaurus, encyclopedia, atlas, almanac)
   □ Journals, magazines
   □ Interview a person
   □ Other: _____

5. Create an outline (on a separate sheet of paper) to show how you will organize your research findings.

6. Create due dates for your research project (outline, Question 1, Question 2, Question 3, bibliography, first draft, second draft, final copy). Write these on a separate piece of paper and get your teacher's signature.

7. Select a product that you will create in order to share with the class what you learned through your research. See Product List page for choices.

   PRODUCT CHOICE: _____

8. Use the Product Rubric in order to create the assessment piece to this product. You get to fill in Requirements for Product & Content Expressed Through Product. Please make sure the teacher signs this rubric.

9. What supplies will you need for this product? List:

(Continued)

Product Planning Page (Continued)

PRODUCT PLANNING PAGE
RESEARCH PROJECT

NAME: _____

10. How will you share this product and your research with your class? How will you present it? Be creative! Explain below.

11. Student Self-Evaluation for Product. Please complete the following AFTER your project is complete. Remember, "Begin with the end in mind."

Answer the following statements on a separate sheet of paper:

1) While completing this project, I used my time wisely. Explain.

2) I struggled with the following tasks the most while completing this project:

3) I feel _____ about my completed work because . . .

4) The most important thing that I learned from this project is:

5) The part I liked best about this project was:

6) I believe I deserve the grade of _____ because . . .

7) I would also like to tell you the following about this project . . .

PRESENTATION RUBRIC

NAME: _____

Student Presentation Skill Goal for This Presentation:			

Evaluator: Please circle the box for each category that best explains the presenter's presentation. Total the number by the section: Grade Summary. Feel free to write comments about the categories within the specific Category Box.

Category	Needs Improvement 1	Good 2	Excellent 3
Organization	Grabber, conclusion, and/or sequence not strong or evident.	Sequence is not logical, but grabber and conclusion are present.	Sequence is coherent and easy to follow; outstanding grabber and conclusion.
Content	Important information was not mentioned; not much purpose to the presentation; standards were not evident; arguments were nonexistent or very weak; main ideas not clear.	Some important information was emphasized; some content goes along with the standards; arguments were a little weak; some main ideas were clear.	Most important information was present; content goes along with the standards; strong arguments were used to support content; main ideas were clear.
Facial Expression	Few or no facial expressions were used.	Some facial expressions were used to keep audience engaged.	Lots of facial expression to show the emotion of the content; facial expressions helped communicate the content better.
Gestures	Few or no gestures were used.	Some gestures were clearly planned and emphasized the content better.	Arms, stance, hands, head, and body movement were used throughout the presentation to convey importance of content.

(Continued)

Presentation Rubric (Continued)

NAME: _____

Eye Contact	Little eye contact with participants; eyes were mostly on notes or elsewhere.	Some eye contact was used in the appropriate places within the presentation.	Eye contact was strong; student knew material well enough to look at audience the majority of the time.
Vocal Expression	Very little vocal expression was used; monotonous voice.	Some vocal expression was used.	Variations in vocal tone, pitch, and speed; encouraged participant engagement.

Student's Strengths:	Some Suggestions:

Feedback About Goal:

Possible Goals for Next Presentation:

Grade Summary: TOTAL Rubric Number: _____

CHOOSING YOUR TASK: STRUCTURED CHOICES

Task 1

If you're not quite sure about today's learning, then choose one of the following:

Choice A - _____

_____

Choice B - _____

_____

Task 2

If you're starting to understand today's learning and feel comfortable practicing it, then choose one of the following:

Choice A - _____

_____

Choice B - _____

_____

Task 3

If you completely understand today's learning and can teach it to another student, then choose one of the following:

Choice A - _____

_____

Choice B - _____

_____

Source: Adapted from Dodge (2005).

PALM PILOT

Problem: _____

_____

_____

_____

A solution to
this problem is:

_____

_____

_____

_____

_____

_____

Other Solutions:

_____

_____

_____

_____

_____

_____

_____

_____

_____

_____

_____

_____

PALM PILOT

Problem: _____

_____

_____

_____

A solution to
this problem is:

_____

_____

_____

_____

_____

_____

Other Solutions:

_____

_____

_____

_____

_____

_____

_____

_____

_____

_____

_____

_____

PALM PILOT

Topic: _____

I learned the following:

_____
_____
_____
_____
_____
_____

Other students learned:

_____
_____
_____
_____
_____
_____
_____
_____
_____
_____
_____
_____
_____
_____

PALM PILOT

Topic: _____

I learned the following:

_____
_____
_____
_____
_____
_____

Other students learned:

_____
_____
_____
_____
_____
_____
_____
_____
_____
_____
_____
_____
_____
_____

STOP-N-THINK

Name: _____ Date: _____

Circle One: Book, Lecture, Video, Other _____

Stop #1

Stop #2

Stop #3

Stop #4

Synthesis of the Stops:

WALKING IN THE SHOES OF ANOTHER

My Name:	Partner's Name:
Topic:	Topic:
My Point of View or Perspective:	His or Her Point of View or Perspective:
Why I have this perspective: (support with facts)	Why do you have this perspective? (support with facts)
I received this information from: (sources)	Where did you receive your information? (sources)
The following fact or idea might change my perspective:	Is there a fact or idea that could change your perspective? If so, list it here.

After the interview, put yourself in your partner's shoes. Explain what you understand, appreciate, or respect about your partner's perspective. Respond on the back of this page.

After considering both perspectives, what is your perspective now? Write on the back of this page.

PERSONAL REFLECTION ON PROCESSING

Topic or Skill: _____

1. How would you rate background knowledge on this topic or skill before the lessons?
   - ☐ I knew a lot
   - ☐ I knew a little
   - ☐ I didn't know much

2. Check all the ways that you processed this topic or skill during the lessons.
   - ☐ Discussed it with one person
   - ☐ Discussed it with several people
   - ☐ Wrote about it
   - ☐ Webbed it
   - ☐ Played a game about it
   - ☐ Created a product about it

3. Check all of the ways that you deepened your understanding of this topic or skill.
   - ☐ Read a book
   - ☐ Read a journal or magazine article
   - ☐ Searched and read on the Internet
   - ☐ Reviewed notes from teacher
   - ☐ Viewed a video or DVD
   - ☐ Read the newspaper
   - ☐ Discussed with others (peers, family, teacher, expert)
   - ☐ Other: _____

4. How do you know that your work/processing is accurate?
   - ☐ Peer editing
   - ☐ Compared it with something
   - ☐ Teacher checked work
   - ☐ Did additional research
   - ☐ Used the following resource: _____

5. What was the most valuable/interesting/surprising aspect of what you learned? _____
   _____
   _____

6. Now that I have processed what I've learned, I think I need to do one of the following:
   - ☐ Ask more questions about the concept in order to improve my understanding.
   - ☐ Continue at the pace I'm going.
   - ☐ Extend my learning because I understand it and want to learn more.
   - ☐ Other: _____
   _____

7. Next time I process, I would like to: (GOAL)
   _____
   _____
   _____
   _____

TELL: A TOOL FOR GROWTH

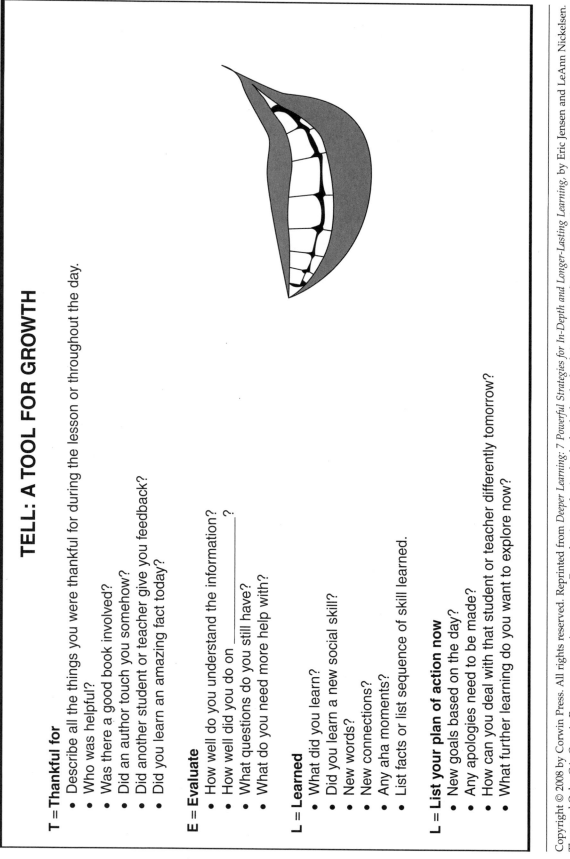

T = Thankful for
- Describe all the things you were thankful for during the lesson or throughout the day.
- Who was helpful?
- Was there a good book involved?
- Did an author touch you somehow?
- Did another student or teacher give you feedback?
- Did you learn an amazing fact today?

E = Evaluate
- How well do you understand the information?
- How well did you do on _____?
- What questions do you still have?
- What do you need more help with?

L = Learned
- What did you learn?
- Did you learn a new social skill?
- New words?
- New connections?
- Any aha moments?
- List facts or list sequence of skill learned.

L = List your plan of action now
- New goals based on the day?
- Any apologies need to be made?
- How can you deal with that student or teacher differently tomorrow?
- What further learning do you want to explore now?

254

Goal-Setting Plan for the Topic of _____

Author of Plan: _____

Dates _____ to _____

Goal:	Benefits of Accomplishing This Goal:

STRATEGY	ACTION PLAN *What I will do this week to make my strategy successful. Write this section in your planner.	RESULT
1.		
2.		
3.		
4.		

The Next Steps After Evaluation:

STOP-SAVE-START

Goal Setting

As I think about my performance, here is one thing I will . . .

Stop:

Save:

Start:

Special thanks to Rachel Billmeyer, trainer and author of *Strategies to Engage the Mind of the Learner* (2003, p. 235), for giving us permission to use this activity.

Part III

Putting It All Together

6

The DELC Lesson Planning Guide

DELC Step 7

Before-Reading Processing

The *Report of the National Reading Panel* (National Reading Panel, 2000) indicated that graphic and semantic organizers and question-generation and question-answering strategies are top ways to improve reading comprehension. Questions allow the brain to automatically focus on what is most important and generate sustained, enriching brain activity. Questioning is the strategy that propels the learner forward. When students have questions they want answered, they're less likely to abandon the text and lesson.

This is your opportunity to use the main headings and the subheadings to generate questions. Use the T-chart on page 291 to create your questions on the left-hand side. Then try to find the answers to these questions and write those answers on the right-hand side directly across from the question that it answers.

For example, under the heading Choices You Need to Make for Processing, the following are questions that could be formed: What kind of choices will I need to make for processing time in my classroom? How will this chapter support me in my decision making?

While reading this chapter, find answers to these questions and write them directly across from the question on the T-chart.

During-Reading Processing

Complete the T-chart with the answers when you come to them. Remember, not all answers to your questions can be found in this book. We hope they will, but the sky is the limit on how you form your questions. Please take the time to research answers to your questions if the book doesn't answer them.

After-Reading Processing

Choices You Need to Make for Processing

1. What type of teacher best describes you and why?

2. What processing activities might you try first based on the above information?

3. How is the Deeper Learning Cycle (DELC) Lesson Plan Template different from the way you learned to write objectives?

4. How is DELC Step 7, Evaluating Student Learning, a three-way system?

5. What components of the lesson plan do you want to learn more about and focus on during your teaching?

6. Why is encoding so important, and which strategies do you want to try out from the ROYGBIV list?

7. How can the 10–24–7 rule of thumb be used to review concepts in your classroom?

This chapter helps put all the pieces in one powerful and practical place: your lesson plan. To do that, you build on what you already have, which is why processing is so critical and how the many strategies support deeper processing. We tie every piece together in this chapter from the DELC model to the Domains for Elaborate and Effective Processing (DEEP). After reading this chapter, you will be able to see how all that you learned from this book comes together so you can implement the strategies toward deeper learning.

■ DELC STEP 7: CHOICES YOU NEED TO MAKE FOR PROCESSING

Good teaching is both science and art. You know the value of planning, so here you construct the lesson plan to facilitate deeper learning for all students. You have to make some choices, which we explore in this book, such as the following:

*   Will the students learn as a whole group, independently, in pairs, or in small groups?
*   How will students process at the beginning of the lesson, during the lesson, or after the lesson? Which domains of processing will I use during my lessons?

- How will they acquire the information I want them to learn? How will they review it?
- How will I preassess and assess my students to check for mastery?
- Will my students choose how they process, or will I challenge them to branch out and use a new processing activity or one that they're less comfortable with?
- How will I differentiate the processing activities for small groups or individuals so that all students are successful?
- How will I activate their prior knowledge on the topic at hand?

Start at Your Comfort Level

First, begin implementing these new ideas based on your comfort level or based on what you already know—your background knowledge and experiences. If people feel they're going to be successful with a strategy, they'll most likely continue to choose that strategy. So feel free to begin where you are—choose the processing strategies that go along with your teaching style.

Educators tend to teach the way they learn best. For example, if you're primarily a kinesthetic learner, you probably plan more kinesthetic strategies in your lesson plan. If you're a more auditory learner, you might talk more to the kids or lecture more. Because there are so many different types of learners in the classroom, you need to make sure that you're using a variety of visual, auditory, and kinesthetic (V-A-K) learning style strategies in every lesson. There should be a message in every lesson to make sure that you're meeting the varied ways the students receive information. Like learning styles, teachers should also make sure that a variety of processing activities are being used in the classroom.

Have you ever categorized the teachers at your school according to their teaching style or personality? We created 10 categories that most teachers fall into (see Figure 6.1). As you read through these categories, you'll probably find yourself in many of them. The key is to find the category of teacher you relate to the *most*. If you had to explain yourself, which phrase would you choose? After choosing a category or two that best explains you, see Start With These in Figure 6.2 for processing activities from Chapter 5 that you'd enjoy implementing first. So which teaching style best fits you? You might want to get an opinion from a teacher on your team.

Now that you know which processing activities you should start with to ease you into implementation of the ideas in this book, focus on how you can branch out with the strategies. People like to try things they feel comfortable with, and to try new strategies that don't fit their personality styles or comfort levels is quite difficult sometimes. There are many processing activities you can try, depending on your purpose for the processing. The Branch Out to These activities (Figure 6.2) are ones that your personality type might not feel too comfortable doing and you would most likely *not* choose to implement.

Once you feel comfortable with the Start With These processing activities (Figure 6.2) and have tried a variety of others based on the purpose of your lesson, go ahead and try one in the Branch Out to These category. Many students are thrilled to have a different type of processing activity than what they usually are involved in.

Where do you place these processing strategies? In your daily lesson plans. You might use anywhere from one to three different processing

Figure 6.1   Types of teachers

1. Keep It Quick & Simple • Lock it in and lock it down • Multitasker • Likes to use timers in the classroom • Never leaves home without a watch • Always on the run and in a hurry • If it works, don't change it • Don't take too much of my time • Likes to delegate • Loves lists and to check them off • Runs into the lounge quickly, grabs a cup of coffee, and leaves promptly • PROCESSING: Would want quick, simple, ready-to-go processing activities	2. Give Me Novelty or It's No Fun • Wants the newest strategies and enjoys putting own twist on them • Reading lots of idea books • Always sharing the latest with other teachers • Always asking to borrow idea books • Always asking where other teachers bought something • Shows excitement in the lounge over new ideas and projects • PROCESSING: Likes to try the unique processing activities that other teachers might stay away from
3. Work That Creative Brain! • Creates many projects for the kids to do • Likes to turn simple ideas into elaborate, creative ideas • Likes to use many supplies to spice up lessons • Takes time to reflect on ideas to make them more creative • Makes the decorations for the lounge • PROCESSING: Would want creative, longer-lasting processing activities that dive into students' creative thinking skills	4. Gotta Have Friends • Always found talking with team and parents • Wants to process with others about new ideas • Volunteers and organizes all social events • Loves volunteers in the classroom • Spends free time on cell phone • Usually plans the teacher parties that occur after school or on holidays • Makes sure that each student has a partner • PROCESSING: Would want cooperative learning processing activities
5. The Lone Ranger Rides Again • Independent—wants to do everything rather than asking for help or delegating • Would rather plan lessons independently than with a team of teachers • Would rather not be involved with team teaching • Doesn't go into the lounge very often; eats alone • Tends to be insecure regarding own abilities • PROCESSING: Would want activities that allow students to reflect internally	6. The Sage Analyzer • Asks the what if questions in faculty meetings • Encourages students to generate their own questions • Challenges others' ideas • Likes to take the time for deep exploration • Wants to learn new perspectives • Usually takes on the facilitator role with the students • Decides to start conversations in the lounge about how education needs to change • PROCESSING: Wants the deep and longer-lasting processing activities

7. Smart, Right on Track & Target	8. The Jokester
<ul><li>Back to the basics</li><li>Very sequential and methodical in teaching</li><li>Might be considered to be a traditional teacher</li><li>Content focused; standards driven</li><li>Reteaching until blue in the face</li><li>Checks off for mastery</li><li>Makes sure to arrive in the lounge on time and leave from the lounge promptly</li><li>PROCESSING: Would want activities that ensure accuracy and can be graded</li></ul>	<ul><li>Fun, fun, fun, and relevant learning</li><li>Kids are moving around and totally involved in the learning</li><li>Silly Putty, oobleck, or goop might be found in this teacher's room</li><li>Brings out the humor in every situation</li><li>Places comics on the lounge bulletin board, forwards funny e-mails, or draws mustaches on people's faces in the lounge</li><li>PROCESSING: Wants processing activities to be fun, active, and energy driven</li></ul>
9. Quiet and Nobody Gets Hurt	10. The Customizer (Miracle Worker)
<ul><li>Doesn't want credit</li><li>Hard worker yet quiet</li><li>Mild mannered</li><li>Wears many hats</li><li>Comes to work and does job without any fanfare</li><li>Very professional</li><li>Not a whiner</li><li>Avoids conflict whenever possible</li><li>PROCESSING: Would select activities that are basic in nature and complete</li></ul>	<ul><li>Wants it to work for every kid, every time</li><li>Understands the importance of processing</li><li>Shares the power and decision making</li><li>Fosters collaboration by promoting cooperative goals</li><li>Clarifies personal values</li><li>Sets an example by aligning actions with shared values</li><li>Applies brain research to all aspects of teaching and learning</li><li>Not concerned with minuscule details; never writes things down; has it all in head</li><li>Knows how to get where he or she is going, but has difficulty articulating the step-by-step process</li><li>PROCESSING: Uses processing for application of higher learning (not rote review or practice); knows the value of matching the processing activity with the student's learning style</li></ul>

activities from Chapter 5 in each daily lesson plan. Use the DELC Lesson Plan Template below (page 292) to help you place these processing strategies in the right places.

DELC Lesson Plan Template: Evaluating the Deeper Learning (DELC #7)

We've explained all the DELC steps so far except Step 7, Evaluating Student Learning. We discuss that step throughout this chapter on the daily lesson plan. Unfortunately, you can't click your fingers and have all students experience deeper learning. Deeper learning must be planned. You've learned about the many strategies in the Domains for Elaborate and Effective Processing (DEEP) that you can use in the daily lesson plan.

Figure 6.2   Which processing activities to start with: Begin where you are

1. Keep It Quick & Simple **Start With These:** Door Pass Countdown Processing Three-Point Summary **Branch Out to These:** WebQuest WebMonster Media Bias Five and Five	2. Give Me Novelty or It's No Fun **Start With These:** Encode It! Spinner Presentations With Pizzazz and Purpose The Six Thinking Hats **Branch Out to These:** Four-Choice Processing Personal Reflection on Processing TELL: A Tool for Growth
3. Work That Creative Brain! **Start With These:** WRITE! Arts Galore! Independent Contract Choices The Six Thinking Hats **Branch Out to These:** Walking in the Shoes of Another Reporter Goes Big Time	4. Gotta Have Friends **Start With These:** Palm Pilot Web-N-Pass Rap & Chant **Branch Out to These:** WRITE! Independent Contract Choices Stop-Save-Start Personal Reflection on Processing
5. The Lone Ranger Rides Again **Start With These:** Goal-Setting Template TELL: A Tool for Growth Independent Contract Choices Personal Reflection on Processing **Branch Out to These:** Stump the Chump Expert Interviews Quality Questioning Strategies	6. The Sage Analyzer **Start With These:** Missing Links Walking in the Shoes of Another Elaborate and Extrapolate (E & E Time) ABS: Association by Scavenging Media Bias **Branch Out to These:** Door Pass HAS Synopsis The Important Book
7. Smart, Right on Track & Target **Start With These:** Countdown Processing Question Top-Down Webbing Quick Writing Response Tools Create Your Own Rubric to Evaluate **Branch Out to These:** WebQuest What's the Biggest Idea? Smash Pics	8. The Jokester **Start With These:** 20 Questions Quick Writing Response Tools Web-N-Pass Rap & Chant **Branch Out to These:** Who's Been There and Done That? Five and Five Processing Notebook TELL: A Tool for Growth

9. Quiet and Nobody Gets Hurt **Start With These:** Super Mooter Who's Been There and Done That? Processing Notebook Door Pass **Branch Out to These:** Presentations With Pizzazz and Purpose What's the Biggest Idea? Missing Links Headlines for Heralding	10. The Customizer (Miracle Worker) **Start With These:** Four-Choice Processing Choosing Your Task: Structured Choices Goal-Setting Template Create Your Own Rubric to Evaluate **Branch Out to These:** Stop-Save-Start Connect Four Virtual Interviews

We explain in this chapter how to place preassessment activities, priming activities, activating prior knowledge activities, acquiring knowledge, and differentiated strategies in the daily lesson plan.

If you teach your students to metacognitively think through skills and thinking processes, then you need to model this skill by writing out or thinking through your lesson plans. We know there isn't much time to write out lesson plans, so we've kept the process simple. Make this a priority for student success. Try it sometime: write out a lesson and see the student success. Then try winging it. Which lesson had less reteaching, less confusion among the learners, more stress on you, more differentiated strategies and assessments that didn't even match the objective, or was there even an objective? To take the time to write out a lesson plan that leads to deeper learning saves time. It's the key to good teaching and good learning. You will have more student success, be less stressed, feel confident that the students are learning what they should be learning, and know that most likely, greater retention of the material will occur. You can also use this lesson plan next year and refine it.

The DELC Lesson Plan Template (page 292) guides you in making A+ lessons for all. This template really doesn't take much time to complete either. It's a matter of taking your brain through the metacognitive tasks to *ensure* that all brain-smart components are thought through and exist for the learner's benefit. We explain the following components that are essential to keep kids enjoying and engaged in the lesson: Objective and Assessment, Preassessment, Student Vesting (Grabber, Activating Prior Knowledge, What's in It for Me [WIIFM]?), Procedures and Processing, Closure, and Teacher Debrief.

Objective

The objective and assessment are crucial to the success of your lesson. We've learned through the years that a well-written objective also has the assessment in it. They go hand in hand, and you can't have one without the other. Writing a good objective and assessment is a part of the DELC. Ensuring that you're writing objectives that are part of your curriculum and standards is of utmost importance. Chapter 2 focused on unit planning, and this section focuses on the details of elaborating on the unit with specific objectives.

The objective should be written out, verbally stated in student-friendly language, posted, and emphasized throughout the lesson. It's very important for visual learners to see what's expected of them during that lesson and what the outcome will be. The brain wants to know what the end will look like and the expectations. You can write out the objective on the dry erase board, or you can state it as an essential question. When learning is stated as a question, the brain wants to try to figure out the answer. We like to transform our objectives into questions, write these questions on the dry erase board, and then tell the students, "You'll be able to answer these three questions before you walk out the door today." You might even see the relief on student faces as if they were thinking, "We're going to be successful today because our teacher just said so."

A good objective has the following components: specific higher-level thinking verb, specific content to learn, how the content will be acquired, and the end product or result of the learning (assessment). The following template assists you in writing your objective and assessment in one statement.

The students will _____
                        (Thinking Verb)

_____
            (Specific Content)
by using _____
            (Acquisition of Content)
to _____
            (Product)

• Thinking Verb = A particular verb to serve as a goal for the students. In this section, you decide how you want the students to think about or process the content. You might want to refer to the DEEP domains in the reproducible on pages 117 through 120, which will give you more verbs to use for lesson planning. You need to decide if you want students to become more aware of your specific content, analyze and synthesize the content, apply the content, or assimilate the content. It'll depend on what your students are ready for and what the curriculum calls for. Here are some thinking verbs to get you started—there are many more:

Compare and contrast

Define and illustrate

List positives, negatives, and ahas

Organize and present

Identify and label features

Understand and analyze

Summarize and critique

Outline and posterize

Discover, list, and show the chronology

Find actions and consequences

Collect and distinguish key facts

Explain, describe, and predict

Collect, connect, and convince

Explain and generalize

Synthesize and simplify

• Specific Content = Specific content to be learned in this lesson. The more specific you are, the easier the assessment becomes. What exactly do you want your students to learn about our democratic government?

• Acquisition of Content = How the students are acquiring the content (lecture, book, video, Internet, cooperative learning groups, other students teaching, experiments, jigsaws, guest speakers, etc.). Be sure to be specific here; for example, which pages from which book will they use or which Web site?

• Product = How the learning is displayed and assessed (paragraph, quiz, graphic organizer, presentation, brochure, etc.). Students should clearly understand what is expected of them and how they'll be evaluated on this product. Refer to Products (pages 240–241) for more ideas. Make sure that this assessment shows that the students understood or learned the objective you just wrote.

Example

The students will *compare and contrast*
        (Thinking Verb)

two branches of government (their choice)
        (Specific Content)

by using *social studies book pages 234–237*
        (Acquisition of Content)

to *complete an H diagram or Venn diagram.*
        (Product)

A well-written, detailed objective guides the whole lesson. It's worth investing the time in creating a quality, specific objective so that the assessment matches your objective expectations. It will also ensure that chosen activities are relevant and support the objective versus just choosing strategies because they're favorite pastimes, fun, or easy to implement. The strategies chosen for the lesson must support the learning of the objective.

Assessment

"Begin with the end in mind" is one of our favorite proverbs. How can you write an objective without stating the assessment piece? A product is what the students produce to show their mastery. It can be anything from a project to a friendly letter or completing a cloze paragraph (fill in the blank). With each product, decide how you're going to grade it. There are many choices for grading:

• Rubrics
• Personal reflection writing
• Tests and quizzes

- Portfolios
- Complete and correct answer checks
- Feedback (formal and informal) (individual, teacher, or peer)

DELC Step 7, Evaluating Student Learning, is a three-way system in which teachers need to evaluate the student mastery of the objective, students need to evaluate themselves and their peers as learners, and teachers need to evaluate their daily lessons to make sure the lessons are geared for deeper learning and the students experience deeper learning at their "just right" level.

In Chapter 5, we gave you examples of rubrics, personal reflection writing, and checklists as assessments. We'd like to elaborate on feedback. With simple learning, very little feedback is needed. It's a simple question of whether something is accurate or not. But virtually no abstract, complex cognitive skills can be learned without feedback. Only through the elaboration process can one ever get some level of mastery. In a way, elaboration is essential for mastery, and the feedback corrects the elaboration. Our brain is not designed to get things right the first time except for exposure to either very simple learning or trauma. Instead it makes what we call rough drafts of the learning. These are sketchy, highly inaccurate representations of the material that are held either in working memory or in the hippocampus (temporary holding area) until there are reasons to either forget the learning or elaborate on it.

Almost universally, data suggest that feedback greatly facilitates improved posttest performance and increased near-transfer performance as well (McCarthy, 1995). Quality classroom activities have feedback built into them. This means students are able to see, hear, and experience the result of what they're doing while they're doing it. It allows them to take in the impartial feedback and adjust. Feedback is most effective when it draws attention to the task itself, not the person doing it (Kluger & DeNisi, 1996). This tells us that teachers should be careful about the type of activity and the type of feedback that students get.

Not only do teachers need to give students feedback on how they're learning the content, they also need to give them feedback regarding the processing. You want students to be ready to process on their own while learning when they're in college (and hopefully before then). For that lifelong skill to be acquired, students need to metacognitively evaluate themselves as processors. We created a series of questions for students to ask themselves and then to ultimately set a processing goal for growth. We recommend that you give this processing evaluation when you feel that students need to improve the quality of their processing. See Personal Reflection on Processing (page 252).

The rubrics, personal reflections in a learning journal, tests and quizzes, portfolios, and other forms of assessment need to be ongoing and part of the three-way system. That means that teachers are assessing students, students are assessing themselves and their peers, and teachers are assessing their daily lessons to make sure that deeper learning is experienced by all students in a successful, differentiated way.

Preassessment

How can you know how to meet your students' needs if preassessment doesn't occur? Preassessment and differentiation go hand in hand, since you can't differentiate well if you don't know where your learners are in their understanding of a concept or their level of readiness for a skill. Once you preassess your students, you're ready to brainstorm the many ways you can differentiate for them. Scatter these differentiated strategies that are best for your students throughout the lesson plan. For example, during Chunk 1, you need a small group of about five students who need more support because their pretest results showed that their background knowledge is not sufficient for Chunk 2.

DELC Step 2 in Chapter 2 is focused on preassessing your students. We explored the many reasons for preassessing your students and the many choices of how to preassess them. You can create a unit preassessment or short, quick preassessments to see where they are on a particular concept. You can observe them and write notes about where they are, or you can check for understanding during the lesson. There are many choices for you to make on how you preassess your students.

The preassessment is valuable because it leads the teacher in making better decisions about the learning. It allows the teacher to know where to start and what to skip based on student background knowledge; what to focus more on based on interests, background knowledge, and questions from students; how to differentiate during the lesson for certain students with special needs; how to group students; which strategies to use throughout the unit or lesson; and how to pull in more support.

Some of the preassessments you can choose from that were mentioned in Chapter 2 are (a) unit preassessment, (b) T or F Quiz, (c) K-W-L, (d) Venn diagram or H diagram, (e) alphabet brainstorm, (f) webbing, and (g) paragraph writing. Once you've chosen a preassessment (write it in the DELC Lesson Plan Template in the section labeled Preassessment) and studied the results, you're ready for the next steps: What are you going to do about those preassessment results? How will you differentiate for your students based on those results?

Differentiated Strategies to Use in the Lesson Plan

Below are several lists of choices available to you to help you decide how you might need to differentiate this lesson for certain individuals or small groups or help unique learners with their struggles. Write your choices down on the DELC Lesson Plan Template in the sections where they belong. Differentiation can happen anywhere in the lesson plan: before, during, or after. These ideas might be quick decisions and actions that you're taking for the students based on your observations of them. This quick, spontaneous, observation-driven type of differentiation happens the most in the classroom, but we can't emphasize enough how important it is to *plan* your differentiated strategies too. Both types of differentiation are important and needed on a daily basis: spontaneous strategies and preplanned strategies.

Strategies to Help Get Students Interested in the Lesson

- Activate and build background knowledge on the topic before you teach the lesson. The more students know ahead of time, the better their understanding of the content in the lesson.
- Find out the child's interests and connect the content to the child's life.
- Read a story or create a personal story that helps the child connect the topic to his or her life.
- Create a concrete representation for the abstract information that is involved in the content.
- Provide feedback throughout the lesson often (comments about discussions and questions). Show positive facial expressions and body language when students show an interest.
- Seat students closer to where you teach; distance affects interest.
- Make sure to answer the WIIFM? questions at the very beginning of the lesson.
- Find a way to blend curriculum with each child's interest (refer back to the Interest Inventory (page 64).
- Show students objects or pictures related to the content.

Strategies to Help Students Monitor Their Time Throughout the Day

- Give a cue to begin the work (thumbs up, quick dance, tap on desk, symbol held up).
- Give work in smaller, more doable chunks. Check for understanding immediately. This approach of teaching a small chunk and checking for mastery on this small chunk is like scaffolding. One skill relies on the other; one layer on top of another.
- Provide feedback on small chunks of work when completed.
- Sequence work so that the easiest problems are first and the most relevant problems are first.
- Explain the assignment in a different way (draw it, write it out step-by-step) so that understanding is enhanced.
- Provide time suggestions for each task and possibly use a timer. Write the schedule out and ask the student to place a check mark when assignments have been completed.
- Give a checklist for each step of the task (for example, long division problems).
- Assign the student who manages time well to assist this student.
- Set a goal to improve students' time management skills and ask students to self-assess when they intentionally use their time well.
- Reduce the amount of work (for example, cut math practice sheets horizontally—child completes one line at a time until mastery occurs; cut math practice sheets vertically to increase the level of difficulty).
- Use a Teach Timer (www.crystalsprings.com) to place over the overhead projector so all students can see how much time is remaining to complete an assignment.

Strategies to Help Students Pay Attention to the Spoken Word

- Give explanations in small, distinct steps, using student-friendly words, and one direction at a time (give direction, then they do it).
- Provide directions in written form too.
- Have students repeat the directions in small groups after directions have been given.
- Provide other sources of information: buddies, tape recordings, and so on.
- Look directly at the student. Make sure the student has eye contact with you while explaining.
- Utilize noise-suppressing headsets or earplugs to block out extraneous noise.
- Background music that is predictable and soothing can block out extraneous noise for some students (Bach, Beethoven, etc.).

Strategies to Help Students Focus Better on Text

- Select a text with less on a page or photocopy the text so smaller chunks are only on one page.
- Give a purpose for the reading and then ask students to highlight important information that will answer the purpose questions.
- Use text-posting symbols to tag the thinking while reading (see Chapter 1, During-Reading Processing activity). Teach students to mark their texts in a way that helps them interact with the text (for example, "?—I don't understand this"; "U—Unknown word—look up").

- Ask students to find headings and subheadings and change them into questions that might be answered in that section. Questions keep the brain more focused than do statements.
- Require students' desks to be cleared of extraneous material.
- Ask students to use twist-up crayons or pencils to highlight text according to what is being read. For example, if the answer to a purpose question is being read, go back and underline this with green twist-up crayon or pencil (only if text is photocopied from a book versus being in the book).
- Find a text written at a lower level—at the child's instructional level.
- Provide graphic organizers to help students organize the information while reading.
- Tape the student's text or go to www.gutenberg.org for books on CD or tape.
- Allow another student or parent to read the text aloud to disabled students.
- Allow for extra time for reading.
- Put the main ideas of subheadings on index cards so that students can keep them in their minds while reading the section of the subheading (they can look at the card every now and then to remind themselves of the big idea).
- Provide speculation and prediction questions; students then have an investment in the subject and read to discover how they did.
- Build the student's background knowledge on the topic by explaining concepts in a concrete way (pictures, models, similes, etc.).
- Enlarge the text on a photocopy machine.
- Use transparent, colored tape to highlight titles, subtitles, and special words and concepts.

Strategies to Help Students Work Better Independently

- Assign a task at an appropriate level (lower the level if needed or make it more complex—depends on pretest results).
- Give an approximate amount of time it might take to complete the assignment. Give students a check-off sheet of what needs to be accomplished during this time.
- Write and say the precise directions.
- Give students packs of Post-It notes to write questions down; they should only give these questions to the teacher after thinking them through or asking another student.
- Praise often when you see a student concentrating.
- Create check-in goals for the assignment (for example, "Come get me when you complete Part One").
- Provide a variety of types of work in the assignment instead of all writing tasks (chart making, drawing, mind mapping, simulations, etc.).

Strategies to Help Students Follow Directions Better

- Use fewer words and words that students understand.
- Provide examples of how to do the assignment.
- Have students repeat or explain out loud.
- Monitor closely as student begins or have a peer check.
- Present both auditory and visual directions.
- Provide graphic organizers to help child organize content (for example, turn lined paper horizontally as a way to facilitate number placement during arithmetic operations; use graph paper for division problems).
- Permit overactive students to stand when they're not working at their desks. Provide ample time for movement—helps them focus better.

Strategies to Help Students Stay More Organized

- Require a three-ring notebook that has folders for each subject or class.
- Have a system for checking the planner and notebook (parent, teacher, or peer).
- Provide assignment sheets in the notebook so students can keep track of their homework.
- Write assignments on the board for students to write on their assignment sheets.
- Provide special privileges for bringing supplies to class.

(Continued)

(Continued)

- Return corrected work promptly and have a certain day when all graded papers are returned home.
- Use tape to mark off a student's personal space around his or her desk—very helpful for students with attention-deficit/hyperactivity disorder (ADHD) or sensory issues.

Strategies to Build Background Knowledge

- Preteach difficult and/or new concepts for those students who need to be eased into learning new concepts (preteach vocabulary before reading any content-area texts).
- Bring virtual museums via the Internet into your classroom.
- Prime the brain by preteaching a few concepts or facts about the unit a couple of weeks ahead of time.
- Show how the concepts of the unit connect to one another—show how the words or concepts relate by creating a web.
- Activate students' prior knowledge before each lesson so that you know where the gaps are and can teach these missing concepts.
- Provide sustained silent reading time—reading across a variety of genres improves background knowledge.
- Make sure homework pertains to the missing pieces of students' background knowledge. Give special assignments before the lesson or unit.

Student Vesting—Grabber

This is the beginning of the lesson—the place where you draw the student into your lesson. This quick activity should make kids want to stay with you the entire lesson. It also provides a sense of direction and purpose for the learning. Remember that the grabber relates to the learning objective, stimulates interest and desire to learn, is brief, and occurs in every lesson at the beginning. The following things should be done during this quick 2 to 5 minutes of the lesson.

Grab the students' attention right away by doing one or more of the following short activities that are totally related to your lesson: read a short book or excerpt from a book, do a short simulation, distribute pictures or books about the topic and have the students take 2 minutes to flip through the book that you've given them, short video clip, startling question or quote, teacher miniskit, picture or story from the teacher, show an object or perform an experiment, share startling research, ask students how a group of artifacts are related to one another, play a song, or have everybody do a certain move.

Student Vesting—Activate Prior Knowledge

Once we learned how important it is to activate students' background knowledge before they acquire the information, we made it a personal goal to ensure that every lesson had an activating prior knowledge activity. It is such an important step to deeper learning that we dedicated Step 4 of the DELC to this concept (see Chapter 3). We listed several priming and preexposure strategies, questioning and discussion strategies, and ideas for how to elicit stronger connections.

You could choose from any of the following ways described in Chapter 3 to activate your students' background knowledge:

- Treasure Chest
- Book Tag
- Peripherals in the Classroom
- Your Ticket In
- Super Sleuth
- IIQEE Strategy
- Spin & Activate
- MAKE Meaning
- Digging Detectives

Student Vesting—WIIFM?

Not only do students need to know what is expected of them to learn from the lesson, they also need to know why they need to learn it or how they will personally benefit from learning the concept or skill. All brains want to know, What's in It for Me?

Educators owe it to their students to explain the WIIFM? for each lesson. We admit that there were tough times when we had to explain how dividing fractions related to the real world, but we still did our best to state the WIIFM? for our students.

The following three questions should be answered in this section and told to the students (or better yet, ask them these questions):

1. Why do you think you need to learn today's concept or skill? How will it help you now and when you're an adult? (purpose)

2. How does today's concept or skill relate to what you already know or have recently learned? (similar to activating prior knowledge) (personal connection)

3. How does today's concept or skill connect with a bigger picture or concept? (bigger connection)

You will see greater student vestment when these three questions are answered after sharing what is expected from them. Put yourself in their shoes. Notice that we included the WIIFM? at the beginning of the book in Chapter 2. We want you to be personally vested in the reading of this book so that implementation occurs. Master teachers are consciously competent— they can explain why they use the strategies they use and why those strategies are so successful. You'll see greater motivation in your students when you share the WIIFM?

Acquiring and Processing Information

The Acquiring and Processing Information section is the largest part of the DELC Lesson Plan. Remember that students can acquire information in several different ways: experiments, research, Internet, small groups, student-led presentations, virtual museums, videos or DVDs, books, journals, magazines, television, or Socratic Seminars. Not all ways of acquiring information in the classroom are as sequential as explicit, direct instruction.

The Acquiring and Processing Information section of the template can look different based on the way students acquire information. For example, if you are teaching (or students are reading) a small chunk of information and then processing it, you might want to write in this section Chunk #1, Processing Activity #1; Chunk #2, Processing Activity #2; and so on. If it's student research you might write the steps in the research model you are using.

This template encompasses many steps for learning that are crucial for mastery. For example, teachers and facilitators need to make sure that the following strategies are used during this section: explicitly defining, giving examples, explaining, connecting, modeling, asking questions for clarification, guiding practice and more practice based on diagnosis, providing independent practice and more feedback, and giving ample time for processing several times within the lesson. Through these strategies, students acquire the information in a direct manner needed to master the objective.

The acquisition could be from teachers, guest speakers, students, cooperative learning groups, videos or DVDs, Internet information, or text from books or journals. These are choices you'll have to make, but keep in mind that when students teach one another, they remember the content better than if you presented all of it. There's a time to do both, but keep in mind the saying, "More of them and less of you." Those who teach the information remember it.

The Acquiring and Processing Information section is important for several reasons:

- The hippocampus remembers information best when small chunks of information are presented and it is given enough processing time to digest the information. The procedure should involve a set of related chunks.
- The brain needs to understand the information that supports the objective.
- The brain needs to see the concepts and labels that are connected to one another.
- The more the information is elaborated through processing, the deeper will be the learning of the objective.

This is the point where teachers must make sure their information is delivered in a coherent sequence that is scaffolded for the ease of connections with each student. Scaffolding is the support you give students to help them understand each chunk of information. Teachers differentiate in many ways during the procedure. You might have the following decisions to make during the procedure:

- I need to give Susan, Mike, and David more time practicing this.
- Terri and Kyle need more challenging work—they mastered this quickly.
- I need yesterday's manipulatives to help Destiny and Jessica understand today's concept.
- I better draw a quick picture of this word—they seem confused.
- I'm going to finish this lesson, but afterward, I need to spend more time with those five students at the learning lab table (reteach table for small groups).
- I need to provide more practice or guided practice time with these students.

Practice and Guided Practice

Allow students to practice and do the objective at hand at the level where they'll be successful. Students should only practice what they understand; otherwise, it could be the first step to failure.

Many times guided practice is left out because of time constraints. That's a big mistake. Without it, you're likely to have more reteaching to do the next day, which takes up more time anyway. This is one of the most important times during a lesson. Teachers guide students through several examples—that means, you're practicing the skill *with* them. Then you have the students practice it on their own. This is where you need to check immediately to see if they're practicing it correctly. During this stage of the lesson, you might want to use a processing activity from the Awareness Activities in Chapter 5, such as the gel boards, to check for understanding on what was just taught. If a student has shown that the content or skill is not mastered, you need to reteach the concept or skill in a different way for that student. This is when you should look at the student's learning profile to know his or her strengths and use those strengths to help the student master the concept or skill.

For example, we had a student, Josh, struggle with multiplication tables. We know how important it is to have multiplication tables become part of automatic memory. So we used Josh's strengths to help him memorize the multiplication facts. Josh was an artist, so we asked him to take his 20 most challenging multiplication facts and embed them into a picture with creativity and color, one fact per page. We asked him to do only one a day but to review all of them every day as he added each new one. He enjoyed the process and was very successful in learning all 20.

Why Encoding Is Critical During the Procedure

For some, encoding has gone out of fashion. But there's no way to get around it: repetition is good for learning and an absolute must for any learner to gain mastery. It's the repetition that tells our brain "It's worth saving—keep this." In fact, recent research suggests it takes repetition for our brain to remember most things (Colicos & Goda, 2001). Whether you're thinking of learning to play the piano, learning to do multiplication in your head, or writing an essay, practice is essential. The human brain works on the principle that more use and more repetition is better for enhancing the memory. Remember, this is more repetition done by the learner, not the teacher.

Now that you know the students have learned the information correctly, have applied it correctly, and have mastered the information, it's time to make sure you cement this learning deeply into the brain by using the best memory strategies out there. The following strategies are powerful memory strategies that allow the newly learned information to make it into long-term memory: (a) tying an emotion to the content, (b) repeating the content four to six times over an extended period of time elaborately and by rote, (c) attaching a rhythm, movement, or music to the learning, (d) showing the big picture or context of the new learning, and (e) using a variety of semantic systems such as chunking, associations, mnemonics, flash cards, and mock tests. This last step ensures that the new learning sticks for application the next time it's brought up.

Some researchers and scientists thought that storage (or memory) was like an audio or video recording. Others thought it was like a camera. We now know those analogies are both wrong and misleading. Researchers have discovered that synapses, the gap between brain cells where learning chemicals are passed on to communicate a message, are not static: they constantly adapt in response to activity (Atwood & Karunannithi, 2002). This means that those so-called pictures in the head aren't fixed entities; they're an ever-changing set of memories of what was learned. Memories aren't fixed (Nadel & Land, 2000), and they can be reactivated, disrupted, and altered during reactivation. But the more we use an idea correctly and the more we activate a skill or practice that same skill, the smoother and faster we will become at it, and the greater the chance will be for its retrieval. Just as important, once a task is repeated, our brain becomes more economical. It uses less glucose to do the same task, so it becomes more energy efficient (Haier et al., 1992).

There are seven powerful ways to encode information for the long term:

1. Repetition

2. Oxygen from activity

3. Yearning for meaning

4. Glucose

5. Bias the attention

6. Intensity of emotions

7. Variety of word tools

Each of these strategies has a significant amount of research behind its effectiveness. You might like to read *The Great Memory Book* (Markowitz, 1999) for more details on these. Some ways you can strengthen memory are on page 277.

You may have noticed that these seven memory strategies are familiar. But avoid letting "the familiar" become the ignored. These are powerful, they're well researched, and they're all easy to use. In fact, to make it easier to use, there is a simple acrostic formula. Remember how we all learned the colors of the rainbow? The letters were R-O-Y-G-B-I-V, for the mythical person named Roy G. Biv. The seven strategies listed above are all in the same order, the first letter matching up with the same letters as our friendly memory reminder, Roy G. Biv. That should help you recall them. In fact, before you go on to the next section, see if you can make the links to encode these in your mind.

Teaching Smarter, Not Faster

We just can't learn at an unlimited speed. All fast learning is either simple learning or priming; it's never complex. The potential speed of learning in our brain is regulated by many internal factors. Even the child prodigies throughout history were notorious for their endless hours of practice to develop mastery. What was as impressive as the skill level of

Repetition

Elaborate rehearsal of concepts, repetition of content through games, flash cards, previews, revisions, preexposure, priming, daily reviews.

Oxygen From Activity and Movement

Act out vocabulary words, simulation of concepts learned, plays, cooperative learning, experiments, hands-on activities with manipulatives, drama, charades, using your arms, hands, and postures to dramatize concepts.

Yearning for Meaning

Make the learning personally relevant to friends, neighborhood, family, emotions, and goals. Choices can help, WIIFM? questions posed and answered with each lesson, connecting content with each student with similes, metaphors, analogies, a good frame given at the beginning of a lesson.

Glucose

Healthy snacks provided on a regular basis. Avoid sugar spikes and sugar lows. Glucose runs the brain, especially memory. Adolescents need glucose replenished every 90 minutes. Please see *Foods That Maximize Learning* on pages 278–279 for the best foods to feed students throughout the day.

Bias the Attention

Use novelty, urgency, and priming. Add state changes and a grabber at the beginning of the lesson to hook them into the learning.

Intensity of Emotions

Learning content through controversy, gross objects or demonstrations, surprises, urgent deadlines, relays, debates, competition, rhythm, and music.

Variety of Word Tools

Graphic organizers, mnemonics, acronyms, rhyming raps, and mind maps. Use flow charts, pictures, stick figures, and acrostics.

artists like Beethoven was the early interest, or passion, that drove the work ethic necessary for such early excellence. At school, educators are not usually concerned with developing the next icon in musical history, but at least they want good learning.

The first of four regulators is working memory. Each student has unique limitations on his or her working memory, which has to juggle the new input while making sense out of it. The old notion was that students could hold seven plus or minus two chunks or bits of information. New research suggests students are lucky to hold just four chunks (Cowan, 2001). Other evidence supports significant limitations on what students can hold in their minds (Callicott et al., 1999; Klingberg, 2000; Lachter & Hayhoe,

Foods That Maximize Learning

"As you eat, so shall you think." Every day people make decisions about what to eat, and these foods have a direct impact on their quality of life. In fact, parents make most of these decisions for their children. Parents have to feverishly create a breakfast, pack snacks, and make lunches before their children rush out the door to school. To save time, maximize children's learning potential for the day, and give them a variety of foods daily, we created the Healthy Food List (Figure 6.3). These are the best foods to give students throughout the day. We hope it helps you as much as it has helped us.

The brain needs certain amounts and specific types of nutrients daily in order to function properly. Too much or too little (deficiency) of any nutrient can negatively affect the brain and thus learning. If parents feed their children the same foods every day, the children might be missing some important nutrients. These nutrients impact which chemicals and how many chemicals are being manufactured in the brain. These chemicals control daily behaviors or states of mind. They can make people more alert and focused, more relaxed, more hyperactive, more attentive, or more sleepy and unfocused.

Breakfast. Feed your children a great brain breakfast because teachers can do amazing things with well-fed brains. This kind of breakfast includes a high-fiber, low-fat, low-sugar carbohydrate along with some protein. Avoid sugary pastries and sugary cereals, because within 30 to 60 minutes, blood sugar drops, leaving children with less energy, more easily frustrated, and with a feeling of hunger. Breakfast enhances cognitive performance, particularly on tasks requiring processing of a complex visual display. Boys and girls showed enhanced spatial memory, and girls showed improved short-term memory after consuming oatmeal, which provides a slower and more sustained energy source and consequently may result in cognitive enhancement compared with low-fiber, high-glycemic, ready-to-eat cereal (Mahoney, Taylor, Kanarek, & Samuel, 2005). It's the most important meal of the day, and the brain can never regain the positive effects that breakfast leaves on it even if a good lunch is eaten. See the Healthy Food List (Figure 6.3) for specific breakfast foods.

Fruit + 100% fruit juice (with calcium) or milk + protein + whole grain = great breakfast.

Snacks. Neurons or brain cells need two main fuels to function: oxygen and glucose. Neurons can't store these fuels, so they use them up quickly. A constant supply of these fuels is required for the brain to function. This means that in addition to eating three balanced meals a day, humans have to eat several small snacks to keep up the supply of glucose for the brain. Children's brains need a refill of glucose about every 60 to 90 minutes. Cognitive performance suffers when blood glucose concentrations are low (Gold, 1995). We believe that children in Grades K–12 need a powerful brain snack either before or after lunch (depending on the time they eat lunch). The following foods are great choices for snacks: nuts of any kind as long as the children have no allergies; bananas, apples, raisins, grapes, oranges, strawberries, blueberries, and other fresh fruits; carrots, celery, red peppers, broccoli, cucumbers, and other vegetables (even pack a dip if kids must have it); whole wheat crackers and real cheese; low-sugar yogurt with no food coloring; whole wheat pretzels; trail mixes; turkey wrapped on pretzel rods; pita bread and hummus as dip; popcorn; and soy or vegetable chips.

Protein + whole grain = great snack.

Lunch. If you pack a lunch, make sure it has a protein, a complex carbohydrate, and very little sugar. Studies by Connors (1989) at the National Institute of Mental Health indicate that when sugar is eaten with a protein, the learner benefits by being more alert. Sugar is utilized differently by the brain when eaten with a protein. After consuming a protein, the brain can be more alert and focused, and it can have longer-lasting stamina. Remember to pack a variety each day rather than the same thing every day. See the Healthy Food List (Figure 6.3) to know the best foods to pack for lunch.

Protein + whole grain + fruit + vegetable + milk = great lunch.

Water. Send a clean water bottle to school with your children every day. Children need the opportunity to drink water throughout the day. Students who are well hydrated are more friendly, well reasoned, attentive, and coherent. A mere 2% drop in body water can trigger fuzzy short-term memory and decrease focusing ability. The brain dehydrates *every 20 minutes. If access to water is restricted, the stress response can kick in. Within 5 minutes of consuming water, there's a marked decline in the stress hormone cortisol. Drinking water reduces the body's physiological response to adverse situations. We believe that water should be readily available for all students to consume when they're thirsty throughout the day.*

Foods have a direct impact on our states of mind, and children need to be in the most alert, focused, positive learning states of mind. By feeding them a variety of healthy foods daily and making sure they're getting the amount of foods listed in the New Food Pyramid (www.mypyramid.gov), you'll maximize your child's learning.

Figure 6.3   Healthy food list

Breakfast Food Ideas	
Fruit + 100% fruit juice (with calcium) or milk + protein + whole grain	
Complex Carbohydrates	**Proteins**
Any fruit (berries, citrus, applesauce, etc.)	Peanut butter (natural)
Oatmeal or cream of wheat	Almond butter
Whole wheat toast, whole grain tortilla	Low-sugar yogurt (less than 15 grams)
Whole grain waffles and pancakes	Eggs (2)
Cereals (6+ grams of protein, 5+ grams of fiber, low fat, and less than 6 grams of sugar):	Turkey bacon
*Shredded Wheat *Cracklin Oat Bran	Low-fat, no-nitrate bacon
*Grape Nuts *Kashi Go Lean	Low-fat milk
*Wheat and Raisin Chex *Optimum	Cottage cheese
*Low-Sugar Granola *Mighty Bites	Chicken sausages (less than 5 grams fat)
*Cheerios (whole grain) *Peanut Butter Bumpers	
*Heritage Brand Cereals	

Lunch Food Ideas		
Protein + whole grain + fruit + vegetable + milk		
Main Dish	**Fruit/Veggie Side—2**	**Fun Snack**
*Sandwiches with whole wheat wraps and breads with low-fat, low-nitrate meats (turkey, chicken, roast beef)	*Fruit ideas: Apple slices, tangerines, dried fruits (raisins, apricots, etc.), berries, applesauce (no sugar added), fruit smoothie (low sugar), banana, grapes, low-sugar fruit cups	*Low-sugar yogurt
*Peanut butter and banana sandwich		*Trail mix
*Tuna on whole wheat crackers		*String cheese
*Healthy, low-salt soups		*Low-fat nachos with salsa
*Hummus and whole wheat crackers or pitas with 2 slices of meat	*Vegetable ideas: cucumber slices with low-fat ranch, dressing carrots, celery with low-fat cream cheese or peanut butter, carrots, sliced red peppers, cherry tomatoes, etc.	*Graham crackers
*Hard-boiled eggs (2)		*Whole grain Fig Newtons
*Grilled chicken fajitas		*Whole grain fruit and nut bar
*Quesadillas (beans, cheese)		*Veggie chips or natural chips
		*Dry granola cereal
		*100% fruit leathers or bars
		*Pretzels
		*Low-fat popcorn
		*Bananas with chocolate peanut butter
		*Nuts and chocolate chips

*Natural means no preservatives or food colorings, little if any enriching or processing, no trans fats, and no artificial sweeteners.

Created by LeAnn Nickelsen. Editor & Contributor: Karen Siclare—MS Nutritionist.

1995). This mental juggling is known as the cognitive load theory. Research suggests that educators should be cautious about the rate of delivery of instructional information (Carlson, Chandler, & Sweller, 2003).

Some types of learning require more time to stabilize than others. In fact, the amount of time needed to connect, stabilize, and strengthen a memory ranges from several minutes (not seconds) to several hours (Dudai, 2004). Just to record and remember where things are, our hippocampal neurons require 5 or 6 minutes of experience to form stable spatial representations (Frank, Stanley, & Brown, 2004). Typically it takes between 15 and 60 minutes for the synapse to form and become stable for most explicit learning. The majority of presynaptic boutons are stable in efficacy and position over a period of 90 minutes (Hopf, Waters, Mehta, & Smith, 2002). We don't mean to overwhelm you with a truckload of science, but you need a realistic sense of learning and memory. It's not magic, and it's not automatic. Learning consumes resources and time and can leave you exhausted or exhilarated.

Most of our complex implicit learning, primarily skill learning, requires up to 6 hours of settling time to solidify (Shadmehr & Holcomb, 1997). Synapses stay intact partly through synaptic adhesion, a process that binds the connecting axon and dendrite together. It's not known at this time whether different learning in different areas of the brain would constitute "competing" stimuli. But it is clear that too much information constitutes an overload similar to rewriting a CD with new information after it's filled with old information.

The third area of the brain that limits new explicit learning is the hippocampus. It seems that nature is more conservative with existing information and prevents content overload from new learning. If the learning isn't emotional or relevant and if it's not heard from again, the hippocampus might not even encode it. But if the new learning is repeated over time, even for just an hour, it's got a better chance of being remembered (Colicos & Goda, 2001). New information may travel the route of working memory to the hippocampus and await further information regarding saliency. The hippocampus becomes the temporary holding and organizing area for all new explicit learning. It looks similar to two small C-shaped structures, each buried in the temporal lobes, one on each side of the brain.

Routinely, the hippocampus holds information for hours, sometimes for weeks, before letting it go or distributing it to the rest of the cortex for long-term memory (Wiltgen, Brown, Talton, & Silva, 2004). But the hippocampus doesn't have unlimited storage space. It learns fast, but it's more like a flash memory stick than a huge hard drive. In fact, its role in the brain is more like a surge protector than a library. Overload the hippocampus and very little new content gets learned. In addition, we need time during sleep to encode our learning, suggesting that too much during the daytime may set the learning system off balance.

From Consolidation to Recall

New learning needs time or breaks in order to consolidate. Memory that lasts days and weeks becomes consolidated over time. "A memory that has become consolidated is robust and resistant to interference. In its initial stages, even memory that would otherwise persist is highly susceptible to disruption if, for example, an attempt is made to learn some other similar material" (Squire & Kandel, 2000). Researchers found that learning a second list of syllables immediately after learning a first list interfered with later recall of the first list. Without disruption, newly formed memories gradually become more stable. The new learning needs time to consolidate. It's consolidated through sleep, processing, and downtime.

To make sure that students are encoding the content or skills learned in your lesson, you need to make sure to use the ROY G. BIV strategies listed above during every lesson toward the end of the procedure, after checking for understanding and much practice. The following ideas will enhance your students' encoding time.

Example of Choices for Review

- *Have a plan for reviewing content.* To really solidify neural networks, there should be a review or closure of what was learned after the lesson (10 minutes afterward, approximately), and then homework could reinforce this new information that night. Another review the next day will help get this neural network established (24 hours later). Don't stop here though. There should be a review that week (7 days later) and that month and for months to come. This reviewing method, the 10–24–7 rule of thumb, is a powerful way to solidify neural networks.

- *Make review fun by putting the content into review games.* There is a Jeopardy game that teachers can create for their students that makes this easy (www.classroomjeopardy.com). Two books that will help you with these games are *Memorizing Strategies and Other Brain-Based Activities* (Nickelsen, 2004) and *Games That Teach* (Sugar, 1998).

- *Friday Creative Review Day.* Assign two students to review every lesson from every day for that week. This means they're aware that they'll have to take special notes throughout the week to emphasize the key points in each lesson. On Fridays, those two students decide *how* to present this review to their class. It could be a new telecast, puppet show, game show, fun quiz, or overhead projector lesson, or whatever way they want. Creativity is the key, and 10 key review points are the requirements.

- *Sleeping aids in the consolidation process.* Both slow-wave and REM sleep are crucial for organizing the memory parts and developing long-term explicit memories (Stickgold, 2006). Help your students learn the importance of a good night's sleep.

- *Make sure not to teach a ton of new information back-to-back.* The hippocampus will feel overwhelmed and most likely not keep any of it. Space out new material—mix it in with information that is being reviewed.

- *Incorporate a review of yesterday's content by doing the following:*
  a. Ask students to activate their prior knowledge and pull up what they learned yesterday. Use the strategies from Chapter 3, DELC Step 4, to activate prior knowledge.
  b. Before students can sit down in their chairs, they have to write three things on a Post-it note that they learned the day before from the lesson. They can get assistance from other students too.

    c. As a way to review and activate prior knowledge, students should list on the chalkboard or overhead projector everything they learned—ask another student to do the writing (whole group or small group).

    d. Ask students to compare and contrast yesterday's information with today's lesson at the end of the lesson using an H diagram.

    e. Use the DEEP activity called Elaborate and Extrapolate in Chapter 5 with yesterday's vocabulary words that were learned.

Questions to Ask Yourself About
How Your Students Review in the Classroom

- Do I plan for review of content in the school day?
- Do I make sure that this review time is not just rote review for simple learning but also elaborate review so that complex learning can occur?
- Do my students enjoy review time? Is it motivating?
- Is the homework I send home a type of review of content learned that day and previous days?
- Am I readily available during practice time, and do I give the students immediate feedback?
- Do my students look overwhelmed and stressed in my classroom? If so, how do I respond to this?
- Do my students have opportunities for brain breaks?
- Do I teach too much too fast?
- How do I encourage my students to get enough sleep?

As mentioned earlier, the Acquiring and Processing Information section is the largest part of the DELC Lesson Plan (page 292). It's important to ensure that the content or skill being taught is coherent, meaningful, memorable, and full of feedback. This is the section where teachers are on full duty as diagnosticians. They are facilitators of the learning but have to make sure to release the responsibility in a doable manner for all students.

Closure

This is your last opportunity to assist the students' meaning making and content consolidation. The closure occurs at the end of the lesson. It's a time when *all* students explain what they learned, restate the essential question with the answer, show the teacher what they learned, or summarize what they learned. The closure usually only takes 2 or 3 minutes, keeps students actively involved, and is a type of assessment for the teacher. It's a critical part of the lesson; don't let your students leave class without doing a closure activity—it's bad science and poor teaching.

There are several opportunities during the procedure for processing to occur. The closure is a very big picture processing activity that puts all the chunks from the lesson together into one summary statement. You could look at it this way: chunk-chew-chunk-chew-chunk-Big Chew.

Several processing activities in Chapter 5, specifically the Awareness Activities, are excellent choices for closures. The one you choose will depend on how much time you have and whether or not it's the sole assessment piece for the lesson and for the purpose of the whole lesson.

One of our favorite closures is the Door Pass (page 222), because it's quick and versatile. Remind students to write their names at the bottom of the Door Pass and to answer the question well. Tell them that you plan to read every Door Pass. They must complete one before walking out of the classroom. Here are some examples of how we've used Door Passes as closures to our lessons:

"Write a sentence that includes all three of these words and explains how they relate to one another: sedimentary, igneous, and metamorphic."

"Write a summary of what you learned today."

"Draw a quick web of how the concepts that you learned about gas, liquid, and matter relate to one another."

"Draw a timeline showing me the sequence of these four events in this historical period of the American Revolution."

"Write down a question that you still have about today's lesson."

"Write the most valuable piece of information that you learned in today's lesson."

"Write about what you want to do next, now that you've learned this information."

The keys to powerful closures are the following: (a) always do them no matter what, (b) all students must participate in the closure, and (c) the teacher needs to make sure the students understand the importance of closures, that is, the teacher needs to give feedback, discuss further, and/or grade the closures so students take them seriously. This valuable strategy ensures active engagement of your students.

Teacher Debrief

As you use any group of strategies, you need to find out if they work. Without knowing what works and what doesn't, you're teaching in the dark. Evaluating deeper learning strategies and activities requires gathering and interpreting meaningful data. This brings us to the third element of DELC #7, Evaluating the Learning Deeply. Not only are we evaluating student learning and students evaluating their own work, teachers need to evaluate *their* work as well. This critical component can't be overlooked. To help a student toward mastery, teachers must evaluate how their lessons and strategies are working toward student success. This constant evaluation allows you to choose the best strategies, differentiate, create lasting positive relationships, and build the needed background knowledge.

You did it! You taught the lesson using the DELC Lesson Plan Template, and now you need to evaluate how it went. The key to growth in any area of life is to reflect on the experience and do something about it. Here are some questions that you should ask yourself about your lesson. The answers to these questions assist you in writing your next lesson plan, changing this lesson for a better one next year, and deciding what steps you need to take tomorrow based on your evaluation of today's lesson.

Questions to Ask Yourself About the Day's Lesson

- What worked well in this lesson? Who was successful because of a strategy I used? What do I appreciate about this lesson?
- What didn't work well in this lesson? Who wasn't successful in this lesson? Why? What can I do to help this student master it tomorrow?
- What could I have done differently during the lesson to ensure a better understanding by all students?
- Did I choose the appropriate processing activities for the chunks of information that were taught in this lesson?

Write on the back of the DELC Lesson Plan Template what you would change next year with this lesson plan so you don't make the same mistakes twice. Write on tomorrow's lesson plan what you need to include or do differently based on your evaluation of this lesson.

■ CONCLUSION

You've learned about each of the powerful components of a lesson plan that result in deeper learning. It has been wrapped in a neat package called the DELC Lesson Plan Template. We have provided three examples of completed DELC Lesson Plans. Two of the completed lesson plans use the Six Thinking Hats Process but in different ways. The Pueblo Indians lesson reflects processing everything that was learned within that unit at the end of the unit (Figure 6.4). The second example, The Lord of the Flies (Figure 6.5), reflects using the Six Thinking Hats Process during the reading of the book. Third, the Rocks lesson (Figure 6.6) shows you specific chunks that were taught and the specific processing that occurred after each chunk. Closures are listed for this 3- to 5-day lesson plan. We provided three examples so that you can see how versatile this lesson plan template is. It was designed for the daily lesson plan but many times incorporates several days of learning because of the strongly connected chunks of information. We encourage you to share your deeper learning lesson plans with your colleagues. Remember to debrief each lesson so that you can improve each year, follow through with particular students' needs, and celebrate the successes that have occurred.

Figure 6.4   DELC Lesson Plan example: Pueblo Indians

Unit: Native Americans	Length: 2–3 days	Topic/Subject: Pueblo Indians/Social Studies

Objective & Assessment:

Students will be able to brainstorm the facts, tell their feelings about, explain the pros and cons, create new ideas and summarize their learning about the Pueblo Indians (from notes) in order to complete the Six Thinking Hats Process

Preassessment:

Unit Preassessment

Materials:

- Variety of hats to wear
- Thinking Hat manipulatives—a set for each child
- Lifesavers nutritional label
- Lifesavers
- 6 hats for teacher to wear—the Set of Six Thinking Hats
- Posters of Six Thinking Hats
- Six Thinking Hats Rhyme

Grabber:

Teacher puts on several different kinds of hats and asks students to explain the reasons for wearing each type of hat. What is the person's role who is wearing this hat? Hats signify what a person is thinking. While wearing the following hats, say the "Words to Use" aloud so students can fill in the blank. Hat ideas: policeman, fireman, chef, soldier, bride, ballplayer, bicyclist, construction worker, magician, fancy hat, etc.

Words to use:

A person wearing a _____ hat would be thinking about _____.

WIIFM? What's in It for Me?

What kind of hat does a person wear when he or she thinks? A thinking hat! Today we're going to discuss how we wear different colors of hats for different kinds of thinking. By learning these six types of thinking, you'll benefit greatly.

How?

- Your ability to focus and elaborate on one type of thinking will be enhanced.
- You will have fun trying on all of the different hats.
- You'll be able to solve problems better by going through this process.
- We'll all have some great discussions.
- Everybody learns a lot! Everybody can participate and succeed!

Activating Prior Knowledge:

The Grabber and WIIFM? sections activate students' prior knowledge.

Differentiation Ideas:

- Students will be heterogeneously grouped (according to readiness levels) assisting one another. They will only focus on one hat after learning them all.

Acquiring & Processing Information:

1. Now we are going to look specifically at each kind of thinking hat through a classroom activity:

   - Distribute class sets of thinking hats.
   - Kids can play with these while you share the Six Thinking Hats Rhyme.

2. Quick Quiz for Memory: (show memory cards) (Encoding the meaning of the colors of hats)

   - White = boring facts
   - Red = heart for emotion
   - Yellow = bright like sun
   - Gray = gloomy sky for problems or negative
   - Green = new grass, tree
   - Blue = sky is over everything! Summary over everything!

3. Do With Each Hat:

   - Teacher puts on the _____ hat. (one of the six hats)
   - Instruct students to take out the _____ hat from the baggie. Either put the _____ hat in front of you or hold it up where we can see it. Place other hats in the corner of the desk to get them out of the way.
   - Point to the bulletin board or poster with all of the Six Thinking Hats. Students point out the hat they will be using and explain their role with that hat on.
   - Everyone eats a Lifesaver. Let's think about a Lifesaver in six different ways using these six colorful hats.

(Continued)

Figure 6.4 (Continued)

4. Using your White Hat thinking: What are some facts about Lifesavers? Record answers on white colored butcher paper (round, hole in middle, hard, sticky, tastes like _____, small, made at a company, see wrapper nutritional facts, made with sugar, letters on them, etc.).

5. Using your Red Hat thinking: How do you feel about eating this Lifesaver and why? Record answers on red colored butcher paper (excited, happy, curious, yucky, depressed, energized, surprised, etc.).

6. Using your Yellow Hat thinking: What are the good points (or benefits) about eating this Lifesaver? Record answers on yellow butcher paper (tastes great!, fun, positive emotion, company who makes it benefits financially, makes a person creative, opportunity to share, breath smells good, etc.).

7. Using your Gray Hat thinking: What are some possible problems (negative) about eating this Lifesaver (choking, sugar, tooth decay, don't like flavor, litter with the package, want more, etc.)?

8. Using your Green Hat thinking: What if there were no hole in the middle of the Lifesaver (could choke more easily, could NOT call it a Lifesaver, would look like all of the other hard candy, could not put a string (necklace) or a pencil (just to be silly) through it, could not look through it, would get more candy for the money, could not try to put tongue through it, etc.)?

9. Drum Roll—Time for Blue Hat thinking: (choice for teachers and/or students)
   (a) Let's create a summary statement about Lifesavers. Use this cloze if you need to:
      Lifesavers are (describe what they are) . . .
      I feel _____ about Lifesavers because _____.
      Lifesavers benefit people by . . . , but they could cause the following problems . . .
                        OR
   (b) What was your most fascinating discovery about Lifesavers during this lesson?
                        OR
   (c) What did you learn about Lifesavers from today's lesson?

10. Everybody place hats in a baggie and stand up when finished. Three students collect the baggies. After baggies are collected, please sit down.

11. Practice the specific unit with Six Thinking Hats (transfer of learning): We will go through the Six Thinking Hats process about the unit at hand.

12. Unit: Pueblos. Students are sitting in groups of 4. I will assign each table a certain hat to focus on for 3 minutes. They are to brainstorm as fast as they can answers to their questions on the colored paper provided. They will need to assign a RECORDER (someone who writes quickly) for each group.
   • What are some facts about the Pueblos?
   • Would you like to live in a Pueblo village? Why or why not?
   • What are the positive things about living in a Pueblo village?
   • What are some problems you might encounter living in a Pueblo village?
   • What if a person from a Pueblo village came to live with you? How do you think that person would respond to your life?
   • What has been the most fascinating piece of information that you learned about the Pueblos?

13. Each group tells the answers aloud. Remind students to listen well, because they will be having to answer all of the same questions independently at home for homework with their social studies book.
      Students will take home the "Writing Out the Six Thinking Hats" (topic = Pueblo Indians) and think six different ways about the topic.
   Requirements:
   1. Complete sentences
   2. At least 1 sentence per hat written out
   3. Complete the page as best you can

Closure:

Six Thinking Hats is a thinking process in which we do different kinds of thinking with each hat so that we can come to some conclusions. The white hat represents _____, the red hat represents _____, the yellow hat represents _____, the gray hat represents _____, the green hat represents _____, and the blue hat represents _____.

Stand up and tell your group what your favorite hat is and why you like that style of thinking.

Teacher Debrief: What worked, what did not work, what would I do differently next time, what can I appreciate about what I did well, any extenuating circumstances this time?

Everything went very well. I don't have any changes. Students' brainstormed ideas went above and beyond.

Figure 6.5   DELC Lesson Plan example: *Lord of the Flies*

Unit: Lord of the Flies	Length: 2–3 Day Lesson Plan	Topic/Subject: Literature

Objective & Assessment:

The students will analyze and synthesize a chapter from the *Lord of the Flies* book by using notes, the book, and other students' perspectives to complete the Six Thinking Hats Process by writing reflections about each hat in paragraph format.

Preassessment:

Middle of book comprehension quiz to assess their level of understanding the details of the book so far (matching, short answer, vocabulary)

Materials:

- Lord of the Flies book
- Lord of the Flies notes
- Paper
- Six Thinking Hats poster (explains what type of thinking each hat is)
- Six Thinking Hats Question Stems

Grabber:

Show the Six Thinking Hats poster and introduce each hat's type of thinking. Explain the rules of the hats and the purpose and benefits of using the hats.

WIIFM? What's in It for Me?

- Helps the brain focus on one type of thinking at a time.
- Allows students to elaborate on the book in a unique manner that enhances comprehension.
- Gives a deeper understanding of the text.

Activating Prior Knowledge:

Teacher asks one question per hat about chapters that have been read so far. Example: Gray Hat—What are some problems that have occurred under Ralph's leadership so far?

Differentiation Ideas:

- Provide a list of question stems that could be asked within each hat.
- Review how to write a powerful paragraph (topic sentence, supporting sentences, conclusion sentence).

Acquiring & Processing Information:

1. Students number off from 1–6 and remember these "home base groups."

2. All of the ones get together in like groups, twos, threes, and so on.

3. Assign one of the hat colors to each of the groups. For example, group one will become the expert on the white hat, group two will become the expert on the red hat, group three will become the expert on the yellow hat, group four will become the expert on the gray hat, group five will become the expert on the green hat, and group six will become the expert on the blue hat.

4. In these expert groups, the students will create a question that is focused on the hat's perspective for the particular chapter just read by all of the students.

   - White hat—Question about the facts from the chapter read
   - Red hat—Question about one of the character's feelings about that chapter
   - Yellow hat—Question about the positive events about that chapter
   - Gray hat—Question about the problem(s) about that chapter
   - Green hat—Question involving a twist; usually a "what if" question about the chapter
   - Blue hat—Question about the big picture of the chapter

5. Each group will brainstorm answers for their agreed-upon question within their expert groups. One student writes all of the brainstormed ideas while the other students are verbally sharing with one another their ideas.

6. Within the expert groups, each student analyzes the answers and composes a synthesis of it all by writing a summary in paragraph format that answers the question. Students may help one another write this summary paragraph.

(Continued)

Figure 6.5 (Continued)

7. Students go to their "home base groups" and share their paragraphs with each member.
8. Students must listen well since they will need to respond to each hat's question in their own words after this "home base group" discussion.
9. Assessment of the paragraph writing: Each hat's question will need to be answered in paragraph format (one paragraph per hat); question must be completely answered and well supported.
Closure: Two days of closures 1. Create two questions (any hat) that you have about the next chapters to be read. 2. What hat did you enjoy answering the best and why? Write these responses on Door Passes.
Teacher Debrief: What worked, what did not work, what would I do differently next time, what can I appreciate about what I did well, any extenuating circumstances this time? 1. Next time, students need to have role cards in their small groups. I would have a Scribe who writes students' brainstormed answers; Facilitator who makes sure they are following the directions; Encourager to ensure participation by all students; Relay Student to show me the question before they brainstorm the answers. 2. I would encourage students to use the list of question stems for each thinking hat to help them form an appropriate question. The students struggled to create a question for the particular chapter within a specified thinking hat.

Figure 6.6   DELC Lesson Plan example: Rocks

Unit: Earth Science	*Length: 3–5 days*	*Topic/Subject: Types of Rocks*
Objective & Assessment: The students will compare and contrast three types of rock (sedimentary, igneous, and metamorphic) by using teacher-delivered information in order to complete and process with a matrix about these rocks. (Matrix includes properties, definitions, location, examples, benefits) **Preassessment:** Cloze activity with the rock vocabulary words provided.		**Materials:** • Rock kit with a variety of rocks labeled • Preassessment about rocks • Spinners for each small group of 3–4 students • Materials ready for the closures (depending on choice) • Glossary of all of the terms learned
Grabber: Show students an example of each type of rock: sedimentary, igneous, and metamorphic. Ask if they know the names of these rocks.		**WIIFM? What's in It for Me?** • To understand what Earth is made up of and how the rocks change over time • To know how these rocks are being used as resources for our benefit today
Activating Prior Knowledge: Activating Prior Knowledge Spinner Topic: Rocks		**Differentiation Ideas:** Provide a list of the rocks and their names so students can remember the ones that were shown. Find pictures to go along with these definitions.

Acquiring & Processing Information:

Chunk #1: Information about the rock cycle (teacher gets information from science book, Internet, files, etc.). Rock Cycle Diagram; Rock Cycle Song

Process: Each student draws the rock cycle and explains it to another student.

Chunk #2: Information about sedimentary rocks, several examples shown, discussion about how these rocks benefit our nation.

Process: Students complete the Matrix section about sedimentary rock.

Chunk #3: Information about igneous rocks, several examples shown, discussion about how these rocks benefit our nation.

Process: Students complete the Matrix section about igneous rock.

Chunk #4: Information about metamorphic rocks, several examples shown, discussion about how these rocks benefit out nation.

Process: Students complete the Matrix section about metamorphic rock.

Chunk #5 & Process: Students use the Matrix to complete a 3-way Venn diagram comparing and contrasting these three types of rocks.

Closure ideas after each day's lesson:

- Quick Draw the rock cycle and explain one part of the cycle in a paragraph on Door Pass.
- Draw and label three different examples of the type of rock taught today on gel board.
- List two or three products that we use on a regular basis that are created from the rocks that were taught today.
- Do an Important Book entry about the type of rock learned today.
- Using the Palm Pilot, have students share what they think was the most important information from today's learning.

Teacher Debrief: What worked, what did not work, what would I do differently next time, what can I appreciate about what I did well, any extenuating circumstances this time?

1. Next time, I would focus more on showing the students REAL items that we purchase from stores that were manufactured using the rocks that were studied. They were very interested in their uses in this day and age.

2. Next time, I will have more reviews over the vocabulary terms that were introduced within each chunk. I will have games that review these words and a unit word wall with all of the words posted for all to see every day.

After-Reading Personal Reflection Questions for Teachers

Answer the following questions to yourself and then make some goals for yourself:

1. Do I take the time to make sure that I'm teaching the concept in the best sequence so that understanding is more clear and coherent?

2. Do I show how the details of my lesson are integrally related to the big picture, theme, or unit of study?

(Continued)

(Continued)

3. Do I take the time to explain how today's lesson relates to other lessons (previous day or in other subjects)? Do I answer the WIIFM? questions well?

4. Do I have the willpower to say no to activities that seem fun and partly relevant to the objective?

5. Do I prime my students' brains by introducing the topic days, hours, or minutes before teaching it?

6. Do I give my students discussion, writing, or thinking time after a chunk of information is taught so it becomes more meaningful to the learner?

7. Do I share the objectives with my students? Can they hear and see it so they know exactly what's expected of them?

8. Do I have an idea of how I'm going to organize my processing activities?

9. Which teacher am I *most* like, and which processing activities from Chapter 5 will I try first? Which ones will be a stretch for me?

T-Chart

Questions	Answers

DELC LESSON PLAN TEMPLATE

Unit: _____   Topic/Subject: _____   Length: _____

Objective & Assessment:

The students will _____

by using _____

to _____

Preassessment:

Materials:

Grabber:

WIIFM? What's in It for Me?

Activating Prior Knowledge:

Differentiation Ideas:

Acquiring & Processing Information:

Closure:

Teacher Debrief: What worked, what did not work, what would I do differently next time, what can I appreciate about what I did well, any extenuating circumstances this time? Write your response on the back of this sheet.

7

Processing
Must-Have Tips

Before-Reading, During-Reading, and After-Reading Processing

See SQ4R (page 300). This reading comprehension strategy is a powerful one. It has been around for years and is usually called SQ3R. The fourth R really deepens the reflection after the reading. It could be a way to tier up for kids who are ready for a fourth R. Some students would do better with only three Rs.

Before reading, use SQ4R and complete Boxes 1, 2, and 3. Then start reading this chapter. Afterward, complete Boxes 5, 6, and 7. You'll see a deeper understanding of the text by using this process.

After-Reading Questions

Please complete the Reflection Questions on the SQ4R graphic organizer and answer the additional questions below:

Organizing and Managing Content Processing

1. What are the benefits of creating processing baskets that have all the processing supplies in them?

2. Which processing inside secrets were most meaningful to you?

(Continued)

(Continued)

> 3. List the Four P's and give reasons why they're so important to processing.
>
> 4. Which of the Four P's comes easily for you during your lessons? Which of the Four P's would you like to develop more?

■ ORGANIZING AND MANAGING CONTENT PROCESSING

Now that you know what processing is, how it works in the brain, the benefits of it, and the Domains for Elaborate and Effective Processing (DEEP) and have 45 specific processing activities and a lesson plan template, it's time to think about how to organize and manage processing in your classroom. To facilitate your students' powerful processing opportunities in each lesson, you should do the following:

- Create a way to organize the processing activities so that you can use them in an instant in your classroom. Processing baskets can be created very easily and maintained by the students. When these are in place, all students can process in a variety of ways in an instant.
- Keep the Four P's in mind while creating your own processing activities. After using the DEEP activities in this book, you'll probably be excited about creating your own. The Four P's are our secret recipe for creating the 45 DEEP activities in this book. We're sharing it so that students have even more choices for growth.

Processing Baskets

Figure 7.1   Principal Jean Hartman of Waynesville Elementary School in Ohio organizes materials using plastic baskets.

You need the materials and processing activities organized and ready to go so processing can be in place quickly. One way to organize them is to have plastic baskets in the middle of about 4 to 6 tables that are grouped together. In these baskets you can place the processing supplies that you use most at the fingertips of your students. If your students don't sit in groups but rather in rows, you can place the baskets on the floor of the last desk in line. The student who sits there will be the basket manager. At the end of the day, students have the responsibility to organize the baskets for the next day. This could mean that they're replenishing supplies as well. Baskets could include any of the following supplies:

Processing Baskets

Specific reproducibles from the Processing Pathway Activities:

Encode It! Spinner	(p. 227)
The Important Book	(p. 219)
Alphabet Brainstorm	(Figure 2.8)
H Diagram	(p. 65)
HAS Synopsis	(p. 232)
Super Sleuth	(p. 94)
Palm Pilot	(pp. 248–249)
Stop-Save-Start	(p. 255)
Door Pass	(p. 222)
Countdown Processing	(p. 223)
Three-Point Summary	(Figure 5.16)

General Supplies From Processing Pathways Activities:

Chalkboards or slates—chalk or dry erase markers
Gel boards
Post-it notes
Brain balls
Paper plates (just to write, draw, or web anything on)
Six Thinking Hats for groups of students
Choice Reflection glued to inside cover of notebook
Mind-mapping markers or twist-up crayons
Large construction paper for mind mapping
Dice
Other: _____

The processing baskets are tried-and-true tools for many teachers. You don't have to have processing baskets to get your students to deeply think, but they do allow you more flexibility during your lesson. You have all the supplies ready for processing at any moment. Best of all, allow your students to be in charge of maintaining the organized processing baskets. You should only have to photocopy the graphic organizers when needed. A school in Waynesville, Ohio, had a Processing Paradise party in which the principal, Jean Hartman, bought all the supplies that were needed for the processing baskets (see Figure 7.1). She also had the spinners made and laminated for the teachers. She had each of the processing activities photocopied for the teachers to choose which ones they wanted copies of for their baskets. She had labeled file folders ready to place these processing activities in for easy use. Teachers created an assembly line and enjoyed creating their baskets for their classrooms while listening to tropical music. These teachers were ready to implement their processing strategies 100%. They were trained on how to use them and tried them out during the training.

If you're a trainer, we don't suggest that you take baskets in your suitcases but rather that you place the supplies in a large ziplock bag. When we travel, we pack brain balls, Post-it notes, spinners, twist-up crayons, and the graphic organizers that are needed for the presentation during processing opportunities. We place one bag per table. We always ask the client, "How many participants will sit at a table." We make sure that the copies are ready to go in the bags. Another idea is to place the graphic organizer processing activities needed during the presentation in the packet.

Pointers

- Make sure to assign a student to be in charge of maintaining the basket (keeping papers straight, throwing away scrap paper, and replenishing the graphic organizers). We kept the graphic organizer copies in a specific place in the classroom for ease of replenishing the files in the baskets.
- Ask the students to label the files and grab the graphic organizers to start out the process.
- Label the supplies with a certain group table number; for example, Brain Ball with the numeral 5 written on it showing that this particular brain ball belongs in Group Basket 5.
- Have two different colored file folders for the baskets: one that represents processing activity reproducibles that can be completed in less than 4 minutes and one for those that take longer than 4 minutes.
- Create a file folder with transparencies of the processing pages just in case you need to give students an example and explanation of how to use them. Place these transparencies near your teaching area so they're ready to go.

Inside Secrets for Making It Work

You could give the same pastry recipe to 1,000 cooks and it might turn out differently (albeit slightly) for each of the end results. Why does that happen? There are dozens of variables that affect a recipe, even when it's just as plain as day. These variables include

The quality of the ingredients

The altitude (sea level or 4,000 feet) of the kitchen

The speed with which the recipe was made

The quality of pans, utensils, and tools

The cleanliness of the kitchen

The weather that day

The mood of the maker

Unfortunately, the lesson here is that the strategies in this book are not foolproof. They require some attitude, some practice, and a few micro-strategies that are usually learned only with years of experience, but you're going to learn them right now. That will save you some frustration, drama, and time on the learning curve.

- Watch your time—know which processing activities can be utilized very quickly and which ones take more time.
- Keep the supplies for processing handy so you always have them as soon as possible.
- Know 8 strategies really well rather than 50 badly.
- Explore every strategy with its variations.
- Avoid jumping to judge too fast—what's not working for you often does work for some students.
- Branch out and try new processing strategies even when your personality may not have chosen that one. Students benefit from a variety of strategies.
- Keep an open eye for improvement, no matter how good a strategy works.
- Have a tool (train whistle, bells, chimes, special clap, etc.) to let the students know it's time to end the processing and prepare for the next chunk of information. Remind them that they had their turn to talk and process and now it's your turn to teach a new chunk of information.
- Give students the job of keeping the processing materials organized and ready to go.
- Keep a timer on hand.
- Be creative and make the processing activities special to your class (see the Four P's).

And finally, here are the Four P's of processing—our secret recipe tips for creating great processing activities. Keep the Four P's in mind while creating your own processing activities. We're sharing them because they constitute the insider knowledge that you need to make all of these cool strategies work. It's not enough that you know the why and how; these extras will give you the shortcuts that virtually guarantee success. The first of them will make these activities so easy and quick, you'll want to get started on them right away.

The Four P's

1. *Purposeful* (both pertinent and relevant)
The processing activity needs to have a purpose—the DEEP processing activities are just some of the most used pathways in a classroom. Make sure the activity you create has a purpose behind it and that it's pertinent to the objective at hand. The processing activity needs to enhance the objective of learning.

2. *Pumped* (you need to be pumped up and excited)
If you're excited about the activity, it has a much better chance of succeeding. Students pick up on the emotions of teachers and teachers pick up on the emotions of staff developers. When students see emotion on the

teacher's face, it stimulates a part of their brain that signals them to express some or all of that same emotion (Gallese, Keysers, & Rizzolatti, 2004). Think about how excited your audience will get. Think of the deeper learning, the engagement, and the interaction. Imagine the students leaving class excited and unable to stay quiet.

3. *Prepared* (be ready for action)

While creating the processing activity, be sure to answer the following questions:

- What will be done with the content? (discussing, writing, thinking, drawing, moving, mind mapping, etc.)
- What materials are needed for this activity? How will the materials be used by the different learners?
- How will the processing activity be done, and where will it take place? (sitting, standing, walking, etc. Location ideas: desks, corner of room, hallway)
- How will the students be grouped? Independently, partner, small group (3–4), large group, and so on.
- How long will it last? Remember to give some flex time. When students process, teachers always give a range of minutes, so if they see that students are on task, they can give them more time. If teachers see that students complete the processing earlier, then they end it.

4. *Positive, Emotional Ending*

There are many reasons for ending your class on an emotional high. First, it's one of the keys to building a positive association between being in your class and loving it. Second, it's a good time to influence the memory formation process before class is out and new memories have a chance to be contaminating. And finally, the research is quite solid: the greater the emotional experience, the greater the strength of the memory (Cahill, 2000).

Recently researchers have uncovered more about the actual mechanisms in place to make those emotional memories happen. You may know that epinephrine, norepinephrine, and cortisol are heavily involved. The ways they influence memory are quite roundabout. One of the eventual triggers for stronger memories is glucose formation. Glucose is not the only memory-making mechanism, but it's a strong one (Blake, Varnhagen, & Parent, 2001). The message here is actually simple: the more exciting and arousing your closure is, the greater the chances your student will recall it. That means less reteaching and more time for other things such as processing for deeper learning.

We've already explained the importance and implementation of building a positive learning culture in DELC Step 3, and now we're going to explain how to end the processing positively. There are several ways to end a processing activity positively:

1. High fives to everyone in the group—From one group member to another group member

2. Affirmations—Let students choose which way they want to affirm that processing. Here are some ideas:
   - Special celebrations created by students
   - Special song in which hand shaking occurs until the song is over

- Pinky shakes
- Backhand slaps
- Criss-cross hand slaps
- Put up a poster above or next to the door that says, "If you learned something new today, give me five!"
- Put a bell, noisemaker, Easy button (from Staples), or gong at the door and tell students to hit it if they learned something new today.
- All students have a special study buddy in a group other than their own. They go up to their buddies and share the highlights from the day and congratulate them.
- Teams create a team cheer that they use to celebrate the positive results of the day.

After the students process, you sound the whistle, chime, bell, song, and so on to let them know it's over, and they affirm one another quickly. Then they immediately go back to their seats for the next chunk of information. This is a habit that teachers want their students to get into. It takes practice, but your students will get it quite soon. Give them continual feedback so they get faster at it.

Keep the Four P's in mind while creating your processing activities: keep the processing activity purposeful and pertinent, make sure it's pre-planned, get pumped about it, and end it positively. You'll see incredible processing occurring with these reminders.

We've discussed how to make the right choices for implementing the processing activities, how to plan for them in your daily lesson plan or with the DELC Lesson Plan, how to evaluate processing, and how to keep all these ideas manageable and organized.

CONCLUSION ■

You now have the tools to successfully implement deeper learning units and lessons on a daily basis for *all* students. Teachers like to practice what they preach, so now it's time to begin with the end in mind by focusing on the big goal for learning. This big goal is a direct result of powerful, deeper processing: loving learning through deeper processing. We hope that you enjoyed the DELC, the daily lesson plan, and the DEEP, along with all the other powerful strategies presented in each chapter. May the love of learning force be with you and the energy to implement these strategies be stronger than ever. You will see deeper learning results among your students, and you'll feel more fulfilled as a teacher.

Now the big questions of the book can be brought forth again.

1. How do you facilitate the progress of students toward in-depth learning?

2. How do you organize your time for deeper learning?

3. How do you differentiate these powerful deeper learning strategies to meet all of the students' needs in a daily lesson plan?

SQ4R

1. Survey Look through the book for headings, subheadings, pictures, diagrams, charts, graphs, maps, etc. Place three Post-it notes on the most intriguing things that you see while going on this walk through the book.	
2. What do I already know about this book or chapter?	**3. What do I hope to learn after reading this book or chapter?**
4. Questions Turn the headings and subheadings into open-ended questions. These questions will be your purpose for the reading.	
5. Read While reading, write down key words and short descriptions of them (after the section). **6. Recite** Actively read the text. Pay attention to information that will answer your questions. Answer the questions that you created above. Use the book only if needed. Use your own words and complete sentences.	
7. Review To a partner, summarize verbally what you read.	
8. Reflect Answer the following questions on the back of this page. • How did this text connect to your life? • What did you learn? • What do you want to learn more about?	

Preassessment Anticipation Guide: After Learning

Go back to Table 1.1, the Preassessment Anticipation Guide on pages 19 and 20, and evaluate in the "After Learning" column whether you agree or disagree with the statements. Compare your responses with the answer key that follows that shows our opinions about the statements and how we support these opinions. Make sure to discuss this valuable learning tool with your small groups or with another teacher who read this book.

PREASSESSMENT ANTICIPATION GUIDE ANSWER KEY ■

Before Learning			After Learning	
Agree	Disagree		Agree	Disagree
		1. Simple learning is a foundational piece for deeper learning. (Ch. 1)	X	
		2. Preassessment results assist deeper learning. (Ch. 1)	X	
		3. Deeper learning is the acquisition of new content or skills that must be learned in more than one step and with multiple levels of analysis or processing so that students may apply the information in ways that change thinking, influence affect, or change behaviors. (Ch. 1)	X	
		4. Taking the time to activate prior knowledge before starting to teach a lesson can facilitate strong connections. (Ch. 1)	X	
		5. Deeper learning is enhanced when students are highly challenged. (Ch. 2) CORRECT: Deeper learning is enhanced when students are slightly challenged.		X

(Continued)

(Continued)

Before Learning			After Learning	
Agree	Disagree		Agree	Disagree
		6. Preassessments are needed in order to create a very meaningful, developmentally appropriate unit that meets the needs of the students. (Ch. 2)	X	
		7. Research suggests that cooperative learning produces better learning when compared with students competing against each other individually. (Ch. 2)	X	
		8. Loving learning does not necessarily equal positive affect. (Ch. 2) CORRECT: They are equal; they go hand in hand.		X
		9. Your overall mood is not as important as other factors when it comes to creating a positive affect. (Ch. 2) CORRECT: Your overall mood is the deciding factor of the students' states of mind.		X
		10. Priming and activating prior knowledge are the same thing. (Ch. 3) CORRECT: Priming is preexposing information to students that will be taught in great detail later. Activating prior knowledge is giving students time to think about what they know or have experienced with a particular topic.		X
		11. The main purpose behind activating prior knowledge is to preexpose the brain to upcoming content. (Ch. 3) CORRECT: We believe the main purpose is to activate existing neural networks for stronger connections.		X
		12. Processing happens automatically so there is little facilitation that must go on from the teacher. (Ch. 4) CORRECT: Processing does happen automatically, but the brain may not be processing the content that was just learned but rather some other extraneous information or distraction. Teachers must facilitate opportunities for processing so that correct connections can be made right after the learning.		X
		13. Rather than think of deeper processing as a taxonomy of thought, teachers should use a variety of processing strategies depending on the purpose for the processing. (Ch. 4)	X	
		14. Processing all begins in the amygdala, the emotional center of the brain. (Ch. 4) CORRECT: Processing begins in the thalamus.		X
		15. Too much too fast will last. (Ch. 4) CORRECT: Too much too fast will NOT last.		X

Before Learning			After Learning	
Agree	Disagree		Agree	Disagree
		16. Bloom's taxonomy explains how students learn, and teachers should make it a priority to lead students through the taxonomy in its proper order. (Ch. 4) CORRECT: Bloom's taxonomy is a way to categorize thinking verbs and types of processing, but it should not be used as a taxonomy, since some "proposed" higher-level thinking verbs really are types of simple learning.		X
		17. We differentiate because everyone comes to the learning situation with different background knowledge, interests, strengths, and growth opportunities. (Ch. 5)	X	
		18. Students can experience deeper learning even though their background knowledge is not well developed. (Ch. 5) NOTE: Yes, they can, but not as many neural networks will be activated to use to increase connections.	X	
		19. There should be about two to four processing opportunities in each daily lesson plan. (Ch. 6)	X	
		20. Because each teacher has different teaching styles, it is recommended that you start using the processing activities that best fit your teaching style. Then it's very important to branch out and try the others so that you're meeting all of your students' needs. (Ch. 6)	X	
		21. Thinking through your daily lesson plans enhances deeper learning. (Ch. 6)	X	
		22. Closures of the lesson are not as important as once thought. (Ch. 6) CORRECT: Closures are extremely important for consolidation of learning and checking for understanding one more time.		X
		23. Student vesting is so important that it needs to be at the very beginning of your lesson every time you teach. (Ch. 6)	X	
		24. One way to manage and implement the processing activities is to create processing baskets for groups of students so they can easily use the supplies needed for the activities. (Ch. 7)	X	
		25. The Four P's (Purposeful, Pumped, Prepared, and Positive Emotions) help you create your own processing activities for your students. They are the secret recipe to a good processing activity. (Ch. 7)	X	

References

Abe, M., Hanakawa, T., Takayama, Y., Kuroki, C., Ogawa, S., & Fukuyama, H. (2007). Functional coupling of human prefrontal and premotor areas during cognitive manipulation. *Journal of Neuroscience, 27*(13), 3429–3438.

Aguado, A. (2002). Learning and memory. *Journal of Experimental Psychology, 32*(4), 373–381.

Altmann, G. T. (2002). Learning and development in neural networks: The importance of prior experience. *Cognition, 85*(2), B43–B50.

Armbruster, B., & Anderson, T. (1991). Improving content-area reading using instructional graphics. *Reading Research Quarterly, 26*(4), 393–416.

Atwood, G., & Karunannithi, S. (2002). Diversification of synaptic strength: Presynaptic elements. *Nature Reviews: Neuroscience, 3*(7), 497–515.

Bechara, A., Damasio, H., & Damasio, A. R. (2003). Role of the amygdala in decision-making. *New York Academy of Sciences, 985,* 356–369.

Billmeyer, R. (2003). *Strategies to engage the mind of the learner.* Omaha, NE: Rachel & Associates.

Bishop, S., Duncan, J., Brett, M., & Lawrence, A. D. (2004). Prefrontal cortical function and anxiety: Controlling attention to threat-related stimuli. *Nature Neuroscience, 7*(2), 184–188.

Blake, T. M., Varnhagen, C. K., & Parent, M. B. (2001). Emotionally arousing pictures increase blood glucose levels and enhance recall. *Neurobiology of Learning and Memory, 75*(3), 262–273.

Bloom, B. S. (Ed.), Engelhart, M. D., Furst, E. J., Hill, W. H., & Krathwohl, D. R. (1956). *Taxonomy of educational objectives: Handbook I. Cognitive domain.* New York: David McKay.

Boling, N., & Robinson, D. (1999). Individual study, interactive multimedia, or cooperative learning: Which activity best supplements lecture-based distance education? *Journal of Educational Psychology, 91*(1), 169–174.

Boscolo, P., & Mason, L. (2000, April). *Prior knowledge, text coherence, and interest: How they interact in learning from instructional texts.* Paper presented at the annual meeting of the American Educational Research Association, New Orleans, LA.

Brown, M. W. (1949). *The important book.* New York: Harper.

Cahill, L. (2000). Neurobiological mechanisms of emotionally influenced, long-term memory. *Progress in Brain Research, 126,* 29–37.

Caine, G., Caine, R., & Crowell, S. (1994). *Mindshifts: A brain-based process for restructuring schools and renewing education.* Tucson, AZ: Zephyr.

Callicott, J. H., Mattay, V. S., Bertolino, A., Finn, K., Coppola, R., Frank, J. A., et al. (1999). Physiological characteristics of capacity constraints in working memory as revealed by functional MRI. *Cerebral Cortex, 9*(1), 20–26.

Carlson, R., Chandler, P., & Sweller, J. (2003). Learning and understanding science instructional material. *Journal of Educational Psychology, 95*(3), 629–640.

Cave, B. (1997). Very long-lasting priming in picture naming. *Psychological Science, 8,* 322–325.

Chesebro, J. L. (2003). Effects of teacher clarity and nonverbal immediacy on student learning, receiver apprehension, and affect. *Communication Education, 52*(2), 135–147.

Chiu, M., & Khoo, L. (2003). Rudeness and status effects during group problem solving: Do they bias evaluations and reduce the likelihood of correct solutions? *Journal of Educational Psychology, 95*(3), 506–523.

Colicos, M., & Goda, Y. (2001). Pictures reveal how nerve cells form connections to store short- and long-term memories in brain. *Cell, 107,* 605–616.

Connors, K. (1989). *Feeding the brain: How foods affect children.* Cambridge, MA: Perseus.

Cowan, N. (2001). The magical number 4 in short-term memory: A reconsideration of mental storage capacity. *Behavioral and Brain Sciences, 24*(1), 87–114.

D'Anci, K. E., Constant, F., & Rosenberg, I. H. (2006). Hydration and cognitive function in children. *Nutrition Reviews, 64*(10/1), 457–464.

Darling-Hammond, L. (2000). Teacher quality and student achievement: A review of state policy evidence. *Education Policy Analysis Archives, 8*(1). Retrieved July 7, 2007, from http://olam.ed.asu.edu/epaa/v8n1/

Davis, M., & Whalen, P. (2001). The amygdala: Vigilance and emotion. *Molecular Psychiatry, 6*(1), 13–34.

Deci, E. L., Koestner, R., & Ryan, R. M. (1999). A meta-analytic review of experiments examining the effects of extrinsic rewards on intrinsic motivation. *Psychological Bulletin, 125,* 627–668.

Dimberg, U., & Thunberg, M. (1998). Rapid facial reactions to emotional facial expressions. *Scandinavian Journal of Psychology, 39*(1), 39–45.

Dodge, J. (2005). *Differentiation in action.* New York: Scholastic.

Dolcos, F., & McCarthy, G. (2006). Brain systems mediating cognitive interference by emotional distraction. *Journal of Neuroscience, 26*(7), 2072–2079.

Dudai, Y. (2004). The neurobiology of consolidations, or, how stable is the engram? *Annual Review of Psychology, 55,* 51–86.

Feldman, J. (2000). Minimization of Boolean complexity in human concept learning. *Nature, 407*(6804), 630–633.

Fonda, J. D., & Russell, C. (Producers). (1953). *You are there* [Television series]. New York: CBS Television.

Frank, L., Stanley, G., & Brown, E. (2004). Hippocampal plasticity across multiple days of exposure to novel environments. *Journal of Neuroscience, 24*(35), 7681–7689.

Gallese, V., Keysers, C., & Rizzolatti, G. (2004). A unifying view of the basis of social cognition. *Trends in Cognitive Sciences, 8*(9), 396–403.

Gazzaniga, M. (2001). Brain and conscious experience. In J. T. Cacioppo et al. (Eds.), *Foundations in social neuroscience* (pp. 203–214). Cambridge: Massachusetts Institute of Technology Press.

Ghaith, G. (2002). The relationship between cooperative learning, perception of social support, and academic achievement. *System, 30*(3), 263–273.

Gillies, R., & Ashman, A. (1998). Behavior and interactions of children in cooperative groups in lower and middle elementary grades. *Journal of Educational Psychology, 90*(4), 746–757.

Ginott, H. (1976). *Teacher and child.* New York: Avon. Retrieved November 8, 2007, from http://www.linbarconsulting.com/Instructional%20tools/Haim%20Ginott.pdf

Ginsburg-Block, M., & Fantuzzo, J. W. (1998). An evaluation of the relative effectiveness of NCTM standards-based interventions for low-achieving urban elementary students. *Journal of Educational Psychology, 90*(3), 560–569.

Glasser, W. (1986). *Choice theory in the classroom.* New York: HarperCollins.

Gold, P. E. (1995). Role of glucose in regulating the brain and cognition. *American Journal of Clinical Nutrition, 61,* 987S–995S.

Gorham, J., & Christophel, D. (1990). The relationship of teachers' use of humor in the classroom to immediacy and student learning. *Communication Education, 39*(1), 46–62.

Gottfried, A. E. (1985). Academic intrinsic motivation in elementary and junior high school students. *Journal of Educational Psychology, 77*(6), 631–645.

Gray, J., Braver, T., & Raichle, M. (2002). Integration of emotion and cognition in the lateral prefrontal cortex. *Proceedings of the National Academy of Sciences, 99*(6), 4115–4120.

Haier, R. J., Siegel, B. V., Jr., MacLachlan, A., Soderling, E., Lottenberg, S., & Buchsbaum, M. S. (1992). Regional glucose metabolic changes after learning a complex visuospatial/motor task: A positron emission tomographic study. *Brain Research, 570*(1–2), 134–143.

Hammer, B. (2002). Recurrent networks for structured data: A unifying approach and its properties. *Cognitive Systems Research, 3*(2), 145–165.

Hart, A., Whalen, P., Shin, L., McInerney, S., Fischer, H., & Rauch, S. (2000). Differential response in the human amygdala to racial outgroup vs. ingroup face stimuli. *NeuroReport, 11*, 2351–2355.

Hayes, B. K., Foster, K., & Gadd, N. (2003). Prior knowledge and subtyping effects in children's category learning. *Cognition, 88*, 177–199.

Hopf, F., Waters, J., Mehta, S., & Smith, S. (2002). Stability and plasticity of developing synapses in hippocampal neuronal cultures. *Journal of Neuroscience, 22*(3), 775–781.

Ilies, R., & Judge, T. A. (2005). Goal regulation across time: The effects of feedback and affect. *Journal of Applied Psychology, 90*(3), 453–467.

Jensen, E. (2003). *Tools for engagement.* Thousand Oaks, CA: Corwin Press.

Johnson, D., & Johnson, R. (1999). *Learning together and alone: Cooperative, competitive and individualistic learning.* Boston: Allyn & Bacon.

Johnson, D. W., Johnson, R. T., & Taylor, B. (1993). Impact of cooperative and individualistic learning on high-ability students' achievement, self-esteem, and social acceptance. *Journal of Social Psychology, 133*(6), 839–844.

Kagan, S. (1994). *Cooperative learning.* San Clemente, CA: Resources for Teachers.

Kieser, J., Herbison, P., Waddell, N., Kardos, T., & Innes, P. (2006). Learning in oral biology: A comparison between deep and surface approaches. *New Zealand Dental Journal, 102*(3), 64–68.

Klingberg, T. (2000). Limitations in information processing in the human brain: Neuroimaging of dual task performance and working memory tasks. *Progress in Brain Research, 126*, 95–102.

Kluger, A., & DeNisi, A. (1996). The effects of feedback interventions on performance: A historical review, a meta-analysis, and a preliminary feedback intervention theory. *Psychological Bulletin, 119*(2), 254–284.

Lachter, J., & Hayhoe, M. (1995). Capacity limitations in memory for visual locations. *Perception, 24*(12), 1427–1441.

Levenson, R. W., Ekman, P., & Friesen, W. V. (1990). Voluntary facial action generates emotion-specific autonomic nervous system activity. *Psychophysiology, 27*(4), 363–384.

Lipsey, M., & Wilson, D. (1993). The efficacy of psychological, educational and behavioral treatment. *American Psychologist, 48*(12), 1181–1209.

Lochman, J. E., Coie, J. D., Underwood, M. K., & Terry, R. (1994). Effectiveness of a social relations intervention program for aggressive and nonaggressive, rejected children. *Journal of Consulting and Clinical Psychology, 61*, 1053–1058.

Lou, Y., Abrami, P., Spence, J., Paulsen, C., Chambers, B., & d'Apollonio, S. (1996). Within-class grouping: A meta-analysis. *Review of Educational Research, 66*(4), 423–458.

Lupien, S. J., & Lepage, M. (2001). Stress, memory, and the hippocampus: Can't live with it, can't live without it. *Behavioural Brain Research, 127*, 137–158.

Magnus, R., & Laeng, B. (2006). Drawing on either side of the brain. *Laterality, 11*(1), 71–89.

Mahoney, C. R., Taylor, H. A., Kanarek, R. B., & Samuel, P. (2005). Effect of breakfast composition on cognitive processes in elementary school children. *Physiology & Behavior, 85*(5), 635–645.

Markowitz, K. (1999). *The great memory book.* Thousand Oaks, CA: Corwin Press.

Martin, A. (2001). Functional neuroimaging of semantic memory. In R. Cabeza & A. Kingstone (Eds.), *Handbook of functional neuroimaging of cognition* (pp. 153–186). Cambridge: Massachusetts Institute of Technology Press.

Martin, A., & van Turenout, M. (2002). Searching for the neural correlates of object priming. In D. Schacter & L. Squire (Eds.), *Neuropsychology of memory* (pp. 239–247). New York: Guilford Press.

Marzano, R. J., & Kendall, J. S. (2006). *The new taxonomy of educational objectives.* Thousand Oaks, CA: Corwin Press.

McCarthy, M. T. (1995). Form of feedback effects on verb learning and near-transfer tasks by sixth graders. *Contemporary Educational Psychology, 20*(2), 140–150.

McGehee, J., & Griffith, L. (2001). Large-scale assessments combined with curriculum alignment: Agents of change. *Theory Into Practice, 40*(2), 137–144.

Mehrabian, A. (1981). *Silent messages: Implicit communication of emotions and attitudes.* Belmont, CA: Wadsworth.

Miller, R. B., Greene, B. A., Montalvo, G. P., Ravindran, B., & Nichols, J. D. (1996). Engagement in academic work: The role of learning goals, future consequences, pleasing others, and perceived ability. *Contemporary Educational Psychology, 21*(4), 388–422.

Mogg, K., Bradley, B., & Hallowell, N. (1994). Attentional bias to threat: Roles of trait anxiety, stressful events, and awareness. *Quarterly Journal of Experimental Psychology: Section A, 47*(4), 841–864.

Murai, T., Hanakawa, T., Sengoku, A., Ban, T., Yoneda, Y., Fujita, H., et al. (1998). Temporal lobe epilepsy in a genius of natural history: MRI volumetric study of postmortem brain. *Neurology, 50*(5), 1373–1376.

Nadel, L., & Land, C. (2000). Memory traces revisited. *Nature Reviews: Neuroscience, 1*(3), 209–212.

National Reading Panel. (2000). *Report of the National Reading Panel: Teaching children to read.* Retrieved January 3, 2007, from http://www.nationalreadingpanel.org/Publications/summary.htm

Nickelsen, L. (2004). *Memorizing strategies and other brain-based activities: Grades 4 and up.* New York: Scholastic.

Nitsche, M. A., Roth, A., Kuo, M. F., Fischer, A. K., Liebetanz, D., Lang, N., et al. (2007). Timing-dependent modulation of associative plasticity by general network excitability in the human motor cortex. *Journal of Neuroscience, 27*(14), 3807–3812.

O'Kane, G., Kensinger, E. A., & Corkin, S. (2004). Evidence for semantic learning in profound amnesia: An investigation with patient H.M. *Hippocampus, 14*(4), 417–425.

Pellegrini, A., & Bohn, C. (2005). The role of recess in children's cognitive performance and school adjustment. *Educational Researcher, 34*(1) 13–19.

Pellegrini, A. D., & Smith, P. (1998). Physical activity play: The nature and function of a neglected aspect of play. *Child Development, 69*(3), 577–598.

Petersen, R. P., Johnson, D. W., & Johnson, R. T. (1991). Effects of cooperative learning on perceived status of male and female pupils. *Journal of Social Psychology, 131*(5), 717–735.

Polacco, P. (1994). *Pink and say.* New York: Philomel.

Roosevelt, E. (1983). *You learn by living.* Louisville, KY: Westminster John Knox Press.

Ryan, R., & Deci, E. (2000). Self-determination theory and the facilitation of intrinsic motivation, social development, and well-being. *American Psychologist, 55*(1), 68–78.

Ryan, R. M., Connell, J. P., & Plant, R. W. (1990). Emotions in non-directed text learning. *Learning and Individual Differences, 2,* 1–17.

Saud de Nunez, G., Rodriguez Rojas, S., & Niaz, M. (1993). Further evidence relating mental capacity, short-term storage space, and operational efficiency. *Perceptual and Motor Skills, 76*(3/1), 735–738.

Shadmehr, R., & Holcomb, H. H. (1997). Neural correlates of motor memory consolidation. *Science, 277*(5327), 821–825.

Shyer, C. (Director). (1991). *Father of the bride* [Motion picture]. United States: Touchstone Pictures.

Simpson, J., Jr., Snyder, A., Gusnard, D., & Raichle, M. (2001). Emotion-induced changes in human medial prefrontal cortex: I. During cognitive task performance. *Proceedings of the National Academy of Sciences, 98*(2), 683–687.

Smees, R., Sammons, P., Thomas, S., & Mortimore, P. (2002). Examining the effect of pupil background on primary and secondary pupils' attainment: Key findings from the Improving School Effectiveness Project. *Scottish Educational Review, 34*(1), 6–25. (ERIC Document Reproduction Service No. EJ654436)

Squire, L., & Kandel, E. (2000). *Memory: From mind to molecules.* New York: W. H. Freeman.

Stickgold, R. (2006). Neuroscience: A memory boost while you sleep. *Nature, 444*(7119), 559–560.

Stipek, D., & Seal, K. (2001). *Motivated minds: Raising children to love learning.* New York: Henry Holt.

Stronge, J. H. (2002). *Qualities of effective teachers.* Alexandria, VA: Association for Supervision & Curriculum Development.

Sugar, S. (1998). *Games that teach.* San Francisco: Jossey-Bass.

Tamblyn, D. (2002). *Laugh and learn: 95 ways to use humor for more effective teaching and training.* New York: American Management Association.

Treffert, D. A., & Wallace, G. L. (2002). Islands of genius: Artistic brilliance and a dazzling memory can sometimes accompany autism and other developmental disorders. *Scientific American, 286*(6), 76–85.

Walberg, H. (1999). Productive teaching. In H. C. Waxman & H. Walberg (Eds.), *New directions for teaching practice and research* (pp. 75–104). Berkeley, CA: McCutchen.

Walsh, J., & Sattes, B. D. (2005). *Quality questioning.* Thousand Oaks, CA: Corwin Press.

Wiggins, G., & McTighe, J. (2005). *Understanding by design* (2nd ed.). Alexandria, VA: Association for Supervision & Curriculum Development.

Williams, A. M., & Ericsson, K. A. (2005). Perceptual-cognitive expertise in sport: Some considerations when applying the expert performance approach. *Human Movement Science, 24*(3), 283–307.

Wiltgen, B. J., Brown, R. A., Talton, L. E., & Silva, A. J. (2004). New circuits for old memories: The role of the neocortex in consolidation. *Neuron, 44*(1), 101–108.

Wolfe, C. R. (2006). Cognitive technologies for gist processing. *Behavior Research Methods, 38*(2), 183–189.

Wood, C. (1997). *Yardsticks: Children in the classroom ages 4–14: A resource for parents and teachers.* Turners Falls, MA: Northeast Foundation for Children.

Yurgelun-Todd, D. A., Killgore, W. D., & Young, A. D. (2002). Sex differences in cerebral tissue volume and cognitive performance during adolescence. *Psychological Reports, 91*(3/1), 743–757.

Zimmer, R. (2003). A new twist in the educational tracking debate. Retrieved January 2, 2007, from http://www.rand.org/pubs/authors/z/zimmer_ron.html

Zull, J. (2002). *The art of changing the brain.* Sterling, VA: Stylus.

Index

CORWIN
PRESS